AF875788

Die Umsetzung der Übernahmerichtlinie in Europa

ILFS

Institute for Law and Finance Series

Edited by

Theodor Baums
Andreas Cahn

De Gruyter Recht · Berlin

Die Umsetzung der Übernahmerichtlinie in Europa

Herausgegeben von

Theodor Baums
Andreas Cahn

RECHT

De Gruyter Recht · Berlin

♾ Gedruckt auf säurefreiem Papier,
das die US-ANSI-Norm über Haltbarkeit erfüllt.

ISBN-13: 978-3-89949-378-8
ISBN-10: 3-89949-378-8

Bibliografische Information der Deutschen Nationalbibliothek

Die Deutsche Nationalbibliothek verzeichnet diese Publikation in der Deutschen Nationalbibliografie; detaillierte bibliografische Daten sind im Internet über http://dnb.d-nb.de abrufbar.

© Copyright 2006 by De Gruyter Rechtswissenschaften Verlags-GmbH, D-10785 Berlin

Dieses Werk einschließlich aller seiner Teile ist urheberrechtlich geschützt. Jede Verwertung außerhalb der engen Grenzen des Urheberrechtsgesetzes ist ohne Zustimmung des Verlages unzulässig und strafbar. Das gilt insbesondere für Vervielfältigungen, Übersetzungen, Mikroverfilmungen und die Einspeicherung und Verarbeitung in elektronischen Systemen.

Umschlaggestaltung: Christopher Schneider, Berlin
Datenkonvertierung/Satz: jürgen ullrich typosatz, Nördlingen
Druck und Bindung: Hubert & Co., Göttingen

Printed in Germany

Vorwort

Die 13. Richtlinie hat eine wechselvolle Geschichte hinter sich. Nach langen Vorarbeiten, die bereits im Jahr 1987 mit dem Vorentwurf der Richtlinie begonnen hatten, scheiterte ihre Verabschiedung am 4. Juli 2001 zunächst im Europäischen Parlament an einem Abstimmungsergebnis von 273:273 Stimmen bei 22 Enthaltungen. Hauptpunkt der Kritik war seinerzeit das übernahmerechtliche Vereitelungsverbot, das nur bestimmte Abwehrmaßnahmen erfasste, andere hingegen unberührt ließ. Einige Mitgliedstaaten befürchteten daher Nachteile für ihre heimischen Unternehmen, weil kein *level playing field* für Übernahmen gewährleistet sei. Die nunmehr verabschiedete, am 20. Mai 2004 in Kraft getretene Richtlinie, die bis zum 20. Mai 2006 von den Mitgliedstaaten umzusetzen ist, enthält zwar wiederum ein übernahmerechtliches Vereitelungsverbot und darüber hinaus eine sog. Durchgriffsregel, nach der satzungsmäßige Beschränkungen der Übertragung von Aktien gegenüber dem Bieter grundsätzlich keine Wirkung entfalten. In der Schlussphase der Beratungen wurden indessen Vereitelungsverbot und Durchgriffsregel durch den neu eingefügten Art. 12 zur Disposition der Mitgliedstaaten gestellt. Dieses Optionsmodell wird durch Wahlmöglichkeiten für die betroffenen Gesellschaften ergänzt, die ihrerseits wieder einem Reziprozitätsmodell folgen. Insgesamt ergibt sich damit ein nicht leicht zu durchschauendes Zusammenspiel von europarechtlichen Vorgaben, nationaler Umsetzung und Satzungsgestaltung auf Gesellschaftsebene. Nicht zuletzt die Frage, ob das petitum eines *level playing field* für Übernahmen durch die Richtlinie in höherem Maße gewährleistet wird als durch den Vorgängerentwurf, war Anlass für ein von der Stiftungsgastdozentur für Internationales Bankrecht ausgerichtetes ganztätiges Symposion am 9. November 2005, an dem ausgewiesene Experten des Übernahmerechts aus sechs Mitgliedstaaten beteiligt waren, deren Referate in dem vorliegenden Band zusammengefasst sind.

Frankfurt am Main, Juli 2006

Theodor Baums *Andreas Cahn*

Inhaltsverzeichnis

Die Autoren

Professor Isabelle Urbain-Parleani
Isabelle Urbain-Parleani is Professor in Commercial Law at the University of Paris V (René Descartes). She is Editor of the *„Revue des Sociétés“* (Dalloz), French oldest and most prestigious corporate law review, and a member of the board of the European Company and Financial Law review. She is also member of the CRDA (Institute of Research in Business Law, University of Paris 1 Panthéon – Sorbonne), and member of the CEDAG (Institute for research on business law and management, University Paris V René Descartes). She is a regular participant in conference in France and Europe. She is a recognized specialist of corporate law, and has published extensively in this field.

Professor Dr. Susanne Kalss
Univ.-Prof. Dr. Susanne Kalss LL. M. (Florenz) habilitierte sich am Institut für Bürgerliches, Handels- und Gesellschaftsrecht im Jahr 2000 an der Wirtschaftsuniversität Wien für Handels-, Gesellschaftsrecht, Bürgerliches Recht und Kapitalmarktrecht. Von 2000 bis 2003 hatte sie eine Professur an der Universität Klagenfurt für Privatrecht inne, seit Oktober 2003 ist sie Professorin für Bürgerliches und Handelsrecht an der Wirtschaftsuniversität.

Rolf Skog
Rolf Skog was for five years (1985–1990) secretary to the Committee on Stock Ownership and Efficiency, Ministry of Industry, Sweden, and for ten years (1991–2001) secretary to the Company Law Committee, Ministry of Justice, Sweden. Today he serves as an expert to the Ministry of Justice in the field of company law and takeover-regulation. He was for many years the Swedish Government' expert and negotiator on the Takeover-directive. He is also the Swedish Government's representative to the OECD on corporate governance issues. He is managing director of the Swedish Securities Council („The Takeover Panel“). Ten years ago he founded the Swedish Corporate Governance Forum to which he is still managing director. He is also founder and co-editor of Nordisk Tidsskrift for Selskabsret (The Nordic Journal for Company Law) and has published extensively in the field of company law and corporate governance. Rolf Skog was in 2004 appointed to the European Corporate Governance Forum expert group set up by the European Commission.

Jonathan Rickford
Jonathan Rickford is a Professorial Fellow attached to the Company Law Centre at the British Institute of International and Comparative Law, and Visiting

Professor in corporate law at the London School of Economics. He was the Project Director of the UK Government's independent Review of Company Law from 1998 to 2001 and a member of the European Commission's High Level Group (the „Winter" Group) on company law in 2001–2002. During a varied career in government, business and academe he has been Director of Corporate Strategy, Director of Regulation and Chief Legal Adviser with British Telecommunications plc and Head of Company Law and The Solicitor (or General Counsel) at the UK Department of Trade and Industry. Early in his career he also taught law at the University of California at Berkeley and the London School of Economics. In 2001 he was made a Commander of the British Empire.

Professor Guido Ferrarini

Guido Ferrarini graduated from the Genoa Law School in 1972, and obtained an LL.M. from Yale Law School in 1978. He is Professor of Business Law at the University of Genoa and Director, Centre for Law and Finance. He is Lead Independent Director of Telecom Italia S.p.A.; Independent Director of Autostrade S.p.A., and Chairman of TLX (an Italian MTF and investment exchange). He is Vice-Chairman of the European Corporate Governance Institute (ECGI), Brussels, and Independent Director of Assogestioni (the Italian Asset Managers Association). He was a member of the Board of Trustees of the International Accounting Standards Committee (IASC), London, from 2000 to 2004. He is the author of various books and articles in the fields of financial law, corporate law, and business law. He was a Visiting Professor at Bonn University, Columbia Law School, Hamburg University, NYU Law School and University College London. He was Commerzbank Stiftung Visiting Professor at the Institute for Law and Finance, Frankfurt University, for the Spring Semester 2006.

Prof. Dr. Andreas Fuchs

Geschäftsführender Direktor des Instituts für Handels- und Wirtschaftsrecht sowie Inhaber des Lehrstuhls für Bürgerliches Recht, Handels- und Gesellschaftsrecht, deutsches, europäisches und internationales Wirtschaftsrecht, Rechtsvergleichung an der Universität Osnabrück (seit 2003), Ordinarius an der Universität Konstanz (1999–2003), Habilitation an der Georg-August-Universität Göttingen (1998), Wissenschaftlicher Assistent an der Georg-August-Universität Göttingen in der Abteilung für Internationales und Ausländisches Wirtschaftsrecht am Lehrstuhl von Prof. Dr. Dr. h.c. Ulrich Immenga (1991–1998), Syndikus in der Rechtsabteilung eines internationalen Industrieunternehmens in Hannover (1989–1991), Zweites Juristisches Staatsexamen (1989), Promotion zum Dr. jur. an der Georg-August-Universität Göttingen (1988), Studium der Rechtswissenschaften an der Georg-August-Universität Göttingen (1978–1983, Erstes Juristisches Staatsexamen 1983) und an der University of Michigan, Ann Arbor (1984–1985, LL.M. 1985). Forschungsschwerpunkte u.a. im Kapitalgesellschafts- und Kapitalmarktrecht, Wettbewerbs- und Kartellrecht.

Dr. Christian Zschocke

Christian Zschocke ist Partner des Frankfurter Büros von Morgan Lewis. Seine Tätigkeit konzentriert sich auf Transaktionen, insbesondere öffentliche Übernahmen, sowie auf europäisches und deutsches Kartellrecht. Christian Zschocke ist ein häufiger Redner auf Seminaren und Verfasser zahlreicher Veröffentlichungen einschließlich eines Kommentars zum deutschen Übernahmekodex. Vor Aufnahme seiner Tätigkeit für Morgan Lewis arbeitete Christian Zschocke im Londoner, Brüsseler und Frankfurter Büro einer in New York ansässigen internationalen Rechtsanwaltssozietät. Herr Zschocke ist seit 1990 als Rechtsanwalt zugelassen. Neben seiner Promotion an der Universität Hamburg erwarb er den Titel eines Licenciado en Derecho nach spanischem Recht.

I. Länderberichte

The Implementation of the Thirteenth Directive 2004/25 Country Report on France*

Isabelle Urbain-Parleani

Gliederung

* This text is current as of November 1ST 2005.

The implementation of the Thirteenth Company Law Directive on Takeover Bids of 21 April 2004 (2004/25/EC) comes at a time marked by an increasing number of acquisitions worldwide.

The legislative process in which the Directive was elaborated was extremely delicate (lasting from 1989 to 2004) not only because the national laws of Member States were very different, but also, and foremost, because regulations on takeover bids affect the nature of country's economic culture.[1] Beyond technical hindrances, the drafting of the Directive was made so difficult because the regulation of takeover bids is a sensitive subject for the national interests of Member States. The threat of global corporate giants, such as those found in the United States, to a lesser extent in Japan, and that soon will be found in China, increases this sensitivity.

The currents that influence French law on takeover bids reflect some ambivalence. France already has an elaborate body of law governing takeover bids. The law is mostly favourable to takeover bids and in compliance with the Directive.

However, this body of law displays a special feature. There are very few legislative provisions governing takeover bids. Some articles of the Commercial Code deal with certain limited aspects of takeover bids and implementation of article 9 of the Directive will bring further amendments to the Code. However, there are only five articles in the Monetary and Financial Code dealing with takeovers. Therefore, French takeover rules are mostly composed of regulations adopted since the 1970s by the securities regulator, the *Commission des Operations de Bourse* (COB), which was replaced in 2003 by the *Autorité des Marchés Financiers* (AMF). Indeed, the law provides in article L. 433-1 of the Monetary and Financial Code that „the AMF General Regulation sets rules governing takeover bids."

1 On the implementation of the Thirteen Directive, n° 2004/25/EC, into French law, *see*: *Couret* la fin d'une trop longue saga: l'adoption de la 13 ème directive concernant les offres publiques d'acquisition, Mélanges Béguin Litec, 2005, p.195; *B. Lecourt* Adoption de la directive 2004/25 du 21 avril 2004 sur les offres publiques d'acquisition, Revue des Sociétés 2005, p.237; *A. Pietrancosta* La directive européenne sur les offres publiques enfin adoptée! RD Bancaire et Financier, n° 5, sept–oct. 2004, p338; *F. Peltier et F. Martin-Laprade* Directive 2004/25/CE du 21 avril 2004 relatives aux OPA ou l'encadrement par le droit communautaire du changement de contrôle d'une société cotée, Bull. Joly Bourse et produits financiers 2004/5, p. 610; *D. Muffat-Jeandet* OPA: l'adoption d'une directive européenne, Revue du Marché commun et de l'Union européenne, n° 480, juillet août 2004, p.455; *P. Servan-Schreiberet W. Grumberg* Défenses anti-OPA, Adoption de la directive européenne sur les OPA et enjeux pour les entreprises françaises, JCP éd. E, 2005, n° 44, p. 1774.

It is surprising that the general principles governing takeover bids are not found in a law, but in article 231-3 of the AMF General Regulation. There are four general principles: the free play of bids and over bids, the equality of disclosure, the transparency and integrity of the market, and loyalty in transactions and competition.

However, if from the seventies to the nineties France was under the influence of the COB, which was unconditionally favourable to takeover bids for the sake of shareholders' democracy and the protection of shareholders, an opposite trend has started to alter this position. In 1992, it was decided that any takeover bid had to be launched for the entire capital of a target company and not be limited to 66.67% of the stock. Increasing the cost of takeover bids obviously limits their number. Furthermore, in 1997 the duration of the bid period was increased (art. 232-2 RG AMF), which gave target companies more time to organize their defence against a hostile takeover bid.

Today, France is clearly engaged in a movement towards greater protection of national companies. Politicians often invoke the term „economic patriotism". For instance, article 34 of the Confidence and Modernization of the Economy Act of July 26, 2005 on the obligation to make takeover bids widens the obligation: the offeror must also launch the takeover bid to the target company's subsidiaries listed abroad, provided that the latter, French or foreign, account for a major part of the assets of the company and that the target company owns more than 33.34% of their capital. This text is seen as a protective measure for Renault, the car manufacturer.[2] Also, a draft regulation intended to protect ten industrial sectors against takeover bids is currently before the Supreme administrative court (*Conseil d'Etat*) for advice and comment, and is also the subject of Brussels' scrutiny.

Thus, it is not surprising that the bill implementing the Directive, which should be adopted by the end of the year and which initially comprised 21 articles, has been presented as a bill against takeover bids.[3] However, this characterization is not really accurate.

Given that defences against takeover bids were at the centre of the debate when the bill was drafted, this paper will first study (A) the implementation of the Directive and the treatment of defences against takeover bids, and then (B) the bidding process.

2 Le Monde, October 20, 2005 .

3 The following analysis will refer to the text of the bill adopted by the Senate, but that version could be amended before it is finally adopted.

A. The Implementation of Directive 2004/25/EC and Defenses against Takeover bids

Three articles of the Directive regard defences against takeover bids. Two articles, articles 9 and 11, display the Directive's initial hostility towards such defences, whereas a third article, article 12, significantly favours these hostile measures.

Article 9 neutralizes the board's powers during the bidding period. The board may not take any defensive measure that has not been approved by the general meeting of shareholders.

Article 11 neutralizes any by-laws restriction on the transfer of securities and voting rights, and also neutralizes contractual agreements between the target company and the shareholders.

These two provisions, however, conflict with the desire of certain Member States to protect their companies against foreign attacks.[4] Faced with the reluctance of Member States, the Directive was saved by a compromise, which was incorporated into article 12.[5] This article makes the implementation of articles 9 and 11 optional and provides for a reciprocity principle that gives the board of directors of the target company the possibility of using a defence if the offeror's Member State does not apply article(s) 9 and/or 11.

France has chosen to implement article 9. [I] Article 10 of the bill on takeover bids – which will be codified in article L. 233-22 of the Commercial Code – implements this article of the Directive. [II] However, France has chosen to implement only two provisions of article, and [III] to implement the reciprocity principle (art. 11 bill codified in article L. 233-33).

4 Professor *Klaus J. Hopt* has perfectly shown Germany's reluctance towards Article 9 and France's to Article 11; *see Klaus J. Hopt* La treizième directive sur les OPA-OPE et le droit allemand, in Mélanges Yves Guyon, Dalloz, 2003, p.536.

5 On the compromise, *see A. Couret* La fin d'une trop longue saga; l'adoption de la treizième directive en matière de droit des sociétés concernant les offres publiques d'acquisition, Mélanges Béguin Litec 2005 p.195, spéc p. 198.

I. The Implementation of article 9 of Directive 2004/25/EC strengthening shareholder democracy (art 10 of the bill)

Current French law does not seem very different from article 9 of the Directive. However, a few observers have highlighted that the implementation of article 9 could drastically change national law. We must therefore 1) examine the nature of the purpose behind the implementation before 2) turning to an analysis of French law after the implementation becomes effective.

1. The purpose behind the implementation of article 9 (Dir.2004/25)

The French legislator had four reasons to implement this optional article

First reason: To reinforce shareholder democracy by returning to the shareholders' general meeting the necessary powers to govern these situations. Shareholders are indisputably the first, if not the only, people concerned by a takeover bid. Building defences against takeover bids means, in theory,[6] depriving the shareholders of the chance to participate in a transaction addressed only to them. In other words, if it is legitimate for a company to try to defend itself against hostile offers for its shares, it can only do so openly in compliance with the shareholders' desires.

Second reason: Preventing or solving conflicts of interests.[7] Conflicts arise when the board members put their interests first, including their interest to retain an executive position in the company at the expense of the company's best interest.

Third reason: Strengthening foreign investors' image of France by showing that France is open and adapted to a global economy.

Fourth reason: Giving French companies the opportunity to use the reciprocity principle.[8] However, the interpretation of the link between article 9 of

6 *See, Ph. Marini* Sénate first lecture, Report n° 20, Finance Commission, 13 october 2005; Report of the committee on the implementation of the Directive on takeover bids, requested by the Minister of Economy, Jean-François Lepetit, 27 juin 2005.

7 *See, A. Viandier* OPA, OPE et autres offres publiques, 2ème éd., Lefebvre 2003 n° 338; adde *D. Schmidt* Les conflits d'intérêts dans la société anonyme, 2ème éd., Joly 2004 p.198.

8 Lepetit Report, supra, p. 15.

the Directive and the reciprocity principle is challenged today as not conforming to European law.[9]

The position in France on implementing article 9 has not been unanimous. A few Representatives and authors[10] at first actively opposed the bill, arguing that an implementation of article 9 would obviously shift the central decision-making power from the board to the shareholders. It would put financial logic before industrial logic. It has also been observed that the legal recognition of a right of the shareholders' general meeting's to take measures against takeover bids during the bidding period could jeopardize well-established securities law principles.

We must then analyze the consequences of the implementation of article 9.

2. The consequences of the implementation of article 9 of 2004/25/EC, art. 10 of the bill

The bill on takeover bids includes in its article 10 a faithful implementation of article 9(2) and (3). This implementation is organized in three subsections.

a) The first subsection of article 10, implementing article 9 of 2004/25/EC provides:

„The board of directors, the supervisory board, the executive board, the Chief Executive Officer (CEO), or one of the officers of the target company, during the bidding period, shall obtain the approval of the shareholders' general meeting before taking any measure likely to make the bid fail, except measures to seek other bids."

This first subsection calls for several remarks.

First remark: Measures decided solely by the board or by the management and likely to make the bid fail are prohibited. The wording of the prohibition, by employing the term „likely", is imprecise and could lead to disputes.

Second remark: The board will not be able to take measures that were theoretically allowed until now, such as distributing exceptional dividends, assets

9 *See* infra p.14.

10 *F. Martin-Laprade,* Transposition de la directive OPA: les sociétés cotées faisant l'objet d'une OPA ressemblent-elles à de simples SICAV? Option finance n° 860, December 5, 2005, p. 35.

transfers, launching a counteroffer, acquiring assets or modifying contractual clauses on control. Thus, this text is more restrictive than current French law. AMF General Regulation article 231-36 only requires that, during the bidding period, the board inform the AMF when they decide to take actions other than management actions, so that the AMF can ensure that the public is adequately informed of its position („*appreciation*"). As a matter of fact, this negative position was widely considered as a *de facto* veto.

The board may, however, under the terms of article 9 of the Directive, seek other bids. Seeking other bids was already possible under French law. This is favourable to the company's shareholders, since the target company's board will look for a higher bid from an undertaking that seems better able than the first bidder to ensure the smooth operation of the company. Nevertheless, when seeking a new bid, the board will have to comply with the principles governing takeover bids,[11] and in particular refrain from any interference with the free play of bids and over bids.[12]

Third remark: With the approval of the shareholders' general meeting the board may take measures likely to make the takeover bid fail. The board's competence is subordinated to the shareholders' general meeting. Thus, the question that should arise is whether the general meeting's competence to approve any measure likely to make the bid fail would also validate defensive techniques that clash with fundamental principles of securities law.

An example frequently cited is the issue of bonds, such as those referred to as „Plavix" in the takeover bid of *Sanofi-Synthélabo* for *Aventis*.[13] Aventis' general meeting voted to approve the issue of such bonds, but the AMF concluded in a press release dated 24 April 2004 that their issue was not in compliance with principles governing takeover bids. Could this be maintained under the amended law in the future?

The future will probably tell us, but I will also venture an answer here. It should be assumed that techniques implemented by the general meeting must remain in compliance with AMF General Regulation article 231-3 establishing general principles that govern takeover bids. The board's powers are merely restricted and these restrictions on the board's powers should not have any

11 The free play of bids and over bids, disclosure equality, transparency and integrity of the market, loyalty in transactions and competition.

12 Paris 1er Ch. April 23, 1993, JCP 1993, éd. E 1993, 457, note *A. Viandier*.

13 *See*, *PH. Conac* „Les bons Plavix et les principes généraux des offres publiques" Revue des Sociétés 2005, n° 2, p. 321.

consequences for the application of securities regulations. Courts have in a few cases implicitly established that these regulations are imperative.[14]

b) The second subsection of article 10 implementing article 9 of 2004/25/EC regards:

„Any delegation granted by the shareholders' general meeting before the bidding period, regarding measures that would be likely to make the takeover bid fail, shall be suspended." The term „any delegation" covers, under French law, delegations of competence and delegations of powers to increase the capital.

This suspension of delegation is drafted in a broader way than the one found in the Commercial Code, which provided for a suspension of delegation during the bidding period only for increases in capital that were not part of the normal activity of the company and that would be likely to make the bid fail. The suspension of delegation in the implementing bill also applies to delegations to decrease capital or to repurchase stock. It must be noted that this does not create a fundamental change. The AMF already subordinated buy-back programs to the approval of the shareholders' general meeting.

c) Third and last subsection of article 10 of the bill implementing article 9(3)

„Any decision that is not completely or partially implemented, if taken before the bidding period and likely to make the bid fail, shall be approved or confirmed by the shareholders' general meeting."

Therefore, only defences that have already been implemented or that are preventive may take effect without the intervention of the general meeting.

The legislator has chosen to implement article 9 of the Directive, but has not implemented article 11 of the Directive.

II. The choice to not implement article 11 of 2004/25/EC

The legislator has decided 1) not to carry all the provisions of article 11 into mandatory French law. However, 2) the legislator has decided that two provisions of article 11, subsections (1) and (4) will be implemented in French law.

[14] *See, A. Viandier* OPA et OPE et autres offres publiques, n° 92 and cited case.

1. First of all, the legislator has decided not to make binding the provisions of article 11 that „lead to suspend private contracts during the bidding period.“[15] This provision is contrary to French securities law and would also work against contractual agreements that enhance the stability of power and capital in a transparent manner. These agreements have to be published (art. 233-11 Commercial Code) under penalty of suspension in the event of a takeover.[16]

French companies may, however, provide in their by-laws that contractual or by-law restrictions do not apply to securities transfers or voting rights pursuant to article 12(2) of the Directive. These companies must then inform the AMF, which will in turn make their decisions public (see arts. 13, 14, 15 of the implementation bill).

2. However, article 12 of the bill, which will be codified in article 233-34 of the Commercial Code, implements two measures within the scope of article 16 of the Directive.

First measure: the suspension of assent and pre-emptive requirements in by-laws during the bidding period. The AMF's position has the effect of law.

Second measure: article 16 of the bill, which will be codified in article L. 225-125 of the Commercial Code, provides that caps on voting rights are suspended for the first general meeting following a successful bid. The Directive provides that a cap would be lifted when the offeror owns at least 75% of the capital with voting rights. Article 16 does not set any threshold, but leaves this task to the AMF.

This provision is not surprising. The COB had already established this principle in its recommendations, and as a consequence, the majority of French issuers had provided in their by-laws that caps on voting rights would be void after a successful bid. Alternatively, we could have imagined a situation in which a company that had acquired an important share of the capital with voting rights subject to a cap could neither modify the charter, remove members of the board, nor appoint new ones.

15 Article 11 provides that multiple-vote securities shall carry only one vote each during the bidding period. This measure does not apply to double-vote securities.

16 *V. Y. Guyon* Traité des Contrats, Les sociétés, Aménagements statutaires et conventions entre associés LGDJ, 5th éd. 2002 p. 312.

III. Equality among the players: the reciprocity clause in art. 12, of 2004/25/EC, implemented in art. 11 of the bill

The implementation of article 9 opens the door to a reciprocity mechanism (1). The implementation bill takes the same stand. However, the implementation of this principle provided for in the bill has been recently subjected to criticism that could have a major impact (2).

1. The implementation of the reciprocity principle

The third paragraph of article 12 of the Directive notes that „Member States may, under the conditions determined by national law, exempt companies which apply Article 9(2) and (3) and/or Article 11 from applying Article 9(2) and (3) and/or Article 11 if they become the subject of an offer launched by a company which does not apply the same Articles as they do, or by a company controlled, directly or indirectly, by the latter.“

The French legislator has implemented this provision in article 11 of the bill so that French companies are not disadvantaged vis-à-vis companies in States where the law allows the board to act during the bidding period or at least does not limit defensive measures against takeover bids. Without this provision, France would have likely been faced with the risk that French corporations would transfer their headquarters to states with more flexible rules on takeover bid defences.[17] This implementation has been drafted as follows: „The provisions in article L. 233-33 do not apply when the company is the target of one or more takeover bids made exclusively by entities which do not apply this article or equivalent measures ...“

The freedom given back to the board is not, however, unlimited. The defensive measures that the target company could implement would have to be approved by the general meeting within eighteen months before the bid (art. 11, subsection 2 of the bill, art. 12(5) of the Directive). Reciprocity then allows the implementation of defensive measures as long as they have been approved by the general meeting,[18] acting in a advance, within the above-mentioned period of time. It will not be necessary to ask for a confirmation of these meas-

17 This reciprocity clause establishes equality between companies in different countries (*see*, Rapport du Goupe d'experts de haut niveau en droit des sociétés sur des questions liées aux offres publiques d'acquisition, Bruxelles 10 janvier 2002, p. 42 to 45).

18 Marini Report, *supra* p. 88 .

ures during the bidding period.[19] Similarly, all the delegations that the general meeting grants to the management will be in effect again (increase of capital, decrease of capital, share buyback program within the limit of 10% of capital). Thus, article 11 of the implementation bill allows a target company to react quickly to the bidder.

Finally, when the principle of reciprocity applies and the conditions of the game are equal, the board will be competent to take defensive measures.

The scope of the reciprocity clause is broad. The principle of reciprocity can apply to companies whose headquarters are in a Member State or to companies whose headquarters are located outside of the European Union.[20] The principle of reciprocity will apply even when the bidding company applies article 9 or equivalent measures, if the company that controls it does not apply equivalent measures. The monitoring provided for in article 11 of the implementation bill may either be exclusive or not.

However, the principle of reciprocity as it is formulated will be a source of extreme complexity in a field where operations should be quick and the legal provisions clear.

The following remarks will illustrate this point.

First remark: the reciprocity principle applies when the offeror company does not apply article 9 or *equivalent measures*. The notion of *equivalent measures* will be difficult to interpret and may slow down takeover bids. The AMF is vested with the power to interpret the notion of *equivalent measures*.

Second remark: Applying the principle of reciprocity will be difficult when the target company is the object of opposing bids from two or more companies, one of which applies article 9 and the other of which does not.

A difficulty has already been noted with respect to the interpretation of article 11 of the implementation bill. According to the Lepetit report, the principle of reciprocity presents no dilemma for the bidder that applies article 9: „the bidder which applies article 9 cannot lose the benefit of its application and therefore could not be the subject of defensive measures.“[21] This interpretation implies a selective system of defences for the target company: a target company will have its freedom of action returned with respect to a bidder that does not apply article 9 and will stay subordinated towards a bidder that does

19 Marini Report, *supra* p. 88.
20 Marini Report, *supra* p. 82.
21 Lepetit Report, *supra* p. 18.

apply article 9 to the limits on shareholder democracy. We can measure the difficulties that will result for the target company.

Another interpretation of the application of reciprocity has been proposed by the reporter of the bill on behalf of the Senate Finance Commission.[22] According to Senator Marini, the principle of reciprocity that is part of the Directive's level playing field conditions must lead to a global application of the principle of reciprocity in the event of opposing bids under different regimes. The reporter highlights that any other interpretation „would allow potential or interested bidders, especially from the United States where the law is more favourable to management to take advantage of this broad application of reciprocity."[23] However, this argument was not heeded, and the desired modification of article 11 of the bill was not made during the approving vote of the Senate of the bill.[24] The official position today is therefore to apply the principle of reciprocity according to the actual situation of the bidder. The solution will be different when a number of bidders take concerted action.

Third remark: Article 11 of the implementing bill also provides for the application of the principle of reciprocity in the case of concerted action. However, unlike what is proposed for the case of opposing bids, the letter of the law strengthened by European legislative history has led to the conclusion that if one of the actors in the concerted action does not apply article 9, the target company can invoke reciprocity against all the actors.[25]

The implementation of the principle of reciprocity will be complex. Furthermore, in France the criticism has very recently been expressed that the implementation of the principle of reciprocity may not conform to European law.[26]

2. Uncertainties about the use of the reciprocity clause

In a recent study, two authors challenge the conformity of the French implementation of the reciprocity clause to European law in the case that Member States decide to impose articles 9 and/or 11. In scrutinizing article 12 of the

22 Marini Report, *supra* p. 85.
23 Marini Report, *supra* p. 90.
24 The Finance Commission had proposed an amendment to take out the term exclusively in the first subsection of article L 233-33 Commercial Code (article 11 bill).
25 Marini Report, *supra* p. 87.
26 *A. Pietrancosta et A. Maréchal* Transposition de la directive OPA, des incertitudes entourant le recours à la réciprocité Lexbase hebdo, n° 189, November 10, 2005.

Directive, these authors state that „the directive seems to limit the use of reciprocity to the particular situation when the companies have decided to voluntarily apply article 9, which excludes the case when the State imposes the measure.“ This statement relies on the study of the structure of the different paragraphs of article 12 of the Directive, on the 21st paragraph of the Directive, and on the note of the Portuguese delegation, which promised to come to the acceptable compromise of the Member States. Thus, these authors join the position adopted by the *Association Nationale des Sociétés par Actions* (ANSA),[27] and then state that „a strict and faithful legal reading of the European intent would consequently lead to prohibit the possibility that a national law imposing article 9 and/or 11 could be accompanied by the reciprocity clause of article 12. The implementing bill is therefore seen as legally risky. Our colleagues Alain Pietrancosta and Mrs Maréchal draw conclusions from this analysis by logically mentioning the possibility that a bidder to whom the reciprocity clause applied „could be tempted to challenge in court its conformity with European law or threaten to do so.“ At the time this text is being written it is not known whether this analysis of the European text will lead the legislator to modify the implementing bill.

B. The Implementation of the Directive and the Bidding Process

The implementation of the Directive has also consequences for the bidding process.[28] This presentation will focus on certain important points and only mention others. The first article of the bill takes into account the case in which several regulated markets in the European Union are affected by a bid, and extends the scope of the AMF's competence.

Article 4 explains the notion of concerted action in the event of a takeover bid.[29] This paper will only cover provisions regarding (I) mandatory takeover bids and the right of squeeze-out, and (II) the improvement of disclosure.

27 The ANSA is a private association established in 1930 in order to protect the interest of listed companies and their shareholders.

28 *See de H. de Vauplane*: La transposition de la directive OPA: bouleversement ou continuité? Revue Banque 2005 p. 92.

29 On concerted action after the implementation, *see de Vauplane, supra* p. 94.

I. Provisions regarding mandatory takeover bids and the right of squeeze-out

The implementing bill provides major innovations with respect to (1) the determination of a mandatory takeover bid price, and (2) the squeeze-out mechanism.

1. Mandatory takeover bid and price: art 5 of 2004/25/EC and art 2 bill

Since 1989,[30] French law has required a mandatory takeover bid to be launched when a certain threshold is reached. The launch of a takeover bid is mandatory when a person acting alone or in concert with others comes to own more than one-third of the target company's stock (art. 243-2 AMF General Regulation). The AMF General Regulation does not set any detailed criterion to determine the price that has to be offered in a mandatory takeover bid. It merely provides that the takeover bid must have terms that can be approved by the AMF (art. 231-23). Experts then use a multi-criteria analysis to determine the acceptability (*recevability*) of the offered price.[31] This analysis was mostly subjective, with the price being set according to financial criteria.[32] This resulted in many financial disputes in which the minority shareholders challenged the price set by the bidder.

Now, under article 5 of the Directive, when the threshold is reached after an acquisition, the bid must have an equitable price determined in accordance with article 5(4) of the Directive. The equitable price is the highest price paid for the same securities by the offeror or others acting with him during a six to twelve month period before the bid.

Article 2 of the bill seeks to implement this price determination provision, but the implementation is actually flawed. Under article 2, „The offered price shall be at least equal to the highest price paid by the bidder acting alone or in a concerted action [...] for a period of time set by the AMF. The AMF may ask for a modification of the offered price under the conditions and terms set by its general regulation." This implementation calls for a few remarks.

30 2 August 1989 law on financial markets' security and transparency.

31 The criteria included: value of assets, profits made, value of stock, subsidiaries, business prospects, market price of stock, and dividends distributed. *See Viandier* takeover bids, public offer of exchange.

32 *See de Vauplane, supra* note 28 at p. 92.

First remark: the bill uses the term „equitable“ price but does not limit it to the case when the threshold is reached after an acquisition.

Second remark: the bill gives the AMF discretion to determine the reference period. The AMF may also ask that the proposed price be modified under the conditions and terms set in its General Regulation.[33] The bill seems to be written in terms that are too broad when compared to the Directive. The Directive provides in its article 5(4) subsection 2 that Member States may authorize authorities to modify the set price, *but* adds „in accordance with conditions and criteria clearly defined.“

This system should succeed in avoiding uncertainties about the price and solving any disputes brought by minorities. Basically, this applies to the mechanism of standing market offers (*garantie de cours*) to takeover bids.

Unlike this provision, the squeeze-out provisions are not designed to protect minority shareholders.

2. The right of squeeze-out

The mechanism of squeeze out has up until now been governed in French law by stringent conditions provided for in article L. 433-4 of the Financial and Monetary Code and articles 237-1 to 237-17 of the AMF General Regulation. This mechanism is, however, not well accepted by minority shareholders, who consider it an expropriation of their property for private utility reasons,[34] even though is has been upheld in Court. Squeeze-outs were possible only when the majority owned at least 95% of the voting rights.

Article 15 of the Directive deals with the different cases of squeeze-out and provides in its second paragraph that „the Member States shall ensure that an offeror is able to require all the holders of the remaining securities to sell him/her those securities at a fair price“. This right of squeeze-out is only possible when the offeror owns at least 90% of the voting rights, but the Directive allows Member States to raise this to 95%.

Article 5 of the bill maintains the current threshold at 95% of the voting rights, and it considerably simplifies the right of squeeze-out. It is no longer necessary for the majority to make a withdrawal offer. The AMF General Regulation will set the conditions under which, following the closing of all takeover bids and the tendering of securities by the minority shareholders, as

33 The directive lists in article 5 the modification cases.

34 *See Ph. Merle* Sociétés commerciales, 10^{éme} éd., Dalloz n° 651-2.

long as they do not represent more than 5%, will be transferred to majority shareholders. The price will be either equal to the bid price or will be determined using the multi-criteria method. Once again, the AMF will specify the details and conditions of the compensation. The amount owed to unidentified persons is deposited in lieu of direct payment.

One remark: on the one hand, the bill reinforces the protection of the minority during a takeover bid, but on the other hand, it weakens their situation by simplifying the right of squeeze-out.

II. The improvement of disclosure

The Directive's implementation has resulted in a strengthening of disclosure obligations that are addressed to either 1) the shareholders or 2) the employees. However, when the Senate passed the bill, the legislator added a new obligation to disclose to the market, colloquially called the „Danone amendment."

1. Disclosure to shareholders, art 6 of the bill

Article 10(1) of the Directive tries to improve disclosure about capital structure. Article 6 of the bill implements this provision. The shareholders will now, independently from any bid, profit from „a periodic X-ray of the social capital structure."[35] Ten, specified disclosure elements must be laid out and presented by the board to the annual general meeting in the annual company report (art. 225-100-2C Commercial Code). Without listing the elements in detail, it is enough to say that they are elements that can serve as defences against takeover bids and are likely to influence a bid.

2. Disclosure to employees, art 7 of the bill

The bill improves disclosure to employees. French law was already a pioneer in this field. Since the law on new economic regulations adopted on May 15, 2001, the offeror of a takeover bid must inform the Works Council (*comité d'entreprise*) of the target company as soon as the bid is made. Now the offeror will also have to inform its own Works Council. This is the only change that the bill makes to current law. The direct dialogue organized by article 432-1 between the Works Council, the target company and the offeror is main-

35 *See A Pietrancosta* La directive européenne sur les offres publiques d'acquisition enfin adoptée RD bancaire et financier, sept–oct 2004 p. 341.

tained. It is up to the Works Council to decide whether they want to talk to the offeror.[36] This involvement of the Works Council in the takeover bid process may be a defensive measure against takeover bids by allying shareholder employees with the board.[37]

3. Disclosure to the market

The implementing bill was amended in the Senate to add a „Danone amendment". During the summer of 2005, French politicians were upset because rumour had it that an American company, Pepsi Co., was about to takeover Danone, the yogurt manufacturer. Thus, the bill provides that any person reasonably considering to launch a takeover bid must disclose his/her intentions to the AMF. A denial of this intention would prevent that person from being able to bid for a certain period of time. The legislator is considering a six-month period. I will conclude on this last point by quoting the French Finance minister who stated that „these new provisions bring together transparency, since a potential offeror could be obligated to disclose its intentions, and flexibility, since the AMF would be able to avoid manipulations without preventing investments."

Conclusion

The implementation of the Thirteen Directive in France will not significantly change well-established principles governing takeovers in France. French law has been developed in this area by the COB and the AMF over the last 35 years. The implementation is currently being undertaken by Parliament, but most of the Directive's detailed implementation will have to be done by the General Regulation of the AMF.

However, the implementation takes place in a context of political concern over hostile takeovers, particularly from the United States. The draft bill

36 A sanction exists in the case of a breach of employers' rights. The offeror would not be able to exercise the rights attached to the securities acquired through the takeover bid. This suspension of the voting rights is not permanent. It will end the day after the council meets.

37 *See* my article, La participation des salaries aux organes de gestion des sociétés anonymes, in Employees Codetermination in the Member States of the European Union, ZGR 2003 p. 47.

strongly reflects this concern. Unusually, the bill is being presented in Parliament well in advance of the European deadline. France has chosen to invoke the reciprocity clause. Therefore, the boards of directors of French companies will be in a better situation to fend off a hostile bid than they were before the Act. Under previous law, the board of directors could not benefit from an ex-ante authorization of the shareholders' general meeting to take defensive measures against a bidder.

Furthermore, the bill included two unexpected corporate goodies, which are the Danone amendment and a provision stating that from the publication of the Act until May 20, 2006, the board of directors was allowed to use delegations to increase capital during a takeover.[38] This temporary situation was more favourable than both the previous and the future law. It could have been very helpful for French companies during this transitional period.

Protectionism obviously seems to be finding its way in France.

38 Art. 21.

Der Anpassungsbedarf im österreichischen Übernahmerecht zur Übernahmerichtlinie

Susanne Kalss

Gliederung

I. Einleitung

1. Status Quo

Die Richtlinie betreffend Übernahmeangebote[1] war bis 20. Mai 2006 in das österreichische Recht umzusetzen. Das Übernahmerechtsänderungsgesetz 2006 trat – rückwirkend – mit diesem Tag in Kraft und stellt das österreichische Übernahmerecht auf völlig neue Grundlagen.[2]

In Österreich ist seit 1. Januar 1999 das Übernahmegesetz (ÜbG) in Kraft,[3] das um zwei Verordnungen der Übernahmekommission[4] ergänzt wurde. Das österreichische Übernahmerecht hat sich in den sechs Jahren seines Bestehens als wesentliches Element des geltenden Kapitalmarktrechts etabliert und ist in der Praxis dem Grunde nach weitestgehend anerkannt. Der unmittelbare Anlass für die relativ frühe Inkraftsetzung eines Übernahmegesetzes war die – damals überraschende und spektakuläre – Übernahme der Creditanstalt durch die Bank Austria im Jahr 1997, bei der die freien Aktionäre gegenüber dem Paketaktionär, nämlich der Republik Österreich, offensichtlich benachteiligt wurden. Das österreichische Recht normiert nicht nur Übernahmeangebote, somit Angebote zur oder aufgrund einer Kontrollerlangung (Pflichtangebot), sondern auch sonstige öffentliche Angebote, wie das Einstiegsangebot bzw das Konzernausbauangebot.[5] Der breite Anwendungsbereich kann und wird daher beibehalten werden.

In der Zeit vom 1. Januar 1999 bis November 2005 wurden 14 Pflichtangebote aufgrund eines Kontrollwechsel durchgeführt. Neben diesen Pflichtangeboten nach Kontrollerlangung wurden 7 freiwillige Übernahmeangebote gem § 22 Abs 11 ÜbG gelegt, die darauf zielten, die Kontrolle in der Gesellschaft zu erlangen (antizipatorisches Pflichtangebot, freiwilliges Vollangebot).

1 RL 2004/25/EG des Europäischen Parlaments und des Rates vom 21. 4. 2004 betreffend Übernahmeangebote; L 142/12.

2 BGBl I 75/2006. Der Beitrag beruht auf dem Stand Dezember 2005.

3 BGBl I 1998/127.

4 1. Übernahmeverordnung – 1. ÜbV, Veröffentlichungsblatt der Wiener Börse AG vom 11. 3. 1999, Veröffentlichung Nr 115; abrufbar unter: www.takeover.at; 2. Übernahmeverordnung – 2. ÜbV, Veröffentlichungsblatt der Wiener Börse AG vom 1. 3. 2000, Veröffentlichung Nr 90; abrufbar unter: http://www.takeover.at/Download/VO2.pdf.

5 S dazu nur *Gall* Angebotspflicht nach dem Übernahmegesetz, 2003, 39; *Diregger/Kalss/Winner* Das österreichische Übernahmerecht, Vier Jahre Übernahmepraxis – ein Gesamtüberblick, 2003, Rn. 16 ff.

Schließlich zeigt die Statistik 11 freiwillige einfache Angebote, bei denen entweder der Bieter bereits die Gesellschaft kontrolliert und eine weitere Maßnahme vorbereitet oder das Angebot gerade nicht zur Kontrolle führen soll, wie bei einem Aktienrückerwerb (zB Baumax).[6] Das volumenmäßig weitaus größte Angebot war jenes der Unicredit an die Aktionäre der BA-CA im Sommer 2005 (Angebotsvolumen von über 2,5 Mrd €), mit deutlichem Abstand gefolgt von der Übernahme der Austria Tabak durch das britische Unternehmen Gallaher und der VA-Tech durch Siemens.[7]

In der Zeit vom 1. Januar 1999 bis November 2005 hatte die Übernahmekommission insgesamt 32 Angebotsverfahren durchzuführen, 48 Verfahren beschäftigten sich mit der Ausnahmegewährung von einer Übernahme trotz Kontrollerlangung (insbesondere Verschiebung in einem Syndikat oder im Konzern); schließlich führte die Übernahmekommission 36 sonstige Verfahren durch, in denen sie sich mit verschiedenen Einzelfragen, wie etwa mit der Verkürzung der Sperrfrist (in dem Fall VA-Tech – Siemens), auseinandergesetzt hat.

Wie bereits ausgeführt war die Übernahmekommission während dieser 6 Jahre am häufigsten damit beschäftigt, Ausnahmen von der Verpflichtung ein Angebot zu stellen, zu gewähren. Davon hatten wiederum 33 Verfahren die Frage von Syndikatsgestaltungen zum Gegenstand, in 8 Verfahren hatte sich die Übernahmekommission mit Sanierungen zu beschäftigen, dreimal lag der Übernahmekommission die Frage vor, ob bei einem nachfolgenden Squeezeout vorher noch ein Pflichtangebot abgegeben werden müsse. Die Übernahmekommission gewährte dreimal eine Ausnahme bei einem unbeabsichtigten geringfügigen oder kurzfristigen Überschreiten der maßgeblichen Schwelle und schließlich fielen zwei mittelbare Kontrollwechsel in die Ausnahmebestimmung von § 25 ÜbG, weil das Volumen im Verhältnis zum unmittelbaren Kontrollwechsel relativ gering war.[8]

2. Aktuelle rechtspolitische Diskussion

Selbst wenn das Übernahmerecht im Gesamten durchaus anerkannt ist und seine Zwecke, nämlich die Gleichbehandlung aller Aktionäre auf dem Kapi-

6 Die Zahlen stammen von *Gall* Vortrag zum Thema „Stand und Entwicklung des österreichischen Übernahmerechts„ am Jahreskongress Wirtschaftsrecht des Instituts für Bürgerliches Recht, Handels- und Wertpapierrecht der Wirtschaftsuniversität Wien am 22. 9. 2005 in Retz (Niederösterreich); Dr *Mario Gall* ist Leiter der Geschäftsstelle der Übernahmekommission; die Zahlen änderten sich seither nicht.

7 Vgl *Gall* ortrag Jahreskongress Wirtschaftsrecht 2005.

8 Vgl *Gall* Vortrag Jahreskongress Wirtschaftsrecht 2005.

talmarkt sowie die Schaffung eines angemessenen Konzerneingangsschutzes, von Wirtschaft und Praxis akzeptiert werden, entwickelte sich während der letzten 12 Monate – ausgelöst durch drei große Fälle, die von der Übernahmekommission zu behandeln waren, nämlich Böhler Uddeholm – Fries-Gruppe,[9] VA-Tech – Siemens[10] und BA-CA – Unicredit[11] – eine grundlegende rechtspolitische Diskussion über die künftige Gestaltung des österreichischen Übernahmerechts. Ursprünglich wurde diese Diskussion vollkommen losgelöst von der Notwendigkeit der Anpassung an die Übernahmerichtlinie geführt. Anfänglich waren betroffene Gesellschaften bzw maßgebliche Emittenten sowie Aktionäre die Träger dieser rechtspolitischen Diskussion, ehe sie vor allem von der Industriellenvereinigung und von der Wirtschaftskammer übernommen wurde.

3. Konkretes Prozedere der gesetzlichen Änderung

Zu Beginn des Jahres 2005 legte die Industriellenvereinigung auf der Grundlage eines Expertengutachtens[12] konkrete Reformvorschläge vor, die vor allem darauf abzielten, das geltende österreichische Übernahmerecht zugunsten von Paketaktionären rückzubauen (vgl sogleich unten bei III). Im Frühjahr 2005 setzte das Bundesministerium für Justiz eine Arbeitsgruppe ein, der neben Vertretern des Ministeriums auch Repräsentanten des Bundesministeriums für Finanzen sowie des Bundesministeriums für Wirtschaft und Arbeit angehören, zudem einige Sachverständige sowie Vertreter von Interessenvertretungen (Industriellenvereinigung, Wirtschaftskammer, Arbeiterkammer) und von kapitalmarktbezogenen Einrichtungen (Übernahmekommission, Finanzmarktaufsicht [FMA]), Kapitalmarktbeauftragter der Republik Österreich). In diesem Rahmen werden nunmehr die rechtspolitischen Vorschläge, die vom Bundesministerium für Justiz bzw einem kleinen Redaktionsteam, das aus Sachverständigen und Vertretern des Bundesministeriums besteht, erarbeitet werden, diskutiert. Im Oktober wurde bereits ein erster Arbeitsentwurf präsentiert und einer ersten internen Diskussion zugänglich gemacht. Im Dezember 2005 ist ein Ministerialentwurf des Bundesministeriums für Justiz zu erwarten, der nach einem Begutachtungsverfahren, bei dem alle Interessierten die Gelegenheit erhalten werden, zu den rechtspoliti-

9 GZ 2004/1/9-112.
10 GZ 2004/3/11-241.
11 Angebotsunterlage vom 26. 8. 2005, abrufbar unter: www.takeover.at.
12 *Jud* Thesen zur Reformdiskussion im österreichischen Übernahmerecht, 2005.

schen Änderungen Stellung zu nehmen, in die Regierungsvorlage mündete, ehe nach weiteren Modifikationen das Gesetz beschlossen wurde.

Der Anpassungsprozess an die Richtlinie ist somit in Österreich nicht Anstoß für die notwendige Änderung des österreichischen Übernahmerechts, sondern vielmehr hat er bremsende Funktion, um schlicht anlassbezogene, rechtspolitische, noch nicht ausgegorene Vorschläge[13] noch einmal zu überdenken und in ein ausgereiftes Gesamtgefüge einzubetten. Das rechtspolitische Anliegen der Novelle zum Übernahmegesetz ist daher ein Dreifaches:

- Umsetzung der Übernahmerichtlinie bis Mai 2006
- Umsetzung der praktischen Erfahrungen mit 7 Jahren Übernahmegesetz
- Umsetzung der rechtspolitischen Forderungen und Grundsatzdiskussion zu zentralen Fragen des Übernahmerechts.

Der notwendige Anpassungsbedarf des österreichischen geltenden Übernahmerechts an die Anforderungen der Richtlinie und die rechtspolitische Grundsatzdiskussion sind nicht deckungsgleich. Zwar bewegt sich die rechtspolitische Grundsatzdiskussion im Rahmen der Regelungen der Richtlinie, die Richtlinie selbst sieht dafür aber keine Vorgaben oder zwingende Regelungen vor.

II. Maßgebliche Grundsatzfragen des österreichischen Übernahmerechts

1. Drei leading cases

Die rechtspolitische Grundsatzdiskussion wurde durch drei Fälle, die die Übernahmekommission intensiv beschäftigten, ausgelöst:

- Böhler Uddeholm – Fries-Gruppe
- VA-Tech – Siemens
- BA-CA – Unicredit

13 S die Kritik bei *Kalss* Übernahmerecht light? Der Standard vom 21. 12. 2004.

a) Böhler-Uddeholm – Fries-Gruppe

An der Böhler Uddeholm AG hatte bis vor kurzem die ÖIAG (österreichische Industrieaktiengesellschaft) noch einen bedeutenden Anteil inne, nämlich 25% der Aktien. Die ÖIAG steht im 100%-igen Eigentum der Republik Österreich, dieser Anteil sollte im Rahmen des Privatisierungsvorhabens veräußert werden. Über verschiedene Gesellschaften baute eine Investorengruppe (= Fries-Gruppe) eine Beteiligung auf, die ein Ausmaß von 25,65% erreicht. Kurz danach vollzog die ÖIAG die Privatisierung, indem sie ihre Anteile über die Börse verkaufte. Nach der Privatisierung verfügte die Fries-Gruppe über eine Beteiligung von 25,65% der Anteile, 70,15% stehen im Streubesitz und schließlich hat die Gesellschaft den Rest der Aktien zurückgekauft. Der Stimmrechtsanteil der Fries-Gruppe wurde daher um rund einen Prozentpunkt höher. Die Fries-Gruppe war somit durch den Verkauf der ÖIAG-Anteile zum deutlich größten Aktionär in der Böhler Uddeholm AG geworden.[14] Im Aufsichtsrat der Gesellschaft waren Vertreter der Fries-Gruppe entsprechend ihrer Beteiligung repräsentiert. Die maßgeblichen Fragen waren, ob ein Aktionär mit einer Beteiligung von 25,65% am Kapital bzw 26,76% der Stimmrechte (wegen der eigenen Aktien der Böhler Uddeholm AG) eine Kontrolle über die Gesellschaft erlangt hat sowie ob das passive Erlangen der Kontrolle ebenso die Abgabe des Pflichtangebots auslöst wie ein aktiver Anteilserwerb, schließlich die Frage der Gestaltung des Verfahrens vor der Übernahmekommission. Die Causa ist nicht abgeschlossen, die zweite Frage ist nunmehr vor dem Verfassungsgerichtshof anhängig.

b) VA-Tech – Siemens

An der VA-Tech AG[15] war die Victory Industrie Beteiligungs- AG, hinter der der Industrielle Mirco Kovacs steht, mit Anteilen von 16% bis 19% beteiligt. Aufgrund der besonderen Konstellation – etwa des Bestehens eines Höchststimmrechts bei 25% – war nicht klar, ob damit schon eine kontrollierende Beteiligung bestanden hatte. Nach einem ersten fehlgeschlagenen Versuch übernahm Siemens das Paket von der Victory Industrie Beteiligungs- AG und legte im Anschluss ein Übernahmeangebot, im Zuge dessen auch die ÖIAG ihre Aktien (14,7%) an Siemens übertrug. Die VA-Tech stellte sich gegen die Übernahme, sodass vom ersten „nicht freundlichen„ Angebot in Österreich gesprochen werden kann. Die Übernahme wurde ursprünglich an die Abschaffung des Höchststimmrechts geknüpft, diese Bedingung wurde aber

14 ÜbK GZ 2004/1/9-112.

15 ÜbK GZ 2004/3/11-241.

wegen Fehlschlagens in der Hauptversammlung aufgegeben. Abgesehen von einigen eher „technischen„ Fragen lag die entscheidende Rechtsfrage darin, wann die Kontrollerlangung bzw der Kontrollwechsel gegeben ist, schließlich die Erlangung der Kontrolle im Rahmen eines Übernahmeangebots.

c) BA-CA – Unicredit

Der Fall BA-CA – Unicredit stellt den österreichischen Arm der transeuropäischen Übernahme der HVB-Gruppe[16] durch Unicredit mit Sitz in Mailand dar. Da die BA-CA eine Tochtergesellschaft der HVB ist, hätte die Übernahme der HVB durch Unicredit nachfolgend zu einem Pflichtangebot in Österreich gegenüber den BA-CA-Aktionären geführt. Um eine derartige Kaskade zu vermeiden, wurden parallel in Deutschland und in Österreich je ein freiwilliges Übernahmeangebot gestellt. Während nach deutschem Recht die Abgabe eines Tauschangebots auch bei freiwilligen Vollangeboten bzw Pflichtangeboten zulässig ist, gestattet das österreichische Recht gem § 22 und § 26 ÜbG für das Pflichtangebot bzw das freiwillige Übernahmenangebot kein alleiniges Tauschangebot, sondern sieht verpflichtend ein Barangebot vor. Neben der dogmatisch schwierigen Frage der Ermittlung des Preises bei einem mittelbaren parallelen Kontrollerwerb, nämlich der HVB-Aktien durch die Unicredit bei gleichzeitigem Angebot an die BA-CA-Aktionäre, stand die rechtspolitische Frage im Zentrum, ob neben dem Barangebot gleichwertig auch ein Tauschangebot für Pflichtangebote bzw freiwillige Übernahmeangebote zulässig sein soll.

2. Zentrale rechtspolitische Fragen

Die zentralen Fragen im Rahmen der rechtspolitischen Diskussion zur Neugestaltung des Übernahmerechts lassen sich vor allem als Ausfluss der grundlegenden rechtspolitischen Diskussion einerseits sowie als Notwendigkeit der Anpassung des österreichischen Rechts an die Richtlinien zusammenführen, wobei in der Gewichtung der Diskussion derzeit vor allem die aus den drei Übernahmen entstammenden zentralen Fragen dominieren.

(a) Zentrale rechtspolitische Grundsatzfragen

(1) Neugestaltung des Kontrollbegriffs:
- materieller versus formeller Kontrollbegriff;

16 Vgl das Angebot der Unicredit, abrufbar unter www.takeover.at.

- Gestaltung der materiellen Ausnahmebestimmungen – Fassung klarer Regelungen;

(2) Art der Kontrollerlangung: aktive oder auch passive Kontrollerlangung;

(3) Gegenleistung für Pflicht- und Übernahmeangebot, Tauschangebot als gleichwertige Alternative;

(4) Neugestaltung der Rechtsdurchsetzung;

(5) Zentrale Fragen der Umsetzung der Richtlinie;

(6) Neutralitätsgebot;

(7) Durchbrechungsregelungen bei einer Kontrollerlangung;

(8) Squeeze-out Regelungen;

3. Sonstiger notwendiger Anpassungsbedarf nach den Vorgaben der Richtlinie

Betrachtet man die österreichische Rechtslage im Lichte der Vorgaben der Übernahmerichtlinien, so zeigt sich, dass allein daraus ein relativ geringer Anpassungsbedarf in maßgeblichen Fragen besteht.

Bevor auf die zentralen Fragen der rechtspolitischen Diskussion eingegangen werden soll, sei auf einige – kleinere – Rechtsfragen hingewiesen, die für den Anwendungsbereich des österreichischen Übernahmerechts im Verhältnis zur Richtlinie eine nicht zu vernachlässigende Rolle spielen. Beispiele sind der Begriff der Beteiligungspapiere, die Einbeziehung des Rückerwerbs eigener Aktien in das Übernahmerecht sowie die Umschreibung der gemeinsam vorgehenden Rechtsträger. Zu ändern sind zusätzlich technische Feinheiten, wie die Dauer des Angebots, die Gestaltung der Zusicherung der Finanzierbarkeit und schließlich die Betonung der zeitgerechten und sachlich fundierten Information der Arbeitnehmer der Gesellschaft.

III. Die Neuregelung des Kontrollbegriffs

1. Richtlinienrechtliche Vorgabe

Die Richtlinie geht in Art 5 Abs 3 von einer Kontrollschwelle aus. Sie lässt den prozentualen Anteil der Stimmrechte, der eine Kontrolle begründet und die Art der Berechnung dieses Anteils den Mitgliedstaat bestimmen, in dem die Gesellschaft ihren Sitz hat. Zwar ist damit implizit von der Richtlinie angeordnet, dass jedenfalls eine Kontrollschwelle durch den Mitgliedstaat festzulegen ist, dennoch legt die Richtlinie eine tatsächliche Kontrollschwelle europaweit gerade nicht fest. Vielmehr formuliert Art 5 Abs 1, dass ein die Kontrolle begründender Anteil der maßgebliche Anknüpfungspunkt ist und überlässt dessen Festlegung den Mitgliedstaaten. Abgesehen von einer Schwelle, die zu normieren ist, heißt dies umgekehrt auch, dass die Richtlinie offen dafür ist, zusätzliche Kriterien zu bestimmen, um den die Kontrolle begründenden Anteil festzulegen. Grundsätzlich ist daher davon auszugehen, dass die Richtlinie nicht zwingend einen formalen Kontrollbegriff verlangt, sondern einen Spielraum für eine materielle Umschreibung der Kontrolle bietet. Die Frage ist somit an den nationalen Gesetzgeber verwiesen, der die rechtspolitische Entscheidung zu treffen hat, ob er sich mit einer formalen Schwelle begnügt oder materielle Kriterien festlegen will.

2. Geltendes österreichisches Recht

Die zentrale Frage der laufenden rechtspolitischen Diskussion stellt die Neuformulierung des Kontrollbegriffs im österreichischen Übernahmerecht dar. Nach dem geltenden österreichischen Recht besteht ein relativ komplexer, zugleich aber auch flexibler, materieller Kontrollbegriff, der maßgeblich auf den Einfluss oder zumindest die Möglichkeit der Einflussnahme abstellt.[17] Dem österreichischen Übernahmegesetz liegt eine Kombination aus qualitativen und quantitativen Kriterien zur Festlegung der Kontrolle zugrunde, bei der auch abseits von widerleglichen und unwiderleglichen Kontrollvermutungen das Bestehen eines beherrschenden Einflusses möglich ist. Gem § 22 Abs 4 ÜbG und § 1 der 1. ÜbV liegt eine unwiderlegliche Kontrollvermutung vor, wenn einer der handelsrechtlichen Control-Tatbestände gem § 244 Abs 2

17 *Huber/Löber* Kommentar zum ÜbG (1999) § 22 Rn. 14ff; *Diregger/Kalss/Winner* Übernahmerecht Rn. 123ff; *Kalss/Oppitz/Zollner* Kapitalmarktrecht § 23 Rn. 118ff.

HGB verwirklicht wird.[18] Eine unwiderlegliche Kontrolle liegt daher vor, wenn ein Bieter über die Mehrheit der Stimmrechte verfügt oder wenn dem Bieter das Recht zusteht, die Mehrheit der Verwaltungsorgane der Zielgesellschaft zu bestellen und/oder abzuberufen und er gleichzeitig Gesellschafter dieser Gesellschaft ist oder wenn er das Recht hat, einen beherrschenden Einfluss auszuüben. Eine kontrollierende Beteiligung ist zu vermuten, wenn der Bieter allein oder gemeinsam mit dem ihm gem § 23 Abs 1 ÜbG zuzurechnenden Rechtsträger über 30% der auf das ständig stimmberechtigte Kapital entfallenden Stimmrechte verfügt. Diese Vermutung kann aber durch den Nachweis widerlegt werden,[19] dass ein anderer Aktionär allein oder gemeinsam mit anderen hinzuzurechnenden Rechtsträgern über zumindest gleich viele Stimmrechte wie der betroffene Aktionär verfügt (§ 2 Abs 2 der 1. ÜbV). Eine weitere widerlegliche Vermutung sehen das Gesetz und § 3 Abs 1 der 1. ÜbV bei einer Beteiligung vor, die zwischen 20 und 30% liegt: Danach gilt ein Aktionär, der über Anteile im Ausmaß von 20%, aber nicht mehr als 30% der auf die ständig stimmberechtigten Aktien entfallenden Stimmrechte verfügt als Inhaber einer kontrollierenden Beteiligung, wenn diese Beteiligung in den letzten drei abgehaltenen ordentlichen Hauptversammlungen jeweils die Mehrheit der anwesenden Stimmen dargestellt hätte. Diese Vermutung kann dadurch widerlegt werden, dass andere Aktionäre im Ausmaß von 10% oder 3 Aktionäre im Ausmaß von 5% vorhanden sind oder jedenfalls ein größerer Aktionär in der Gesellschaft besteht. Zudem ist auch eine sonstige Widerlegung zulässig, etwa dass überhaupt keine Einflussnahme auf Organebene besteht.[20] Gem § 27 Abs 1 Z 1 ÜbG iVm § 22 Abs 5 ÜbG kann die Kontrollschwelle durch Satzungsbestimmung auf bis zu 20% herabgesetzt werden. Auch diese Schwelle ist aber widerleglicher Natur, sodass sie – ebenso wie die anderen Kontrollvermutungen – widerlegt werden kann.[21]

Darüber hinaus ist es nach ganz hL anerkannt, dass diese Regelung der Kontrollvermutungen nicht abschließend ist, sondern auch abseits der Kontrollvermutungen ein beherrschender Einfluss bestehen kann. Dabei ist vor allem an besonders heikle Situationen zu denken, bei denen ein Bieter Anteile von nicht einmal 20% inne hat, aber über zusätzliche Einflussrechte verfügt (Entsendungsrechte in den Aufsichtrat, Nominierungsrechte), die einen be-

18 ErlBem zur Regierungsvorlage des ÜbG 1276 BlgNR 20.GP 39.

19 S dazu im einzelnen *Zollner* Kontrollwechsel und Kontrollerlangung im Übernahmegesetz, 2002, 202ff.

20 *Kalss/Oppitz/Zollner* Kapitalmarktrecht § 23 Rn. 122; *Zollner*, Kontrollwechsel 215f.

21 *Diregger/Kalss/Winner* Übernahmerecht Rn. 129; *Kalss/Oppitz/Zollner* Kapitalmarktrecht § 23 Rn. 123.

herrschenden Einfluss etablieren. Auch in einem derartigen Fall kann der übernahmerechtliche Kontrollbegriff verwirklicht werden.[22]

3. Rechtspolitische Diskussion

Aufgrund der Anlassfälle Böhler Uddeholm – Fries-Gruppe und VA-Tech – Siemens brach die rechtspolitische Diskussion um die Neugestaltung des Kontrollbegriffs auf.[23] Von Seiten der Wirtschaft in Gestalt der Industriellenvereinigung wurde der materielle Kontrollbegriff massiv in Frage gestellt und dessen ersatzlose Streichung und Ersetzung durch eine formale Kontrollschwelle von 30% verlangt.[24] Als maßgebliche Argumente[25] für die Etablierung eines quantitativen Kontrollbegriffs einerseits und der Festlegung der 30%-Schwelle sprechen vor allem (i) die Rechtssicherheit und (ii) die Plan- und Vorhersehbarkeit für die Marktteilnehmer, die auf dem sensiblen und Rechtssicherheit verlangenden Kapitalmarkt unbedingt erforderlich ist. Ein quantitativer, nur auf Stimmrechtsschwellen abstellender Kontrollbegriff habe umgekehrt den Vorteil, dass er die für den Kapitalmarkt notwendige Transparenz schafft. (iii) Aufgrund der offen formulierten Vermutungen und der Möglichkeiten der Widerlegung, vor allem aber auch wegen des allgemeinen Generaltatbestands der Beherrschungsmöglichkeit erlange die Übernahmekommission eine unverhältnismäßig große Einflussposition bzw Machtstellung bei der Beurteilung, ob die Kontrolle tatsächlich vorliegt oder nicht. Bieter und Zielgesellschaft haben daher insofern keine gesicherte Entscheidungsgrundlage, umgekehrt laufen sie Gefahr, dass sie bei Nichtabgabe eines Pflichtangebots trotz Erfüllung des materiellen Kontrolltatbestands mit Verwaltungsstrafen belegt werden bzw ihre Stimmrechte gem § 34 ÜbG ruhen. (iv) Die Übernahmekommission entscheide grundsätzlich als einzige Instanz. Ein ordentliches Rechtsmittel ist gegen ihre Entscheidungen nicht vorgesehen, dem betroffenen Gesellschaftern bzw Bietern steht jeweils nur die Beschwerde an den Verfassungsgerichtshof offen.[26] (v) Die Festlegung eines ma-

22 *Kalss/Oppitz/Zollner* Kapitalmarktrecht § 23 Rn. 124; *Diregger/Kalss/Winner* Übernahmerecht Rn. 124.

23 S nur ÜbK, Presseaussendung Wirtschaftsblatt online vom 8. 11. 2005; *Hügel* Aktien statt Bargeld: Gefahr für Börse Wien, Der Standard, 8. 3. 2005.

24 Vgl *Jud* Thesen zur Reformdiskussion im österreichischen Übernahmerecht, 2005.

25 S etwa *Fichtinger* Tageszeitungen haben hochstilisiert, Wirtschaftsblatt Online 11. 11. 2005; *Fichtinger* Übernahmegesetz neu: Für mehr Rechtssicherheit, Börsekurier, 17. 11. 2005.

26 *Kalss/Oppitz/Zollner* Kapitalmarktrecht § 23 Rn. 192.

teriellen Kontrollbegriffs verlangt zudem die Gewährung von Ausnahmebestimmungen, um die Kontrollfälle, bei denen nur eine geringfügige Änderung bzw ein vorübergehendes Erlangen oder eine Verschiebung innerhalb einer Gruppe vorgenommen wird, nicht mit den allgemeinen Rechtsfolgen, nämlich der Veranlassung eines Pflichtangebots, zu belegen. Um dem qualitativen Kontrollbegriff entsprechend sachgerechte Ausnahmebestimmungen festlegen zu können, sind diese ihrerseits wieder als materielle Tatbestände zu fassen, was bei deren Beurteilung wiederum einen weiten Entscheidungsspielraum der Übernahmekommission öffnet. Die Kontrollvermutungen und Ausnahmetatbestände legen dem Bieter jeweils die Beweislast auf, sich von der Vermutung frei zu beweisen und dies der Übernahmekommission gegenüber deutlich zu machen, insofern wird die Position des Bieters gegenüber der Übernahmekommission verschlechtert. (vi) Im internationalen – jedenfalls europäischen – Vergleich werden überwiegend formale Stimmrechtsschwellen als kontrollbegründende Anknüpfungspunkte festgelegt; daher sei es aus der Vergleichssituation geboten, auch in Österreich eine formelle Kontrollschwelle festzulegen. (vii) Letztlich sollen *österreichische* Kernaktionärsstrukturen gefördert werden, um die positiven Folgewirkungen österreichischer Eigentümer für Unternehmen mit einem heimischen Standort zu sichern.

Auf den ersten Blick könnte man meinen, dass die Übernahmekommission als vollziehende Behörde einen formalen Kontrollbegriff befürworten müsste, würde doch auch ihr die Rechtssicherheit bei den Entscheidungen zugute kommen und hätte sie klare und einfach handhabbare und vollziehbare Regelungen. Die Übernahmekommission, die ein maßgeblicher Verfechter des materiellen Kontrollbegriffs ist, erkennt und anerkennt zwar durchaus den Vorteil der einfachen Vollziehbarkeit einer Regelung, weist aber umgekehrt in der Diskussion auf die Schwächen eines formalen Kontrollbegriffs deutlich hin. Insbesondere wird die Notwendigkeit eines eigenständig gestalteten Kontrollbegriffs aufgrund der Besonderheiten der österreichischen realen wirtschaftlichen Situation herausgearbeitet. Folgende Argumente[27] lassen sich für einen materiellen Kontrollbegriff anführen: (i) Auszugehen ist vom eigentlichen Zweck des Übernahmerechts,[28] nämlich die Gleichberechtigung der Marktteilnehmer sicherzustellen und (ii) bei einer Kontrollerlangung bzw einem Kontrollwechsel den Anlegern die Ausstiegsmöglichkeit zu gewähren, damit sie nicht unfreiwillig einem neuen kontrollierenden Aktionär gegen-

27 Vgl schon *Kalss* Der Standard vom 21. 12. 2004.

28 ÜbK, Presseaussendung Wirtschaftsblatt online vom 8. 11. 2005, abrufbar unter www.takeover.at.

überstehen. Bei einer schlichten Festlegung eines quantitativen Kontrollbegriffs würde vielfach trotz eines realen Kontrollerwerbs ein Pflichtangebot nicht unbedingt abgegeben werden müssen. (iii) Gerade in den Fällen, in denen die Kontrolle nicht durch einen unmittelbaren Erwerb erlangt wird, sondern durch Umgestaltung auf übergeordneter Ebene, ist eine formale Kontrollschwelle allein kein taugliches Instrument, den übernahmerechtlichen Kontrollbegriff festzulegen. So können etwa Verschiebungen innerhalb eines beherrschenden Syndikats mit oder ohne formaler Änderung des Syndikatsvertrags ebenso wenig bewältigt werden wie die Kontrollerlangung oder Einflussgewichtung über eine Privatstiftung bzw die nachfolgende Änderung von Einflussverhältnissen in der Privatstiftung.

Bei einem indirekten Kontrollerwerb durch den Kauf von Geschäftsanteilen einer – naturgemäß nicht börsenotierten – GmbH, die ihrerseits die Kontrolle über eine börsenotierte Gesellschaft hält oder Verschiebungen innerhalb einer Holding GmbH greift der formale Kontrollbegriff nicht. Schließlich sind Fälle denkbar, dass eine Beteiligung an einem ausländischen Rechtsträger erworben wird, der wiederum die Kontrolle über die börsenotierte Zielgesellschaft hält.

Betrachtet man den mehrfach in die Diskussion gebrachten Schwellenwert von 30%, so sprechen insbesondere folgende Argumente gegen die Festlegung dieses Werts: Echte Publikumsgesellschaften sind in Österreich rar. Überwiegend werden – auch – börsenotierte Gesellschaften von einem oder einer syndizierten Gruppe von Gesellschaften dominiert und ist der Streubesitz tendenziell relativ gering. Nur in einigen wenigen Gesellschaften sind die Aktien mehrheitlich im Streubesitz oder liegt er zumindest bei der Hälfte des Kapitals. Im Durchschnitt liegt die Präsenz des Streubesitzes bei Hauptversammlungen (relative Anwesenheit) in Österreich bei Gesellschaften des Prime Markets der Wiener Börse bei rund 12,5%, bei den Gesellschaften des ATX insgesamt bei rund 15,5%. In England liegt die durchschnittliche Hauptversammlungspräsenz hingegen bei über 50% des stimmberechtigten Kapitals.

Kombiniert man nun die typische Gestaltung der Gesellschaften mit einem dominierenden Aktionär mit der geringen Hauptversammlungspräsenz des Streubesitzes, so zeigt sich, dass ein Kernaktionär mit mehr als 20%, aber deutlich weniger als 30% in fast allen Hauptversammlungen die einfache Mehrheit hat, womit er früher oder später den Aufsichtsrat allein besetzen kann. Verfügt er etwa über 29%, so hat er auch eine sichere qualifizierte Mehrheit. Dies bedeutet, dass es einem Aktionär mit einem Anteil von 20–30% in Österreich ungleich leichter möglich ist, die Gesellschaft zu beherrschen als in vergleichbaren ausländischen Rechtsordnungen, da dort der Anteil des Streubesitzes generell höher ist und zudem der Streubesitz typischerweise stärker in der Hauptversammlung vertreten ist. In England kann ein Aktionär, der weniger als 30% der Anteile hält, typischerweise die Gesellschaft nicht kontrollieren, sodass die 30%-Schwelle in England auch eine passende Grenze darstellt,[29] die nicht mechanisch in das österreichische Recht übernommen werden kann. Bei einer Kontrollschwelle von 30% wäre die Übernahme der faktischen Beherrschung der meisten österreichischen Gesellschaften möglich, ohne den Mitaktionären aber das übernahmerechtliche Instrument des Pflichtangebots bzw der Ausstiegsmöglichkeit einräumen zu müssen. Damit würde der maßgebliche Zweck des Übernahmerechts, nämlich die Gleichbehandlung der Marktteilnehmer zu sichern sowie den Ausstieg der Aktionäre bei einem Kontrollwechsel zu ermöglichen, vereitelt werden.

Naturgemäß müssen auch bei Vorliegen von Kontrolltatbeständen Möglichkeiten bestehen, diesen Kontrollbestand einerseits vollkommen zu widerlegen, andererseits von der Hauptrechtsfolge der Erlangung der Kontrolle, nämlich der Abgabe des Pflichtangebots abzusehen und eine Ausnahmebestimmung zu gewähren. Genau dies geschieht im österreichischen Recht; gem § 24 ÜbG bestehen Legalausnahmen; gem § 25 ÜbG kann die Übernahmekommission auf Antrag des Bieters eine Ausnahme von der Angebotspflicht gewähren, die dabei zu einer Anzeigepflicht mutiert. Die Anzeigeverfahren gem § 25 ÜbG machen demgemäß auch einen Großteil der Arbeit der Übernahmekommission aus. Bisher wurden 48 Verfahren im Rahmen der Gewährung von Ausnahmen gem § 25 ÜbG durchgeführt.[30]

Die Negierung der Ausstiegsmöglichkeit führt umgekehrt zu einer deutlichen Anhebung des Schutzes und zugleich zu einer Privilegierung des verkaufswilligen Paketaktionärs, zumal dieser ohne weiteres seine Aktien bis zu 30% verkaufen kann, ohne dass ein Pflichtangebot ausgelöst wird, womit er einen deutlich höheren Preis allein für sich erzielen kann, muss doch dieser Preis nicht mit allen anderen Aktionären geteilt werden. Damit stellt sich eine starre Kontrollschwelle von 30% als verlässlicher Schutz von verkaufswilligen Paketaktionären dar, unabhängig davon, ob diese österreichischer oder ausländischer Provenienz sind. Allein eine Schutzstellung österreichischer Kernaktionäre ist damit nicht erreicht, naturgemäß werden auch Aktienpakete in der Hand ausländischer Investoren dem gleichen Schutzinstrumentarium unterworfen. Zudem besteht kein weiterer Anreiz bzw Schutzmechanismus, der

29 So ausdrücklich auch *Rickford* in der Diskussion.
30 *Gall* Vortrag Jahreskongress Wirtschaftsrecht 2005.

verhindert, dass österreichische Paketaktionäre an ausländische Interessenten verkaufen. Es kann nicht sichergestellt werden, dass private österreichische Paketaktionäre jedenfalls dauerhaft das Paket halten, ihnen kann durch gesetzliche Regelung nicht untersagt werden, die Aktien nicht doch an ausländische Interessenten zu veräußern. Wenn der Preis „stimmt„ und die Marktlage dementsprechend ist, wird sich kein österreichischer Aktionär einer derartigen Möglichkeit endgültig entziehen können. Die einseitige Schutzausrichtung zugunsten der Paketaktionäre könnte auch zu einem Verlust in das Vertrauen des österreichischen Kapitalmarkts bzw der kapitalsuchenden, somit emittierenden österreichischen Gesellschaften führen. Die internationalen Investoren haben im Vertrauen auf ein bestehendes und funktionierendes Übernahmerecht investiert, nämlich mit dem Wissen, bei einem Kontrollwechsel bar aus der Gesellschaft aussteigen zu können. Wird nunmehr das Pflichtangebot durch diese starre 30%-Schwelle praktisch unterlaufen, wird auch die ehemalige Erwartungshaltung der sicheren Ausstiegsmöglichkeit untergraben, womit das Vertrauen in den österreichischen Kapitalmarkt auf funktionierende Regelungen unterminiert wird. Werden somit auf der einen Seite verkaufswillige Paketaktionäre geschützt und privilegiert, so wird diese Besserstellung der Kernaktionäre auf dem Rücken der freien Aktionäre, insbesondere der institutionellen Aktionäre, ausgeführt. Eine derartige Regelung könnte auch an verfassungsrechtliche Grenzen stoßen.

Die Richtlinie verlangt, dass bei typischer Betrachtung die maßgebliche Fälle des Kontrollwechsels in einem Land erfasst werden. Da in Österreich mit der 30%-Schwelle die typischen Fälle der Kontrollerlangung angesichts der realen wirtschaftlichen Situation gerade nicht erfasst werden können, würde somit durch eine derartige Regelung die Festlegung der Kontrolle iSv Art 5 Abs 3 iVm Art 5 Abs 1 innerstaatlich gerade nicht geleistet werden. Schließlich lässt sich nicht pauschal und mechanisch auf internationale Regelungsvorbilder verweisen, vielmehr ist das typische wirtschaftliche und politisch soziologische Umfeld bei einem Rechtsvergleich mit einzubeziehen.[31]

Den Argumenten der Rechtsicherheit muss somit jenes der Zielgerichtetheit des gesetzgeberischen Anliegens, bei einem Kontrollwechsel tatsächlich eine Ausstiegsmöglichkeit zu gewährleisten, gegenüber gestellt werden. Mit einem materiellen Kontrollbegriff wird Gewähr dafür geboten, dass die Kontrollsituation im konkreten Einzelfall beurteilt und auf die konkreten Ein-

31 S dazu bezogen auf das Gesellschaftsrecht *Kalss/Burger/Eckert* Die Entwicklung des österreichischen Aktienrechts. Geschichte und Materialien, 2003, 25; allg. *Zweigert/Kötz* Einführung in die Rechtsvergleichung³, 1996, 33f.

flussmöglichkeiten in sachgerechter Weise eingegangen werden kann, selbst wenn damit zumindest temporäre Unsicherheiten bestehen. In absehbarer Zeit wird sich zudem eine gefestigte Spruchpraxis der Übernahmekommission herausbilden, die die Vorhersehbarkeit steigert, was allerdings die lückenlose Veröffentlichung der Entscheidungen verlangt. Spricht für die formale Schwelle somit die Rechts- und Planungssicherheit und Vorhersehbarkeit, so lassen sich für den materiellen Begriff gerade die typische Treffsicherheit der Regelung, die Sicherung der Verfolgung des zentralen Zwecks des Übernahmerechts, nämlich der Ausstiegsmöglichkeit bei einem Kontrollwechsel, sicherzustellen, anführen, sodass der Gesetzgeber abzuwägen hat, welche Interessen und welche Rechtsgüter er stärker gewichtet.

Mögliche Regelungsszenarien

Derzeit werden drei verschiedene Varianten zur Bewältigung des Spannungsverhältnisses zwischen dem materiellen und formellen Kontrollbegriff diskutiert.

(i) Eine Position besteht in der Festlegung einer starren 30%-Schwelle, unter der eine Kontrolle stets abgelehnt wird, bei bzw über der jedenfalls eine Kontrolle angenommen wird, die ein Pflichtangebot auslöst. Die Übernahmepflicht bzw Angebotspflicht besteht jedenfalls, sobald die Schwelle erreicht wird, selbst wenn im Einzelfall eine Kontrolle nicht ausgeübt werden kann.

(ii) Als weitere Variante wird diskutiert, eine Kontrollvermutung bei 30% der Anteile einzuziehen, über diesem Schwellenwert wird im Regelfall die Kontrolle vermutet. Bei Unterschreiten dieses Werts wird grundsätzlich das Nichtvorliegen der Kontrolle vermutet, allerdings sollte es der Übernahmekommission möglich sein, bei berechtigten Interessen der Beteiligungspapierinhaber einschreiten und besondere Rechtsfolgen anordnen zu können. Jedenfalls sollte ein Pflichtangebot bei einer Kontrolle, die durch eine Beteiligung von weniger als 30% erreicht wird, gerade nicht erforderlich sein, vielmehr sollten nur sonstige begleitende Maßnahmen durch die Übernahmekommission angeordnet werden können. Die Konzerneingangskontrolle durch eine wirksame Ausstiegsmöglichkeit der Streubesitzaktionäre mutiert somit in eine Art *Konzernzustandskontrolle*. Das österreichische Übernahmerecht würde somit mit dieser Lösung einen Paradigmenwechsel vornehmen und bei bestimmten Kontrollerlangungstatbeständen die kardinale Rechtsfolge von § 22 ÜbG, nämlich die Anordnung eines Pflichtangebots, aufgeben. Der Übernahmekommission soll dabei die Aufgabe zugewiesen werden, darüber zu wachen, dass die Mehrzahl der Aufsichtsratsmitglieder vom kontrollierenden Aktionär unabhängig ist,[32] dass keine weiteren Aktien erworben werden und dass bestimmte Maßnahmen der Übernahmekommission vor ihrer Durchführung anzuzeigen sind. Im Wesentlichen werden damit die Entscheidungslinien, wie sie die Übernahmekommission im Fall Böhler Uddeholm – Fries-Gruppe[33] entwickelt hat, in gesetzliche Form gegossen. In der Satzung sollte es möglich sein, die Ersetzung der Konzernzustandskontrolle auszuschließen und stattdessen zwingend die Abgabe des Pflichtangebots vorzusehen.

(iii) Schließlich wird eine sogenannte Floor-Lösung vorgeschlagen, wonach die Schwelle etwa bei 25% liegt und darunter der Bieter die Sicherheit hat, dass die Kontrolle bei Erwerb von Anteilen bis zu 25% jedenfalls nicht erlangt wird und damit kein Pflichtangebot ausgelöst wird. Über der Schwelle von 25% soll der materielle Kontrollbegriff weiter gelten und zwar nicht bloß, um Konzernzustandskontrollmöglichkeiten zu gewährleisten, sondern um bei einem Kontrollwechsel tatsächlich den Ausstieg zugunsten der Streubesitzaktionäre sicherzustellen. Die Floor-Lösung hat den Vorzug, dass sie einerseits bei einem Schwellenwert, der viel deutlicher an der wirtschaftlichen Realität der österreichischen börsenotierten Gesellschaften anknüpft, die Kontrolle etabliert und bei darunter liegen die Sicherheit gibt, dass ein Kontrollwechsel nicht stattfindet.[34] Bei Anteilserwerben über 25% ist die Möglichkeit gewahrt, im Einzelfall zu beurteilen, ob die Kontrolle doch tatsächlich erlangt wurde.

Die Umschreibung des Kontrollbegriffs sowie die Festlegung der Rechtsfolgen bei Bejahung der Erlangung der Kontrolle ist somit noch offen. Am sachgerechtesten erscheint eine behutsame Floor-Lösung bei einem Schwellenwert von 23% bis 25%, um tatsächlich einen wirksamen Schutz aller Marktteilnehmer iSe Gleichbehandlung sowie der Sicherung der Ausstiegsmöglichkeit bei einem Kontrollwechsel zu gewährleisten.

32 S dazu allg. *Reiter* Die Beachtung der Unabhängigkeitsbestimmungen des GesRÄG 2005 durch den Aufsichtsrat, Aufsichtsrat aktuell 4/2005, 9.

33 GZ 2004/1/9-112.

34 Naturgemäß fallen damit Kontrollerlangungen bzw -wechsel mit einem Anteil von knapp über 20%, die in der Realität durchaus vorkommen, aus dem Anwendungsbereich des ÜbG (Pflichtangebot) heraus.

IV. Art der Kontrollerlangung

Der Fall Böhler Uddeholm – Fries-Gruppe rückte zusätzlich die Frage der Art der Kontrollerlangung in das Blickfeld der Diskussion. Insbesondere wurde die Frage aufgeworfen, ob auch die passive Kontrollerlangung die übernahmerechtlichen Rechtsfolgen der Angebotspflicht auslöst. Unter passiver Kontrollerlangung versteht man den Vorgang, dass ein Aktionär ohne ein unmittelbares zeitliches Zutun eine kontrollierende Beteiligung erlangt.[35]

Die Richtlinie spricht in Art 5 bloß vom Halten der kontrollierenden Beteiligung. Die Art der Kontrollerlangung wird nicht genauer umschrieben, sie ist jedenfalls auch offen für die passive Kontrollerlangung. Nach geltendem österreichischem Recht kommt es auf die Art und Weise, wie der Bieter die Kontrolle erlangt, nicht an.[36] Fälle der passiven Kontrollerlangung sind etwa die Erlangung einer Beherrschungsmöglichkeit durch das Aufleben der Stimmrechte aus stimmrechtslosen Vorzugsaktien, die Änderung einer syndikatsvertraglichen Willensbildung, die Auflösung eines Syndikatsvertrags oder insbesondere auch der Abverkauf von Aktien des bislang kontrollierenden Aktionärs.[37] Die Einbeziehung der passiven Kontrollerlangung ist aus der Sicht der durch den Kontrollwechsel betroffenen Beteiligungspapierinhaber konsequent, ist es doch unerheblich, ob sie nunmehr einem neuen dominierenden Aktionär gegenüberstehen, der durch aktives Verhalten in diese Position gekommen ist oder die Kontrolle aufgrund eines passiven Vorgangs erlangt hat.[38] Umgekehrt werden die Vermögens- und Eigentumsinteressen des Bieters bei einer passiven Kontrollerlangung ungleich stärker berührt und ist es ihm auch aus verfassungsrechtlichen Gründen nicht unbedingt zuzumuten, dass er bei einer Kontrollerlangung, die vollkommen ohne sein Zutun passiert ist, allen Aktionären ein Angebot zu machen verpflichtet ist.

Schon nach geltendem Recht ist abzuwägen, inwieweit ein Bieter die Art der passiven Kontrollerlangung beeinflusst hat und ob die Angebotspflicht dem verfassungsrechtlichen Verhältnismäßigkeitsgebot genügt.[39]

35 ÜbK GZ 2004/1/9-112, S 128; *Kalss/Oppitz/Zollner* Kapitalmarktrecht § 23 Rn. 117.
36 S nur ErlBem zum ÜbG 1276 Blg zu den stenografischen Protokollen des Nationalrats 20. GP 39.
37 *Diregger/Kalss/Winner* Übernahmerecht Rn. 134; *Gall* Angebotspflicht 267f; *Zollner* Kontrollwechsel 107; *Kalss/Oppitz/Zollner* Kapitalmarktrecht § 23 Rn. 117.
38 *Zollner* Kontrollwechsel 108f.
39 Vgl *Kalss* Übernahmerecht light? Der Standard 21. 12. 2004.

Die Pflicht zur Abgabe des Angebots hängt davon ab, inwieweit dem nunmehr kontrollierenden Aktionär die Erlangung der Kontrolle zuzurechnen ist, dh inwieweit er etwa die Kündigung eines Syndikatsvertrags nicht verhindert hat und wieweit es ihm finanziell zumutbar ist, Handlungen zu unterbinden. Das Gesetz ist bereits nach der geltenden Rechtslage offen für eine abgewogene Entscheidung, ob und inwieweit diese Pflicht tatsächlich besteht. Das Gesetz eröffnet schon jetzt auf der Grundlage der in § 25 ÜbG (Anzeigepflicht für Ausnahmetatbestände) enthaltenen Wertungen eine angemessene und interessenausgleichende Lösung mit hohem Realitätsbezug, selbst wenn grundsätzlich von der Angebotspflicht bei passiver Kontrollerlangung ausgegangen werden muss.[40]

Sachgerecht ist es jedenfalls, unterschiedliche Fälle der passiven Kontrollerlangung zu differenzieren und insbesondere die Formen der passiven Kontrollerlangung von der Angebotspflicht auszunehmen, die unbeabsichtigt passiert sind und diese bloß mit einer Anzeigepflicht gem § 25 ÜbG zu belegen.[41]

In diese Richtung laufen auch die Vorüberlegungen zur künftigen Gestaltung der Kontrollerlangung, nämlich dass der Fall der unbeabsichtigten passiven Kontrollerlangung ausdrücklich als schlichter Anzeigetatbestand gem § 25 ÜbG definiert wird, der somit von der Angebotspflicht trotz Erlangung der Kontrolle ausgenommen wird. Situationen, bei denen die völlige Passivität des Bieters nicht gegeben ist und die passive Kontrollerlangung wenn nicht betrieben, so doch jedenfalls über einen längeren Zeitraum geduldet worden ist, fallen im Umkehrschluss somit nicht unter diese Privilegierung und würden daher die Angebotspflicht auslösen.

V. Tauschangebote

Gem Art 5 Abs 5 der RL kann ein Bieter als Gegenleistung Wertpapiere, eine Geldleistung oder eine Kombination aus beiden anbieten. Die Richtlinie ist somit offen für ein alternatives Anbieten von Geld- oder Wertpapieren. Sie gestattet den Mitgliedstaaten allerdings ausdrücklich zwingend vorzusehen, dass in allen Fällen zumindest wahlweise eine Geldleistung angeboten werden muss, dh dass bei einem Übernahmeangebot jedenfalls ein Barangebot

40 *Kalss* Übernahmerecht light? Der Standard 21. 12. 2004.

41 ÜbK GZ 2004/1/9-112, 28 ff; *Diregger/Kalss/Winner* Übernahmerecht Rn. 135; *Kalss/Oppitz/Zollner* Kapitalmarktrecht § 23 Rn. 117.

gemacht werden muss. Wertpapiere können bloß zusätzlich angeboten werden. Konkretisierend verlangt die Richtlinie, dass bei nicht liquiden Wertpapieren jedenfalls wahlweise eine Geldleistung anzubieten ist, ebenso in dem Fall, in dem während der letzten 12 Monate mindestens 5% der Aktien in bar erworben wurden.

Nach dem geltenden österreichischen Recht ist gem § 22 Abs 8 ÜbG bei einem Pflichtangebot bzw einem freiwilligen Übernahmeangebot iSd § 22 Abs 11 ÜbG jedenfalls eine Barabfindung anzubieten. Wertpapiere können daneben nur zusätzlich angeboten werden. Das Barangebot ist allein maßgeblich und muss im Einklang mit den Preisbestimmungen des Übernahmegesetzes stehen. Das zusätzliche Wertpapierangebot kann – sofern das Barangebot der gesetzlichen Anforderung entspricht – durchaus attraktiver sein als das Barangebot.[42] Allein wenn es sich um ein freiwilliges, einfaches Erwerbsangebot iSd §§ 4 ff ÜbG handelt, steht es dem Bieter frei, auch ausschließlich Wertpapiere anzubieten.[43]

Die eben abgeschlossene Übernahme der BA-CA durch Unicredit hat, abgesehen von der Preisermittlung bei einem mittelbaren Kontrollerwerb, die rechtspolitische Frage, ob für ein Pflichtangebot ein reines Tauschangebot zugelassen werden soll, ins Zentrum gerückt. Während etwa in Deutschland das Angebot der Unicredit an die HVB-Aktionäre ausschließlich in Aktien besteht, konnte Unicredit in Österreich gegenüber den BA-CA-Aktionären nicht bloß ein – attraktives – Tauschangebot legen, vielmehr war Unicredit gem § 22 Abs 8 iVm § 22 Abs 11 ÜbG auch verpflichtet, unbedingt ein Barangebot zu legen. Zwar war dieses im Verhältnis zum Börsenkurs und auch im Verhältnis zum Tauschangebot wenig attraktiv, dennoch musste es den Mindestpreisanforderungen gem § 26 von Abs 1 iVm Abs 3 ÜbG entsprechen. Gerade die Differenzierung bei einer einzigen Transaktion, die sich über mehrere Länder erstreckt, sowie der Umstand, dass es sich um eine Übernahme im Bankenbereich handelt, zeigen die Brisanz der rechtspolitischen Frage nach der Zulassung des Tauschangebots.

Gegen die Zulässigkeit eines reinen Tauschangebots bei Pflichtangeboten oder Übernahmeangeboten spricht der Umstand, dass allein eine Geldleistung den Aktionären einen echten Ausstieg und eine volle Alternative ihres Investments bietet. Allein durch eine Geldleistung kann ein vollwertiger

42 S nur *Kalss/Oppitz/Zollner* Kapitalmarktrecht § 23 Rn. 164; *Diregger/Kalss/Winner* Übernahmerecht Rn. 183.

43 *Diregger/Kalss/Winner* Übernahmerecht 102; *Kalss/Oppitz/Zollner* Kapitalmarktrecht § 23 Rn. 87.

Konzerneingangsschutz gewährt werden, zudem ist das Geld als Gegenleistung leicht zähl- und bewertbar. Die Angemessenheit des Werts nur der einen Aktie muss ermittelt werden.

Gegen ein Tausch-(Papier-)angebot[44] spricht auch die Überlegung, dass die angebotene Gegenleistung in Aktien oder sonstigen Papieren (GmbH-Anteilen) schwer dahingehend überprüfbar ist, ob diese Papiere tatsächlich werthaltig sind und ob daher das angebotene Umtauschverhältnis angemessen bzw jedenfalls den Mindestanforderungen der Preisfestlegung für ein Pflichtangebot gem § 26 ÜbG entspricht. Dabei sind Schwierigkeiten der Prospektkontrolle für die angebotenen Aktien des Bieters ebenso zu bedenken wie mögliche Änderungen nach dem erstmaligen Anbieten, sofern sich das Angebot bzw die geplante Transaktion über etliche Monate hinzieht. Schließlich ist ein wirtschaftspolitisches Argument zu berücksichtigen, wonach die zwingende Barangebotspflicht österreichische Unternehmen insofern schütze, als die Aufbringung der notwendigen Mitteln schwieriger wird und daher bestimmte Übernahmen mangels Leistbarkeit verhindert werden und daher österreichische Unternehmen tendenziell weniger übernommen werden. Die wirtschaftspolitische Diskussion zum Schutz heimischer Unternehmen wird somit in Österreich an dieser Stelle, und deutlich weniger am Institut des Neutralitätsgebots der Zielgesellschaft geführt.

Für ein Tauschangebot und gegen die ausschließliche Zulässigkeit von Barangeboten spricht gerade umgekehrt die schwere Leistbarkeit von Barangeboten, die es verhindern, dass sinnvolle Übernahmen und Strukturbereinigungen durchgeführt werden. Gerade auf internationaler Ebene zeigt sich, dass ab einer bestimmten Größe Barangebote wegen der hohen Belastung der Bilanz für Bieter nicht durchführbar sind und die Finanzierungskosten untragbar werden.[45] Die hohen Kosten erschweren es nicht nur ausländischen Unternehmen, sondern auch österreichischen Unternehmen, andere österreichische Unternehmen übernehmen zu können.

Die Verneinung der Zulässigkeit von Tauschangeboten bei Pflichtangeboten zeigt auch ein gehöriges Maß an Misstrauen gegenüber dem Kapitalmarkt, insbesondere gegenüber Gesellschaften mit ausreichend liquiden Papieren, da diese nach der gesetzgeberischen Wertung nicht als vollwertige Gegenleistung anerkannt werden. Zwar ist ein allfälliger Liquiditäts- und Transaktionskostenabschlag bei reinen Papierangeboten durchaus zu berücksichtigen, dennoch spricht die Möglichkeit, ein vollkommen liquides, jederzeit

44 *Hügel* Aktien statt Bargeld, Der Standard, 8. 3. 2005.
45 *Hügel* Aktien statt Bargeld, Der Standard, 8. 3. 2005.

veräußerbares Papier als Gegenleistung zu erhalten, nicht gegen das Tauschangebot. Weiters könnte durch die Zulässigkeit eines Tauschangebots die Spekulationsgefahr, die durch das bloß kurzfristige Einsteigen institutioneller Anleger gefördert wird (insbesondere Hedgefonds), die nur darauf zielen, innerhalb weniger Wochen bzw Monate den Vorteil und Kursanstieg der Übernahmephantasie eines Papiers zu lukrieren, zumindest in andere Papiere gelenkt und daher gebremst werden.

Entschließt man sich – entgegen den bisherigen Planungen des Justizministeriums für die Zulässigkeit eines Tauschangebots, so ist jedenfalls sicherzustellen, dass es sich um liquide Papiere handelt. Die Festlegung der Notierung an einem Geregelten Markt gem § 2 Z 37 BWG ist dafür wohl nicht ausreichend, vielmehr sollten ausgewählte Marktplätze bzw Börsen genannt und zudem eine bestimmte Mindeststreuung verlangt werden, die über die Notierungsvoraussetzungen der Börsenzulassungsrichtlinie (Kapitalmarktpublizitätsrichtlinie) bzw von § 66 BörseG hinausgeht.[46] Überdies sollte festgelegt werden, dass die Gegenleistung nicht aus Papieren einer Konzerngesellschaft des Bieters besteht, sondern dies jedenfalls Papiere oder sogar zwingend Aktien der Bietergesellschaft sein müssten, sofern diese die Konzernspitze ist oder sonst die Papiere der Konzernobergesellschaft. Damit wird sichergestellt, dass die Aktionäre der Zielgesellschaft, die sich für den Tausch entschließen, Aktionäre der konzernleitenden Bietergesellschaft oder der sonstigen konzernbestimmenden Gesellschaft werden.

VI. Rechtschutz vor der Übernahmekommission

Ein weiterer wesentlicher Diskussionspunkt ist die Frage der Gestaltung des rechtlichen Verfahrens vor der Übernahmekommission, insbesondere auch die Frage, ob gegen Entscheidungen der Übernahmekommission eine Berufung an eine weitere Instanz ermöglicht werden soll. Für die Etablierung eines derartigen Instanzenzuges spricht schlicht die allgemeine rechtsstaatliche Überlegung, dass Entscheidungen von Behörden überprüfbar sein sollen. Gegen eine derartige Möglichkeit lässt sich der hohe Zeitaufwand geltend machen. Zugleich spricht der ungeheure zusätzliche Aufwand einer weiteren Behörde bzw Etablierung einer Beschwerdestelle gegen eine derartige Maßnahme. Sachlich gerechtfertigt ist es gewiss, bestimmte verfahrensrechtliche Aspekte klarzustellen bzw deutlicher auf die Sondersituation in Übernahme-

46 Vgl dazu *Kalss/Oppitz/Zollner* Kapitalmarktrecht § 12 Rn. 65 ff; Tabelle S 350.

verfahren zuzuschneiden, insbesondere sind die Fragen der Amtsverschwiegenheit und Informationsweitergabe auszuleuchten, zugleich auch Fragen der Transparenz des Verfahrens und der Offenlegung der ergangenen Entscheidungen.

VII. Durch die Übernahmerichtlinie indizierte maßgebliche Fragen

1. Preis des Pflichtangebots

Die Richtlinie sieht in Art 5 Abs 4 eine Festlegung des Preises für das Übernahmeangebot bzw das Pflichtangebot vor. Bereits das geltende Recht entspricht nach seiner Regelung in § 16 sowie § 26 ÜbG weitgehend Art 5 Abs 4 der Richtlinie. Zwei Änderungen sind aber erforderlich: Nach geltenden Recht ist es dem Bieter erlaubt, dem Paketveräußerer mehr als 15% im Vergleich zu den übrigen Aktionären für das Paket zu bezahlen. Aufgrund des rigorosen Gleichbehandlungsgebots nach der Richtlinie ist dieser 15%-Abschlag zu Lasten der Streubesitzaktionäre in § 26 Abs 1 ÜbG ersatzlos zu streichen. Das Gesetz sieht eine zweifache Untergrenze vor, nämlich einerseits den durchschnittlichen Börsekurs während der letzten sechs Monate vor **Abgabe des Angebots sowie den höchstbezahlten Preis während eines Zeitraums von 12 Monaten, beide Werte sind maßgeblich für die Festlegung des Endzeitpunkts der Frist, somit des Rückrechnungszeitraums.** Der maßgebliche Tag bei Pflichtangeboten ist der Tag der Kontrollerlangung. Bei freiwilligen Übernahmeangeboten ist der maßgebliche Tag jener der Bekanntmachung der Angebotsabsicht bzw der Bekanntmachung von Überlegungen ein Angebot zu stellen.[47] Die Richtlinie geht von einem Vorerwerb maximal 12 Monate vor dem Angebot aus. Da nicht genau umschrieben wird, was unter Angebot anzusehen ist, wird die Umsetzung dahingehen, dass die Anzeige des Angebots maßgeblich ist, und nicht mehr – wie bisher – die Überlegungen, wodurch die Frist später ausgelöst wird.

[47] *Kalss/Oppitz/Zollner* Kapitalmarktrecht § 23 Rn. 166; *Diregger/Kalss/Winner* Übernahmerecht Rn. 200.

2. Neutralitätsgebot

Eine der heftigst umstrittenen Regelungen der Richtlinie ist Art 9, der die Pflichten des Leitungs- bzw Verwaltungsorgans der Zielgesellschaft und somit das Neutralitätsgebot oder Vereitelungsverbot für die Organträger der Zielgesellschaft normiert. Die schwierige Kompromissfindung für die Textierung der Richtlinienbestimmung zeigt sich vor allem darin, dass Art 9 nicht zwingend gilt, sondern es den Mitgliedstaaten freisteht, sich vorzubehalten, das in Art 9 Abs 2 und 3 festgelegte Neutralitätsgebot den betroffenen Gesellschaften nicht vorzuschreiben.[48] Die Regelungen über das Neutralitätsgebot und dessen Umsetzung in österreichisches Recht stehen derzeit überhaupt nicht im Zentrum der rechtspolitischen Diskussion.

Der österreichische Gesetzgeber wird nach den derzeitigen Überlegungen von der Opt-out-Möglichkeit gem Art 12 Abs 1 der Richtlinie nicht Gebrauch machen und das Neutralitätsgebot für alle Angebotsarten einheitlich beibehalten. Das Neutralitätsgebot, wie es in § 12 ÜbG normiert ist, entspricht im Wesentlichen den Vorgaben von Art 9 für Übernahmeangebote. Das österreichische Recht ist für alle Angebote, nicht bloß für Übernahmeangebote, anzuwenden. Das Neutralitätsgebot (Verhinderungsverbot) bedeutet, dass dem Vorstand und Aufsichtsrat der Zielgesellschaft – ab Bekanntwerden der Absicht des Bieters ein Übernahmeangebot abzugeben, bis zum Ende der Annahmefrist – sämtliche Maßnahmen untersagt sind, die das Angebot vereiteln könnten.[49] Nur präventive Abwehrmechanismen, die bereits vor Bekanntwerden einer konkreten Übernahmeabsicht ergriffen werden, unterliegen nicht dem übernahmerechtlichen Verhinderungsverbot. Unzulässig sind Maßnahmen, die objektiv zur Verhinderung des Erfolgs eines Übernahmeangebots geeignet sind, unabhängig davon, ob eine Verhinderungsabsicht besteht oder nicht.[50] Unzulässig sind daher etwa der Erwerb eigener Aktien, Kapitalerhöhungen, die Veräußerung von für den Bieter besonders interessanten Unternehmensteilen, die Veräußerung von Tochtergesellschaften oder das Einge-

48 S dazu nur *Maul/Muffert-Jeandet* Die EU-Übernahme-RL – Inhalt und Umsetzung in das nationale Recht (Teil II), AG 2004, 310; *Kalss/Oppitz/Zollner* Kapitalmarktrecht § 23 Rn. 71.

49 S dazu nur *Kalss/Oppitz/Zollner* Kapitalmarktrecht § 23 Rn. 67 ff; *Winner* Die Zielgesellschaft in der freundlichen Übernahme. Pflichten von Verwaltungsorganen und Sachverständigen nach dem Übernahmegesetz, 2002, 87 ff; *Diregger/Kalss/Winner* Übernahmerecht Rn. 68 ff.

50 *Huber/Löber* ÜbG § 12 Rn. 8; *Kalss/Oppitz/Zollner* Kapitalmarktrecht § 23 Rn. 69.

hen von Managementverträgen, die bei einem Kontrollwechsel außergewöhnlich hohe Abfindungszahlungen enthalten.[51]

Zwar soll nach dem derzeitigen legislativen Vorhaben § 12 neu formuliert werden, um den Wortlaut der Richtlinie klarer in österreichisches Recht umzusetzen, im Wesentlichen wird aber das Neutralitätsgebot sachlich nicht geändert. Wie bisher greift das Neutralitätsgebot bereits ab dem Zeitpunkt, ab dem Überlegungen bezüglich eines Angebots bekannt sind. Stellungnahmen und Äußerungen der Verwaltungsorgane sind zulässig, sofern der Pflicht zur vollständigen und wahrheitsgemäßen Information entsprochen wird. Ausdrücklich soll die Suche nach einem konkurrierenden Angebot für zulässig erklärt werden; Vorratsbeschlüsse, dh Ermächtigungen im Vorhinein, sind nicht zulässig. Eine Zustimmung der Hauptversammlung kann nur zu konkreten Maßnahmen vorgenommen werden. Außergewöhnliche Maßnahmen des Vorstands und Aufsichtsrats bedürfen bei noch nicht begonnener Umsetzung der nochmaligen Zustimmung der Hauptversammlung, sofern sie über den gewöhnlichen Geschäftsverlauf hinausgehen und eine Vereitelungseignung haben. Geschäfte, die bereits vor Bekanntwerden der Übernahmeabsicht beschlossen wurden, sind zulässig, sofern bereits ein nach außen hin wirksamer Akt gesetzt wurde.[52] Die Umsetzung bedarf somit einer Konturierung und Darstellung im Detail, im Wesentlichen wird aber nur eine Formulierungsanpassung ohne gravierende sachliche Änderung vorgenommen. In der rechtspolitischen Diskussion ist die Beibehaltung der Neutralitätspflicht der Zielgesellschaft anerkannt, allenfalls könnte überlegt werden, die Neutralitätspflicht in einigen Jahren zu überdenken, sofern alle anderen europäischen Staaten von der Opt-out-Möglichkeit Gebrauch machen[53] und damit österreichische Gesellschaften benachteiligt werden.

3. Durchbrechungsregelungen

Art 11 der Richtlinie sieht die Durchbrechungsregelungen vor. Durchbrechung bedeutet, dass Beschränkungen betreffend die Übertragung von Wertpapieren, die in der Satzung oder in vertraglichen Vereinbarungen unter den Aktionären oder mit der Zielgesellschaft und den Aktionären vereinbart sind,

51 *Huber/Löber* ÜbG § 12 Rn. 7 ff; *Kalss* in Fleischer/Kalss, Das neue Wertpapiererwerbs- und Übernahmegesetz, 2002, 164.

52 *Kalss/Oppitz/Zollner* Kapitalmarktrecht § 23 Rn. 70.

53 So der einhellige Tenor bei einer rechtspolitischen Podiumsdiskussion zur Neugestaltung des Übernahmerechts am 21. 10. 2005 in Rust (Burgenland).

gegenüber dem Bieter während der Angebotsfrist nicht gelten. Durchbrechung bedeutet weiters, dass die Stimmrechtsbeschränkungen, die in der Satzung der Zielgesellschaft oder in Gesellschaftervereinbarungen festgelegt werden, bei der Beschlussfassung über Abwehrmaßnahmen nicht greifen. Schließlich umfasst die Durchbrechungsregelung auch die Aufhebung von Stimmrechtsbeschränkungen sowie von Sonderrechten von Gesellschaftern bei Ernennung und Abberufung der Mitglieder des Aufsichtsrats[54] in der ersten Hauptversammlung nach einem erfolgreichen Übernahmeangebot, sofern der Bieter mehr als 75% der Stimmen erlangt hat.

Den Mitgliedstaaten steht es frei, die Durchbrechungsregelung generell für alle Gesellschaften vorzuschreiben oder dies der Satzung der Zielgesellschaft zu überlassen. Da eine generelle Durchbrechung eines derartig zentralen Elements der österreichischen realen Wirtschaftsordnung, nämlich der Syndikatsverträge,[55] nicht abschätzbare Folgen bewirkte, ist an einen generellen Eingriff nicht gedacht. Die rechtspolitische Diskussion sowie die Regelungsintention des Justizministeriums laufen dahin, der Gesellschaft die Entscheidung zu überlassen, ob sie für sich die Durchbrechungsregelung in der Satzung festschreibt oder nicht. Dabei soll zur Sicherung der Transparenz nur die generelle Anerkennung der Durchbrechungsregelungen vorgesehen werden können und nicht bloß eine teilweise (nur Paketlösung). Der Vorteil der Wahlmöglichkeit durch die Zielgesellschaft liegt darin, dass sie sich dem Kapitalmarkt und möglichen Bietern gegenüber attraktiver präsentieren kann. Umgekehrt kann ihr, wenn sie als Bieter auftritt, nicht die in der Richtlinie vorgesehene Ausnahme von der Durchbrechung wegen mangelnder Reziprozität gem Art 12 Abs 3 der Richtlinie entgegengehalten werden.

Entscheidet sich eine Gesellschaft für die Anwendung der Durchbrechungsregelungen, so hat sie dies in ihrer Satzung festzulegen und unverzüglich der Übernahmekommission mitzuteilen. Fraglich erscheint die Normierung einer Entschädigungsregelung für die durch eine derartige Durchbrechungsregelung betroffenen Aktionäre. Der Schuldner einer derartigen Entschädigungsleistung müsste wohl der Bieter sein, der letztlich von der Durchbrechung profitiert. Zu beachten ist dabei allerdings, wann die Entschädigung tatsächlich anfällt und sie zu leisten ist. Fraglich ist, ob bereits die Etablierung einer Satzungsbestimmung, die die Durchbrechung vorsieht, eine Ent-

54 S zu diesem Sonderrecht nach österreichischem Recht nur *Kalss* in Doralt/Nowotny/Kalss Kommentar zum AktG, 2003 § 88 Rn. 1 ff.

55 Allein 32 Verfahren der ÜbK beschäftigten sich mit Syndikatsverträgen von börsenotierten Gesellschaften; vgl allg. zu Syndikatsverträgen *Tichy* Syndikatsvertrag (2002); *Tichy* in Doralt/Nowotny/Kalss, AktG Exkurs zu § 114 Rn. 86 ff.

schädigungspflicht auslöst oder ob diese erst im konkreten Übernahmefall anfallen würde. Für letzteres spricht grundsätzlich der Umstand, dass nach österreichischem Recht eine Entschädigung für die zulässige Etablierung von Satzungsbestimmungen nicht zu gewähren ist, sofern Aktionäre nur mittelbar betroffen sind. Allein wenn eine unmittelbare Betroffenheit, etwa bei einer Einführung eines Höchststimmrechts besteht (Aktionär wird durch ein Höchststimmrecht von 20% in seinen aktuellen Stimmrechten „gekappt"), ist über eine entsprechende Entschädigungszahlung unmittelbar durch die Satzungsbestimmung nachzudenken.[56] Die Aufhebung einer Vinkulierungsbestimmung führt nicht zu einer Entschädigungspflicht der nunmehr freigestellten Aktionäre.[57] Eine Entschädigung könnte allenfalls tatsächlich bei Durchbrechung von Syndikatsverträgen anfallen, die vom Bieter zu leisten ist.[58]

4. Squeeze-out

Der Ausschluss von Minderheitsaktionären bildet ein auch durch die Richtlinie gefördertes wichtiges Thema der aktuellen rechtspolitischen Diskussion. Die Neugestaltung des Squeeze-outs ist aber ohnehin eine seit langem erhobene rechtspolitische Forderung.[59] Die kürzlich ergangene Entscheidung des Verfassungsgerichtshofs,[60] die den Rechtschutz im Rahmen der Squeeze-out-Spaltung als verfassungswidrig erkannte, setzt den Gesetzgeber auch unter Zugzwang eine verfassungskonforme Regelung zu schaffen. Gem Art 15 der Richtlinie müssen Mitgliedstaaten im Anschluss an ein Übernahmeangebot Regelungen über den Ausschluss von Minderheitsgesellschaftern vorsehen, sofern der Bieter nach Abschluss des Übernahmeverfahrens über 90% des stimmberechtigten Kapitals und 90% der Stimmrechte der Zielgesellschaft verfügt oder über 90% des stimmberechtigten Kapitals sowie 90% der vom

56 S dazu *Kalss* Das Höchststimmrecht als Instrument zur Wahrung des Aktionärseinflusses (1992) 88 ff.

57 *Micheler* in Doralt/Nowotny/Kalss, AktG § 62 Rn. 10; *Koppensteiner* in Koppensteiner, GmbHG² (1999) § 77 Rn. 1 f.

58 Vgl *Kalss* Aktienrecht im Licht der Kapitalverkehrsfreiheit, Die Rechtsprechung des EuGH zu den Goldenen Aktien und die Auswirkungen auf das nationale Recht, JRP 2005, 41.

59 S nur *Kohlhausser* SWI 2001, Squeeze out – Eine Neuregelung in Sicht?, 224; *Diregger/Kalss/Winner* Übernahmerecht Rn. 221 ff; *Kalss* in Fleischer/Kalss, Wertpapiererwerbs- und Übernahmegesetz 191.

60 VfGH am 16. 6. 2005, G 129/04, abrufbar unter http://www.vfgh.gv.at/cms/vfgh-site/entscheid.html?periode=this.

Angebot betroffenen Stimmrechte. Nach der Richtlinie ist es zulässig, die Schwelle von 90 auf einen höheren Wert anzuheben, unter 90% darf dieser Wert nicht abgesenkt werden.

In Österreich besteht nach geltendem Recht keine §§ 327aff dAktG vergleichbare Regelung, die unmittelbar die Übernahme von Aktien des 90%-Gesellschafters gegenüber Minderheitsgesellschaftern normiert. Nach geltendem Recht bestehen nur zwei Funktionsäquivalente aus dem Bereich des handelsrechtlichen Umgründungsrechts, nämlich die verschmelzende Umwandlung gem § 2 UmwG und die nicht verhältniswahrende Spaltung gem § 8 Abs 3 SpaltG. Beide Strukturmaßnahmen sind aber dadurch gekennzeichnet, dass nicht allein ein Anteilstransfer auf Aktionärsebene vollzogen wird, sondern vielmehr und primär findet ein Vermögenstransfer auf Gesellschaftsebene statt; der Ausschluss der Aktionäre ist nur eine Folge davon.[61] Nach der geltenden Rechtslage stehen diese Strukturmaßnahmen allen Kapitalgesellschaften und nicht nur börsenotierten Aktiengesellschaften zur Verfügung. Die rechtspolitische Diskussion um die angemessene Neugestaltung eines Squeeze-outs oder Ausschlussrechts von Minderheitsgesellschaftern erstreckt sich daher auf alle Kapitalgesellschaften und zugleich auf Maßnahmen, die unabhängig von der Übernahme durchgeführt werden können.

Die verschmelzende Umwandlung ist Erbstück der reichsrechtlichen Regelung aus dem Jahr 1934 und dadurch gekennzeichnet, dass der Hauptgesellschafter, der mindestens 90% der Anteile der Kapitalgesellschaft hält, die Maßnahme, unter Einhaltung der allgemeinen verschmelzungsrechtlichen Regelungen (insbesondere Umwandlungsplan, Umwandlungsbericht, Umwandlungsprüfung, frühzeitige Information) beschließen kann. Die Rechtsfolge einer verschmelzenden Umwandlung liegt darin, dass das Vermögen der übertragenden Gesellschaft auf den Hauptgesellschafter übertragen wird und dass die sonstigen Anteilsinhaber der übertragenden Gesellschaft – somit alle mit Ausnahme des Hauptgesellschafters – nicht mit Anteilen, sondern in bar abgefunden werden.[62] Die derart ausgeschlossenen Gesellschafter haben einen Anspruch auf eine angemessene Barabfindung.[63]

61 Vgl dazu *Diregger/Kalss/Winner* Übernahmerecht Rn. 214ff; *Kalss* in Fleischer/Kalss, Wertpapiererwerbs-, und Übernahmegesetz 191f.

62 Vgl dazu nur *Kalss* Kommentar zur Verschmelzung-Spaltung-Umwandlung, 1997, § 2 UmwG Rn. 3f; *Schummer* in Helbich/Wiesner/Bruckner, Handbuch der Umgründungen[6], 2002, Art II Umwandlung – Handelsrecht Rn. 20ff.

63 *Schummer* in Helbich/Wiesner/Bruckner, Umgründungen[6] Art II Umwandlung – Handelsrecht Rn. 32ff.

Bei der nicht verhältniswahrenden Spaltung sind die Anteilsinhaber, die an der übertragenden Gesellschaft vor der Spaltung beteiligt sind, nach Durchführung der Spaltung nicht mehr zu gleichen Teilen an den an der Spaltung beteiligten Gesellschaften (= neue oder übernehmende Gesellschaften), sondern in unterschiedlichem Ausmaß beteiligt. Diente das Instrument der verhältniswahrenden Spaltung nach der eigentlichen Intention des Gesetzgebers vor allem dazu, Unternehmen zu entflechten und klare Beteiligungsstrukturen zu schaffen, so hat die Praxis dieses Instrument sehr rasch nach seiner Einführung 1996 im Rahmen des EU-GesRÄG[64] als Vehikel zum Ausschluss von Gesellschaftern entdeckt.

Aufgrund der Spaltungsfreiheit gem § 2 SpaltG steht es der spaltenden Gesellschaft frei, nur Geld oder sonstige Vermögenswerte auf eine Gesellschaft zu übertragen.[65] Bei einer nicht verhältniswahrenden Squeeze-out-Spaltung werden die Minderheitsgesellschafter in eine Gesellschaft weggespalten, die mit Barwerten (Cash-Box) oder sonstigen Papieren ausgestattet ist. Jedenfalls werden sie aus der Kerngesellschaft entfernt. Im Regelfall ist die neue oder übernehmende Gesellschaft darauf ausgerichtet, den weggespaltenen Gesellschaftern nur vorübergehend die Mitgliedschaft zu gewähren, vielfach sind diese Gesellschaften nur befristet errichtet und Vorkehrungen für die Auflösung und Abwicklung sind schon getroffen.[66] Die weggespaltenen Gesellschafter haben gem § 9 SpaltG ein Recht auf Austritt gegen angemessene Abfindung. Jene, die das Austrittsrecht nicht wahrnehmen, werden bei Liquidation der übernehmenden Gesellschaft bar abgefunden.

Von maßgeblicher Bedeutung war der im Vergleich zur verschmelzenden Umwandlung eingeschränkte Rechtschutz, da ein Gesellschafter, der der Spaltung nicht zustimmte, zwar das Austrittsrecht hatte, die Angemessenheit der dafür angebotenen Barabfindung war aber bis vor kurzem nur von einem Gesellschafter überprüfbar, sofern dieser über 1% bzw € 70.000,– Nominalwert der Anteile inne hatte, bei der Hauptversammlung anwesend war und Widerspruch zur Niederschrift erklärt hatte. Das Quorum von 1% bzw € 70.000,– wurde wegen faktischer Abschneidung des Rechtschutzes und in Übereinstimmung mit der überwiegenden Lehre[67] kürzlich vom Verfassungs-

64 S nur *Kalss* Verschmelzung-Spaltung-Umwandlung, Vorbemerkungen zu SpaltG Rn. 3, § 8 SpaltG Rn. 10.

65 *Kalss* Verschmelzung-Spaltung-Umwandlung, § 2 SpaltG Rn. 15.

66 S dazu *Dorda* Squeeze out durch Spaltung, RdW 1999, 185.

67 S nur *Bachner* Bewertungskontrolle bei Fusionen (2000) 99; *Rüffler* Lücken im Umgründungsrecht, 2002, 183 ff; *Diregger/Kalss/Winner* Übernahmerecht Rn. 221 ff; *Kalss* in Fleischer/Kalss, Das neue Wertpapier-, Handels- und Übernahmegesetz 191 ff.

gerichtshof aufgehoben, sodass dieses Quorum nun nicht mehr erforderlich ist.[68]

Die maßgeblichen rechtspolitischen Defizite liegen somit in der Kompliziertheit des Vorgangs sowie in Unzulänglichkeiten des Rechtschutzes bei der Spaltung. Künftig wird eine Squeeze-out-Regelung nicht an der Übertragung von Vermögen der Gesellschaften, sondern schlicht an der Übertragung der Anteile der Minderheitsgesellschafter an den Hauptgesellschafter anknüpfen. Die künftige Gestaltung des Squeeze-out-Rechts wird durch folgende Charakteristika geprägt sein:

Der Gesellschafterausschluss (Squeeze-out) beschränkt sich nicht auf börsenotierte Gesellschaften bzw Aktiengesellschaften sowie auf Maßnahmen in unmittelbarem zeitlichen Anschluss an eine Übernahme, vielmehr soll sie allen Kapitalgesellschaften, dh Aktiengesellschaften und GmbHs, offen stehen. Die konkrete Gestaltung wird sich deutlich an §§ 327a ff dAktG orientieren. Sie kann unabhängig von einer vorgeschalteten Übernahme durchgeführt werden. Vergleichbar dem deutschen Recht wird der Ausschluss von Gesellschaftern an die Beschlussfassung in der Hauptversammlung gebunden, was den Vorteil der Öffentlichkeit und der Klarheit des Zeitpunkts für sich hat, umgekehrt stellt dies einen nicht zu unterschätzenden Formalismus dar, der überdies dazu einlädt, rechtsmissbräuchlich Rechtsbehelfe zu erheben.[69] Der Hauptgesellschafter muss allein über die 90%-Schwelle verfügen, ein Zusammenrechnen iSv § 23 ÜbG als gemeinsam vorgehender Rechtsträger soll für den Ausschluss der Gesellschafter gerade nicht möglich sein.

Wie bisher wird sich der Gesetzgeber auf die 90%-Schwelle festlegen. Eine allfällig höhere Schwelle ist an eine entsprechende Satzungsänderung gebunden. Der Satzung der Gesellschaft soll es freistehen, die Schwelle für den zulässigen Ausschluss anzuheben oder überhaupt das Ausschlussrecht zur Gänze auszuschließen.

Wie bereits bisher ist der Ausschluss an die Gewährung einer angemessenen Barabfindung geknüpft. Die Sicherung der Angemessenheit wird vergleichbar dem Verschmelzungs- und bisherigen Umwandlungsrecht normiert. Einerseits soll ein Vorwegschutz durch ausreichende und frühzeitige Information über den Ausschluss sowie die Höhe der dafür angebotenen Barabfindung und eine entsprechende Vorbereitung der Beschlussfassung geschaffen

68 VfGH vom 16. 6. 2005, G 129/04-17, G 63/05-3, G 64/05-2, G 65/05-2, G 66/05-2.

69 Vgl die Kritik zu § 327a dAktG; *Grunewald* in MünchKomm zum AktG² (2004) vor § 327a Rn. 9 ff.

werden, ergänzend soll die gerichtliche Überprüfbarkeit der Angemessenheit der Barabfindung etabliert werden, indem das verschmelzungsrechtliche Überprüfungsverfahren gem §§ 225c ff AktG auch auf die Frage der Angemessenheit der Barabfindung im Rahmen eines Ausschlusses ausgedehnt wird. Wird ein Ausschlussverfahren nach einem erfolgreichen Übernahmeangebot durchgeführt, so ist die höchste Gegenleistung des Angebots als Untergrenze für den angemessenen Wert der Barabfindung anzusehen. Die höchste Gegenleistung im Rahmen eines Übernahmeangebots gilt auch als angemessener Wert für die Barabfindung. In einem derartigen Fall ist somit aufgrund des Markttests die Angemessenheit bereits sichergestellt, sodass für die gerichtliche Überprüfung der Angemessenheit wenig Raum bleibt, soll doch die Angemessenheit bereits im Gesetz selbst festgeschrieben werden.[70]

Die verschmelzende Umwandlung sowie die nicht verhältniswahrende Spaltung sollen weiterhin als Gestaltungsinstrumente zur Vermögensübertragung im Wege der Gesamtrechtsfolge zur Verfügung stehen. Wie ihre Ausgestaltung im Detail aussehen wird, nämlich ob die Maßnahmen weiterhin mehrheitlich mit hohem Beschlussquorum beschlossen werden können oder es einer einstimmigen Beschlussfassung bedarf, ist noch Gegenstand der endgültigen rechtspolitischen Entscheidung.

Zusammenfassende Würdigung

Die Anpassung des österreichischen Übernahmerechts an die Übernahmerichtlinie bietet den Rahmen für eine umfassende und grundlegende rechtspolitische Diskussion über das Übernahmerecht. Die herausragenden Themen sind die Umschreibung des Kontrollbegriffs (materiell oder formell) und die Rechtsfolgen nach Kontrollerlangung in Gestalt des Pflichtangebots oder alternativer Konzernzustandsmaßnahmen sowie die Rechtsfolgen bei unterschiedlichem Erlangen der Kontrolle (passiv oder aktiv), schließlich die Frage, ob ein Tauschangebot bei einem Pflichtangebot alternativ zum Bargebot zugelassen werden soll. Gerade in der zentralen Frage der Festlegung des Kontrollbegriffs besteht derzeit noch kein politischer Konsens. Im Rahmen der Anpassung an die Richtlinie wird weniger das Neutralitätsgebot, sondern die Durchbrechungsregelung von Satzungs- und Syndikatsvertragsbestimmungen diskutiert, deren Anordnung nicht durch Gesetz, sondern bloß für jede einzelne Gesellschaft durch Satzungsbestimmung vorgenommen werden

70 Vgl dazu *Zottl/Tauböck* Neue Regeln für Squeeze out, Der Standard, vom 27. 9. 2005.

soll. Hohe Aufmerksamkeit richtet sich auf die neue Squeeze-out-Regelung, soll sie doch wesentlich rechtstechnisch vereinfacht werden. Daneben sind alle notwendigen Änderungen im Übernahmerecht vorzunehmen. Aller Voraussicht wird der österreichische Gesetzgeber den Umsetzungsstichtag 20. Mai 2006 halten und fristgerecht das österreichische Recht ändern und an die Richtlinie anpassen.

The Takeover Committee's proposal for the implementation of the EC Takeover Directive in Swedish law

Rolf Skog

Gliederung

In June 2005 the Takeover Committee presented its proposal for the implementation of the EC Takeover Directive in Swedish law. The proposal has been submitted for consideration and the Swedish Government is presently drafting a Government Bill. Rolf Skog was secretary to the Committee and is the author of this account of the proposal.

1. Background

Following many years of negotiations, the EU Member States and the European Parliament agreed in 2004 on a directive harmonising the regulation of company acquisitions through public bids for shares – takeover bids.[1] The Directive is to guarantee a fair and equitable treatment and to facilitate so called sound restructurings on the markets for publicly listed companies. The Takeover Directive had to be implemented by the Member States by 20 May 2006 at the latest.

To a large extent the Takeover Directive is modelled on the British takeover regulation – The City Code on Takeovers and Mergers – which was developed

1 Directive 2004/25/EC of the European Parliament and of the Council of 24 April 2004 on Takeover Bids.

at the end of the 1960s within the framework of the self regulation of the UK equity market. In the light of the British experience, the Directive can be implemented not only through regulation by law but also through self-regulation.

In the spring of 2004 the Swedish Government appointed a special investigator with the task to put forward a proposal for the implementation of the takeover Directive in Swedish law. Göran Schäder, Justice of the Supreme Administrative Court, was appointed investigator. The investigation body, which was named „The Takeover Committee", also included experts nominated by The Confederation of Swedish Enterprise, The Swedish Securities Dealers Association, The Institutional Shareholders' Association for the Regulation of the Equity Market, The Swedish Shareholders' Association, The Swedish Bar Association, The Institute of Authorised Public Accountants, The Swedish Financial Supervisory Authority and the Ministries of Justice, Finance and Industry, Employment and Communication.

The Takeover Committee started its work in September 2004 and submitted its report to the Government in June 2005.[2]

2. The current Swedish takeover regulation

Takeover bids have been common in the Swedish economy for a considerable time.[3] In addition, Sweden is among those countries where takeover rules were developed at an early stage. As early as 1971, the *Näringslivets Börskommitté* (NBK) – the Swedish Industry and Commerce Stock Exchange Committee – issued rules on public offers for shares, modelled on the British rules. These rules have been gradually developed over the years and adjusted to the needs of the economy and international developments. The most recent update was made in 2003.

2 *Ny reglering av offentliga uppköpserbjudanden* (New regulation of public takeover bids), SOU 2005:58.

3 During 1990–2004 a total of 358 takeover bids were made for Swedish listed companies, and 293 of these bids were successful. Consequently, on average 20 listed companies were acquired each year through a takeover bid, or on average 7 per cent of all Swedish listed companies were acquired every year through such bids. This represents a higher rate of takeover activity than in most European countries.

The NBK Takeover Rules regulate the practices and processes in connection with takeover bids. Similar to the British rules the NBK rules determine, among other things, the circumstances under which a takeover bid is allowed to be made, the information that must be given in connection with such a bid, the conditions that may be attached to the bid and the actions that the target company is allowed to take during the offer period. There are also rules to the effect that a shareholder who reaches an equity stake of 30 per cent or more of the votes in a listed company must, under certain circumstances, make a bid for the remainder of the shares in the company, a so called mandatory bid. Finally, there are rules on the required contents of the takeover prospectus.

Another body, the *Aktiemarknadsnämnden* (AMN) – the Swedish Securities Council – promotes good practice on the stock market by making *in casu* statements on the interpretation of the takeover rules and by handling requests for exemptions from the rules. Today the activities of the AMN are dominated by issues related to takeovers.

The NBK's Takeover Rules express the perceptions of good practice in takeovers held by a wide array of interested parties in the Swedish commercial community. The Rules are not binding per se but provide that bidders confirm that the NBK Takeover Rules and the AMN rulings on the interpretation and application of those rules are applicable to the offer. This places a contractual obligation on the bidder in relation to the shareholders of the target company to observe the NBK Takeover Rules and the AMN rulings concerning those Rules. Moreover, the NBK Takeover Rules are incorporated in the listing agreements of the Stockholm Stock Exchange, the Nordic Growth Market (NGM) and AktieTorget (the Equities Market Place) and thus binding for bidders and target companies listed on those markets. Specific takeover legislation has so far not been deemed necessary in Sweden.

3. The form of the new takeover regulation

A basic task for the Takeover Committee has been to discuss and evaluate the suitable form of the new regulation of takeovers in Sweden. The Directive does allow continued self-regulation, but presumes that the self-regulation reflects public regulation. This means that self-regulation must be based on law (Article 1). In addition, effective sanctions must be imposed for infringements of the rules (Article 17).

The Committee considered three alternative forms for the new regulation; i) law, ii) law and implementing directives, and iii) law, implementing directives and self-regulation.

Regulation in the form of law would satisfy the requirements of the Directive and have the additional advantage of being in conformity with the forms of civil law regulation established by the Swedish Riksdag (Parliament). Such rules could also be combined with traditional sanctions such as penalties. However, regulation in the form of law would have disadvantages, not least in connection with the interpretation of the rules. Today it is typical for the interpretation of the takeover rules that the purpose of the rules is of great importance. As in the Directive (and modelled on the British regulation) the opening section of the NBK Takeover Rules contains general principles which form the basis of the more detailed rules. These principles serve as guidance for interpretation and application of the rules. Such a form of regulation would hardly be possible in regulation by law. Another very serious negative consequence would be that regulation by law would in effect preclude the possibilities for the parties to obtain binding advance rulings on the interpretation of the rules. Within the framework of the current regulatory system, the AMN continuously issues rulings on the interpretation of the Takeover Rules. In the case of regulation by law, interpretation would essentially be left to the supervisory authority, which would hardly be able to issue binding rulings on the interpretation of the rules with the exception of some clearly specified issues. Disputes regarding the interpretation of the rules would have to be referred to courts of law, which have limited practical and up-to-date experience of business life or the stock market. In addition, the use of administrative or judicial proceedings would probably lead to a considerable lengthening of handling times compared with the current handling by the AMN. Judicially formulated doctrine might also become split.

A combination of law and implementing directives would be a possible alternative to regulation by law only. A fairly brief law would lay down certain basic rules on takeover bids and the Government or an authority appointed by the Government would be authorised to issue more detailed, implementing provisions. Such manner of regulation would satisfy the requirements of the Directive and have the advantage of being both clearly in line with the rule of democracy and quickly adaptable to changes in business practice. Traditional sanctions, such as penalties, could be imposed for infringements of the rules. A serious obstacle to takeover regulation by a combination of law and implementing directives is that it would be in conflict with the Swedish Constitution for the Government or authorities to rule on issues of the kind that are typical in takeovers. According to the Swedish Constitution, rules on personal and economic relationships between individuals – essentially those found in civil law – can only be laid down by law.[4] In civil law, the Government cannot, with some exceptions, execute its normative powers by other means than by issuing notices of enforcement.[5] In practice this means that it is impossible to implement the Takeover Directive in Sweden through the combination of a relatively brief law and one or more comprehensive, implementing directives.

The third option for regulation is to create a legal basis for a continued self-regulation that in substantive terms is adapted to the Directive. This is the regulatory model for implementing the Directive that will be used by the United Kingdom, which, like Sweden, currently uses self-regulation in this context.

Based on an overall assessment of the pros and cons of the alternative regulatory models, the Takeover Committee concluded that the best solution among the aforementioned options would be the latter.

The Committee proposed to build the new takeover regulation through a combination of law and market rules. Stock exchanges and authorised markets will be obliged by law to issue takeover rules, and all bidders making a takeover bid for shares listed on such a market will be obliged by law to undertake to observe those rules. The law is to be combined with sanctions to the effect that a takeover bid can be prohibited if the bidder does not undertake to follow the rules.

Anyone who acquires shares in a listed company to such an extent that his holding is equivalent to 30 per cent or more of the voting power of the company's outstanding shares must, as per the current NBK Takeover Rules, make an offer for the remaining shares of the company. The Committee proposes that such a mandatory bid rule be regulated by law and made more stringent in some respects. This rule by law is to be combined with sanctions such as penalties and a prohibition to exercise the votes of the acquired shares for a bidder who does not observe the mandatory bid rule.

4 The Instrument of Government Article 8, 13 paragraph.
5 The Instrument of Government Article 8, 2 paragraph.

4. The substantive elements of the new takeover regulation

Stock exchanges and authorised stock markets will be required by law to adopt takeover rules. The Takeover Committee has presumed that those rules will initially consist of the NBK Takeover Rules. These rules satisfy essentially the requirements of the Takeover Directive even though they will need revision or addition on some points.

Regarding the most controversial parts of the Takeover Directive – the regulation of defensive measures (Articles 9, 11 and 12) – the Committee took the following view.

Where regulation of so called post-bid defences is concerned, the Swedish rules satisfy the requirement that the Board of the target company may not, at least after the bid is made, take defensive measures aiming to frustrate the bid. This rule is well established and the Committee recommends that it be retained. Consequently, Sweden as a Member State should introduce rules equivalent to Article 9 („opt in") as mandatory law.

The situation is different regarding pre-bid defences. The so called breakthrough rule has no equivalent in Swedish takeover regulation and would probably have serious negative consequences for the possibilities of corporations to issue shares with differentiated voting rights. Sweden should thus, as a Member State, not introduce mandatory law equivalent to Article 11 („opt out") but offer such rules as an option for corporations to introduce in their articles of association.

Sweden should neither, according to the Committee, introduce any reciprocity rules as provided for in Article 12.

The provisions of the Swedish Company Act on the squeeze-out of minority holdings satisfy the requirements of Article 15 and 16.

5. The future supervision

The Swedish Financial Supervisory Authority is responsible for the supervision of the securities market. The new takeover regulation will, however, emphasize its supervisory role in connection with takeovers.

Through the introduction of a mandatory bid rule into law, the Financial Supervisory Authority will be given competence to decide in individual cases whether a bid is mandatory or not and to allow exemptions to the mandatory bid rule. The Financial Supervisory Authority may, however, delegate the handling of such issues to a body consisting of representatives of business and commerce such as the AMN.

Stock exchanges and authorised securities markets will be obliged by law to adopt takeover rules. Consequently, it will to a large extent rest with the markets to supervise the observance of the rules. The relevant market, or a body appointed by such market, shall also have the right to interpret and to grant exemptions from the rules in the same manner as the AMN does today.

6. The continued legislative work

The proposal of the Takeover Committee has been subject to consultation with about fifty authorities, organisations and other bodies. The reactions from these bodies have been positive, and the Swedish Government is now drafted a Government bill on takeover bids that it presented to Parliament in the beginning of 2006.

The Takeover Committee proposed that the new regulation enter into force by the time that the Takeover Directive is to be implemented by the Member States, i.e., 20 May 2006.

Takeovers in Europe – Shareholder Decisions and Open Markets – a UK perspective

Jonathan Rickford[1]

Gliederung

1 Director, The Company Law Centre, British Institute of International and Comparative Law. Visiting Professor, London School of Economics and Political Sciences. An earlier version of this paper was published as Chapter 4 in J Grant Ed., European Takeovers –The Art of Acquisition, Euromoney, London, 2005.

1. Introduction: Regulating Takeovers – Property Rights and Wider Objectives

This paper[2] offers a perspective from a British point of view on the „breakthrough“ provisions of the European Directive on Takeovers[3] and their relation with the provisions on shareholder decision-making and board neutrality. These provisions sit at the centre of a highly charged policy debate about the desirable shape and structure of the markets for capital, corporate control and corporate management services within the EU.

The policy considerations supporting the regulation of mergers[4] fall into two sets – the protection of investors and the facilitation (or impeding) of mergers. The case for the former is largely uncontroversial. But the latter raises rival imperatives. On the one hand regulators may favour industrial restructuring

2 This paper covers part of the ground first reviewed in a paper for the Oxford Roundtable on Corporate Governance in March 2003 (before EU Directive adoption) published as J Rickford, The Emerging European Takeover Law from a British Perspective, (2004) 15 EBLR 1379 („Rickford 2004 EBLR“), which discusses these issues in a wider perspective.

3 Directive 2004/25/EC of 21. 4. 04 on takeover bids, OJ L142/12, 30. 4. 2004 („the Directive“). The Directive is to be brought into force through implementing domestic legislation in each EU and EEA state by 20 May 2006, art. 21(1). Articles referred to without attribution are articles of this directive.

4 „Merger“ is usually used in English to denote business combinations both by takeover (i. e. offers by one company – the bidder – for the shares, or sufficient shares to confer control, in another – the target) and by transactions with similar effect (such as by agreed transfer of target's undertaking). Core policy considerations are the same for both types; UK takeover regulation applies to both. But the Directive, and proposed UK implementing provisions on breakthrough (see below), only apply to takeovers.

and liquid markets in corporate control and management services. But on the other rival policies are in play. These include mercantilist and protectionist policies (misguided or not) favouring company continuity of management and ethos, conservation of control of corporate resources (whether at management, shareholder, or political level) and conservation of employment, within national or state jurisdictions.[5]

The relevant market failures to be addressed by regulation are not controversial in the case of investor protection. These are primarily: inadequate information and time, leading to pressured and ill-judged decisions by target shareholders; preferential bidding excluding weaker investors/outsiders; harassment of company operations by bidders; and interference with the market process by conflicted managers in both bidders and targets.

But opinions may differ on what market failures are to be addressed in the case of policies impeding or facilitating mergers. In particular, national economic objectives may require protection of claimed legitimate externalities. A degree of obstruction of, or at least slowing, of market processes may thus be regarded as necessary to achieve a legitimate public good. But these arguments are open to serious objections based on the Treaty provisions on free movement of capital and establishment, which are designed precisely to oppose many such assertions of national (and nationalist) economic policy.[6]

All these conflicting considerations underlie the new EU merger regime.

The two main models of merger regulation are described below. Both tend to be characterised by reference to the investor protection objective. While the facilitation dimension is inevitably addressed by all systems and there is a trade-off between it and investor protection, that dimension tends to be less specifically addressed.[7] However in the case of the European regime it is explicitly stated as an objective.[8] It was recognised as such throughout the de-

5 What connecting factors „locate" corporate control for this purpose is a debatable question, normally lost in the nationalist rhetoric. But it lies beyond the scope of this chapter.

6 *See* for example the „Golden Share" cases e.g. *Commission v Portugal*, referred to in more detail below.

7 *See Davies/Hopt*, in chapter 7 of The Anatomy of Corporate Law, ed *R Kraakman* et al, Oxford, 2004, making a similar point and drawing a similar distinction and *P Davies*, The Notion of Equality in European Takeover Regulation, in J Payne Ed., Takeovers in English and German Law, Hart, Oxford 2002, 9, 26, 27.

8 Though only in the preamble, (3), (19),(20), (24), but cf. (25), rather than the body of the text.

velopment of the directive and in particular from the revival of the financial services and corporate law action plans, which were triggered by the Lisbon Council declaration on competitiveness in 2000.[9]

The two possible existing models of merger regulation available to Europe were the British („City Code") model and the US model – Europe opted for the former. This relies on continuous a priori regulation of mergers by an expert, hands-on regulator, shareholder freedom of decision making with full information, within a regulated timetable, and its necessary correlative, target board neutrality. The US model, on the other hand, relies, for target shareholder protection, on the exercise by boards of essentially their normal operational powers. Shareholders and other investors and bidders must intervene through the courts to discipline these boards' activities and in particular to secure protection against the inevitable conflicts of interest for directors seeking to protect their own position or extract rents from the transaction.

The British emphasis on shareholder decision-making has much in common with the traditional Continental European approach to the governance of restructuring, through consensual mergers, which is also based on strong versions of such decision-making rules.[10] On the other hand, the British emphasis on freedom of property and contractual rights for target company shareholders conflicts with widespread, if perhaps vague, Continental theories favouring the stakeholder orientation of company governance. These regard such governance as in part designed to serve a wider public good. Such theories are also, perhaps surprisingly, reflected in US theory, which regards the company board as in some sense an independent mandatory of the state with a wider stakeholder oriented remit.[11]

9 Lisbon European Council, Presidency Conclusions, 23–24 March 2000, paragraphs 20–22.

10 E.g. 3rd Directive on mergers of public companies 78/885/EEC, article 7, 6th Directive on divisions of public companies 82/891/EEC, article 5, European Company Statute Council Regulation 2157/2001, articles 17, 32, 37.

11 *See* e.g. *L Bebchuk/A Ferrell* Federalism and Corporate Law, The Race to Protect Managers from Takeovers, (1999) 99 Col LR 1168. The US „stakeholder statutes" are designed to allow, or even oblige, boards to obstruct bids at the expense of shareholders where in the directors' view necessary to protect e.g. employees or local community interests. The statutes were enacted through a combination of local political, trades union and management interests to obstruct the perceived damage to state interests from restructuring and relocation of assets, employment and corporate control. Even in states with no stakeholder statute, e.g. Delaware and other states with laws based on the Model Business Corporations Act (MBCA) the directors' fidelity duty, to serve the interests of „the company", can be invoked to similar

The Directive is perhaps somewhat ambiguous on this critical question, in that it incorporates, as a key overriding principle („general principle (c)"), that

„the board of an offeree company must act in the interests [sic] of the company *and* must not deny the holders of securities the opportunity to decide on the merits of the bid".[12]

But the overall investor protection philosophy of the Directive is clearly based on the first principle, shareholder decision-making, set out in Report of the Commission's advisory High Level Group (known as the Winter Report after its chairman),[13] from which these Directive provisions derive, and thus on freedom of contract and freedom of property rights for shareholders. This principle emerges both in general principle (c) and in the neutrality rule in article 9 of the Directive. That article provides that boards may, during a bid period, only take actions which may result in frustration of the bid with the prior authorisation of a general meeting of shareholders, often referred to as the meeting to authorise „defensive measures".

However the Winter Report was also animated by the need to achieve takeover facilitation,[14] which required that where contractual and property rights were exercised in ways which inhibited „legitimate" bids these rights should be broken through. Thus the breakthrough provision embodies an enhanced, idealised, or paternalistically imposed, freedom of shareholders based on a defined optimal redistribution of rights, described as a breaking through of „restrictions". This is intended to achieve, in takeover situations, the second Winter principle of proportionality, (sometimes simplistically described as „one share: one vote"). Thus the „successful" bidder (defined broadly as a bid-

purpose – see for example MBCA, ABA 1999 Ed., section 8.30 and commentary at 8-41(2).

12 Article 3(1)(c), emphasis added. Does the article imply that the two things cannot conflict? Cf. article 9(5): the board is to publish its opinion of the bid and its effects „on all the Company's interests and specifically employment". Article 3(1)(c) governs implementation of the whole of the directive, including articles 9 (neutrality), 11 (breakthrough) and, crucially, 12 (optionality).

13 This group appointed by the Commission in September 2001 to recommend a way forward after the deadlock in the European Parliament in July 2001, based itself on two principles – shareholder decision making , which requires board neutrality, and proportionality of risk and control, which leads to a breakthrough regime for disproportionate governance rules. See High Level Group of Company Law Experts, Report on Issues Relating to Takeover Bids, EC Brussels 10 January 2002, 20–23.

14 Ibid. 19.

der who has, wholly or in part by virtue of the bid, achieved a 75% holding)[15] should be able to exercise the rights over the company which would have accrued to him if the cash-flow rights, or risk, which he has acquired were reflected in proportionate control. This in its ideal form requires that all „disproportionate restrictions" should therefore be broken, or rather replaced with proportionate provisions. These must operate both during the takeover period (to ensure that defensive measures are only authorised on the basis of a proportionate authority) and after the threshold of success has been achieved by the bidder. At this stage a special meeting (the „post-breakthrough meeting") can be called by the bidder to put in place his preferred control mechanisms.

This principle, proportionality, even in its pure form as proposed by Winter, raises a number of fundamental difficulties.[16] It is also adopted in the Directive in a severely curtailed form and made optional, giving rise to further difficulties and uncertainties. Both the curtailment and the optionality show less than full commitment by the EU legislature to takeover facilitation and the Winter principles.

Thus the investor protection mechanisms, of shareholder decision-making and board neutrality, and the merger-facilitating, breakthrough, policy emerge in the directive against an ambivalent background. There is ambivalence not only on company purposes and the legitimacy of ultimate shareholder control, but also on the facilitating of mergers in open, state and inter-state, markets.

The remainder of this chapter examines the effects of this modified implementation of the breakthrough principle (sometimes called „mini-breakthrough") and its inter-play with the neutrality, or shareholder decision-making, component of the new EU regime.

2. Breakthrough: Restrictions and Threshold

We have noted that breakthrough is characterised as the breaking of the target's restrictions on proportionality of cash-flow rights and control rights when a certain threshold of success has been achieved by the bidder.

15 Acquisition of „control" by other means requires a mandatory general bid – see article 5.

16 For detailed discussion see *Rickford* 2004 EBLR above, 1385 and ff.

The definitions of the restrictions to be broken and of the threshold when they are fully broken are found in article 11. Some restrictions are to be broken for any meeting called to authorise defensive measures, some for the post-breakthrough meeting when the successful bidder is empowered to reorder the company, some for the whole of the offer period and some for that period and thereafter. Article 11 also indicates the threshold of success, when on-going breakthrough is to be achieved.

2.1 „Restrictions“

As for restrictions, broadly speaking (Article 11(2)–(4)):

- Restrictions on free transfer, (including, apparently, limits on holdings) of target company securities, whether incorporated in the articles or in certain contracts[17] are all suspended „vis-à-vis the offeror“,[18] both during the offer period and thereafter if the offeror has achieved the threshold (article 11(2) and (4)),
- „Restrictions on voting rights“, included in the articles, or such contracts, are also suspended and „multiple voting securities“ carry one vote only, for the relevant meetings – i.e. the defensive measures authorisation and post-breakthrough meetings (article 11(3) and (4)).
- „Extraordinary rights“[19] of shareholders to appoint, or remove, board members are not to apply at any time after the bidder achieves the threshold (article 11(4)).

17 I.e. any contract to which the company and the security holder is a party and any other contract between securities holders entered into after adoption of the directive (21. 4. 2004) – art. 11(2), 2nd sentence.

18 This seems to leave such restrictions enforceable *inter partes*, but the effect must presumably be to disapply the restrictions in relation to transfers to the offeror. Apparently even if the threshold is not achieved the bidder remains entitled to securities acquired in this way.

19 Not defined. Presumably these are rights which depart from normal default rules. Under UK standard default articles (Table A 1985 article 73) the board is first appointed in the constitution, the board itself fills casual vacancies, the whole board is replaced at the first annual general meeting by ordinary resolution and one third retire and are similarly replaced at each subsequent AGM. This can be overruled by a special resolution (75% majority). Special rights to appoint directors are sometimes conferred by the articles and they could apparently be by contract with the company (both I believe unheard of for listed companies). The ordinary rule on dismissal is

Various anomalies emerge in the way these provisions relate to multiple voting securities, non-voting securities and securities carrying preferential rights.

2.1.1 Multiple Voting Securities

„Multiple voting securities" are to carry only „one vote each"[20] at both defensive and post-breakthrough meetings. But it seems that only a limited range of voting distortions is covered by this provision. To qualify as „multiple voting securities" securities must be of a „distinct and separate" (sic) class – an unexpected result, achieved not in article 11 but in the definitions in article 2(1)(g). Thus, for example, the typical French „ceiling" or „time lapse voting" shares, which are only fully enfranchised after a holding period, are not caught, because while the voting rights of such shares will vary from time to time, according to the contingency of the duration of a holding, they remain of the same class.[21] This device is sometimes justified on the grounds that it rewards „loyal" or „long-term" shareholders. But the effect is to entrench boards and incumbent shareholders. It clearly infringes the proportionality principle and inhibits takeovers, rendering them more costly and commercially unattractive (typically ensuring that the bidder acquiring such a share obtains a diluted control right unless he is able to wait for up to 4 years for the shares to be fully enfranchised).

But separate classes of multiple voting shares of the kind common in Scandinavia and not unknown in the UK (often referred to as Class A and class B shares) are broken.[22] It is not entirely clear how multiple vote shares of different classes are to be enfranchised – for example suppose that there are two classes of share of £1 nominal with one vote and of £3 nominal with 6 votes are the latter to carry 1 vote, or 3? The proportionate approach seems clearly right in principle but it is not consistent with the language of the directive („one vote each").

Companies Act 1985 section 303 – any director is always dismissable without cause by ordinary resolution.

20 Article 12(3), 3rd paragraph and (4), second phrase.

21 Confirmed by the Commission position in its proposal of 2 October 2002, see Explanatory Memorandum, OJ C45E 25. 2. 2003, at 9. For a description of such „actions à droit de vote double du droit francais" see J Simon, OPA: Divine Surprise ou Faux Semblant?, EUREDIA 2003/3, 329, 340.

22 *See U Bernitz* The Attack on the Nordic Multiple Voting Rights Model (2004) 15 EBLR 1423, and *R Skog* The Takeover Directive, the 'Breakthrough' Rule and the Swedish System of Dual Class Common Stock, ibid, 1439.

2.1.2 Non-voting securities

Non-voting shares are apparently not subject to the breakthrough principle. It is clear that non-voting equity contravenes proportionality. To satisfy the principle it needs both to count as risk capital for assessing the bidder's achievement of the threshold and it needs to be appropriately enfranchised to carry its proper weight at both meetings, both in the hands of the offeror and in the hands of others, whether sympathetic to the offeror or not. Threshold issues are considered below, but as to the second of these needs, enfranchisement, it is reasonably clear that it is not met.

There are a number of reasons for this conclusion. First, as matter of language, it is hard to regard the absence of a vote as a „restriction on voting rights" to be overridden under article 11(3). Voting rights on non-voting securities are not „restricted" – they are just absent (and have never arisen). Second, if it was intended to include non-voting securities, provision would be needed to indicate how many votes non-voting shares should get if, as will normally be the case, they are of a different class from voting shares. Perhaps however this deficiency could be remedied by adopting a proportionate approach, as suggested above for multiple voting securities. But third, and most conclusively, such an outcome seems impossible to reconcile with the Directive definition of „securities" as limited to voting securities in article 2(1)(e). The Directive is full of provisions providing protection only to holders of such „securities". Most significantly in the context of breakthrough, restrictions on transfer, including limits on holdings, are broken through only for such „securities" – i.e. such restrictions on non-voting securities are not overridden. The restrictions on voting rights in the articles appear at first sight possibly (the language point apart) to be breakable whether the securities in question are voting or not, because there is no express linkage to „securities" in article 11(3), first sentence, which governs this. But those in contracts are quite clearly broken only if they are on voting securities – see article 11(3) second sentence, which requires the contracts in question to be with „holders of securities". The inevitable (for the sake of consistency), though surprising, conclusion seems to be that „restrictions on voting rights" can, as the language indeed suggests, only arise on voting securities. The combination of these 3 arguments seems conclusive. Non-voting securities do not, therefore, get the benefit of the breakthrough provision in the sense of having votes conferred upon them, even though they may carry cash-flow risk.

Thus non-voting securities are not enfranchised in the hands of the offeror in the post breakthrough meeting, nor can the offeror, or others sympathetic to the offer, exercise votes on such shares in the meeting called to authorise defensive measures. A company which renders itself bid-proof by keeping voting shares in the hands of the board and its supporters and issuing non-voting equity to others is not vulnerable to breakthrough in that respect.

I understand that securities that are not shares, and therefore can carry no votes, but carry equity risk, through a right to participate in profits, are common in some countries. Thus „enjoyment rights“ (Genussrechte)[23] are increasingly used in Germany and constitute a means of avoiding the one share/one vote principle which applies now to almost all German public companies.[24] These too are apparently, because they are not voting securities, not subject to breakthrough though they may require annual disclosure under the special control disclosure regime in article 10.[25]

2.1.3 Securities with preferential rights

Article 11(6) excludes certain preference-type securities from certain breakthrough provisions. It provides that securities to which breakthrough rules on voting restrictions apply – i.e. for the purpose of adjusting rights during the offer period and/or removing restrictions once the breakthrough threshold has been achieved – do not include „securities where the restrictions on voting are compensated for by specific pecuniary advantages“. It seems that a company can in this sense continue to be bid-proofed by issuing equity with limited voting rights and with, for example, a dividend preference, however small.[26] It is less clear whether acceptances of an offer for such preferential equity will count towards the breakthrough threshold; however I am now in-

23 Art 221(3) Aktiengesetz.

24 *See* Art 12(2) prohibiting „multiple voting rights“ and Art 134(1), (2), prohibiting a ceiling of votes in listed companies. Both provisions were introduced by the Gesetz zur Kontrolle und Transparenz im Unternehmensbereich 6 March 1998 (KontraG), BGBl I 1998 786.

25 Article 10(1)(f) requires disclosure of „systems whereby, with the company's cooperation, the financial rights attaching to securities are separated from the holding of securities“. This seems designed to deal with cases where securities and votes are vested in depositary banks and depositary receipts carry cash-flow rights. Quaere whether Genussrechte are to be disclosed under this provision.

26 Such „preference“ shares need not necessarily be excluded from equity exposure. Similarly the German provision in Aktiengesetz Article 139, for departure from 1 share/1 vote for preference shares, allows substantial departure from the proportionality principle. Restrictions on transfer of such securities in the articles or in relevant agreements are broken through during the bid period but (apparently) not post-breakthrough – article 11(6) disapplies (3) and (4), but not (2).

clined (in agreement with the UK Government's announced intentions on the threshold – see below) to believe that it will.[27]

2.2 Threshold

There are also problems on the definition of the threshold for breakthrough and the concept of risk capital in that connection. Article 11(4) merely provides that „where the offeror holds 75% of the capital carrying voting rights" this allows the offeror to call the post-breakthrough meeting. This makes it quite clear that acceptances of offers for non-voting shares do not count towards achievement of the breakthrough threshold (consistently with the analysis of restrictions above). But it is not clear how the 75% share of voting capital is to be determined where there are more than one class of voting share.

Perhaps the most obvious possible criteria are nominal value or voting power. A third, less objective and orthodox, criterion is market value. As to the first two possibilities, if multiple voting shares and single voting shares have the same nominal value is the achievement of 75% to be assessed by reference to their aggregate nominal value or rather to the aggregate of voting rights acquired? Presumably it would not be consistent with the directive for member states to implement it by treating „75% of the capital carrying voting rights" as meaning either (i) „capital carrying 75% of the voting rights", or perhaps even (ii) „capital carrying 75% of the voting rights at the post breakthrough meeting". Yet weighting the capital acquired by reference to nominal value seems to lead to the anomaly that in determining whether the 75% threshold has been achieved a French „ceiling" share can be treated as weighted according to its nominal value, but at the post breakthrough meeting its actual voting power is to remain restricted, because it is not a „multiple voting right" share. Arguments of consistency point towards interpretation (ii) above, but it is probably unsustainable.

27 Cf. *J Rickford* (2004) EBLR, above, at 1392. Article 11(6) provides that (3) and (4) shall not apply to „*securities* where the restrictions on voting rights are compensated for ...", etc. (4) defines the threshold as where the offeror „holds 75% or more of the *capital* carrying voting rights". If (6) is construed narrowly and literally, as is appropriate for an exception, it does not exclude preference shares from the general reference to „capital" but only from „securities" in (4). This means, anomalously, as with the French case above, successful bidders may pass the threshold but not command 75% of the votes at the post threshold meeting. But this objection is hardly conclusive, particularly given that precedent.

This is amongst the issues to be resolved by member states when they come to implement. The UK government proposes to adopt the third possible approach mentioned above – i.e. to define the threshold by the value of the voting securities acquired (including shares such as preference shares, which carry the right to vote only in certain circumstances, such as when a preferential dividend is in arrears).[28] This seems to be permitted by the directive.[29] It is arguably also the interpretation most consistent with the theory underlying the proportionality principle (on the basis that market values reflect future cash-flow rights). It will however give rise to valuation problems at the margin, at least where a class of voting shares is not quoted. It will also again produce the anomalous result, mentioned above for the nominal value approach, in some cases – i.e. where voting preference shares count towards the threshold but do not count towards the votes available to the bidder, whether at the defensive measures or at the post threshold meetings.

2.3 Conclusions on Restrictions and Threshold

By way of conclusion on the Directive definitions of the restrictions to be broken through and the threshold to be achieved to allow such breakthrough, it seems fair to reflect that the rules seem to be complex, arbitrary, obscure and highly imperfect in achieving the desired result.[30] Arguably they discriminate unfairly between different devices with equivalent effect which operate in different member states. A cynic might conclude that the larger states, France, Germany and the UK, successfully exempted their national practices – de-

28 *See* clause R26(2) and R29(1) in the DTI Company Law Reform announcement, 19 July 2005 <http://www.dti.gov.uk/cld/clauses.htm> („DTI Announcement").

29 *See* the discussion of the preference shares exception, above.

30 For completeness it should be added here that article 11(6) disapplies article 11 from securities which confer special rights on member states where „compatible with the Treaty" and for other such rights (including, presumably, special rights conferred on states otherwise than as shareholders and on others, whether as shareholders or not). This exempts lawful „golden shares" and the like. European Court of Justice jurisprudence substantially reduces the scope for such internal market distortions. See cases C-367/98, C-483/99, C-503/99, C-463/00, C-98/01 and C-174/04 (Commission v Portugal, France, Belgium, Spain, UK and Italy, respectively). Member states may take advantage of this provision to treat such companies as conforming with the breakthrough regime – i.e. disregarding such offending provisions (with consequent benefits as bidders as well as targets – see below. But the UK clauses, DTI Announcement, above, simply prevent such companies „opting in" to article 11 – clause R24(4)).

layed ceiling voting, preferential and non-voting shares respectively – while Scandinavian countries, where multiple voting shares in separate classes are common, failed to achieve a similar escape. The proposed UK implementing measures do not generally adopt a position on the difficulties of interpretation mentioned above. They simply require that before a UK company can opt in to breakthrough its constitution must satisfy the directive requirements, either in all circumstances, or at least in circumstances where the Directive applies.[31]

3. Breakthrough – Compensation, Jurisdiction and Mandatory Bids

The other main issues on the content of the breakthrough regime relate to compensation for loss of restriction rights, the implications of the Directive rules on jurisdiction – i. e. which national authority is to regulate the various aspects of a takeover with international characteristics – and the effect of the enhanced rights of bidders as a result of breakthrough on the mandatory bid regime, which is a central part of the investor protection provisions of the directive.

3.1 Compensation

Article 11(5) provides a right to „equitable compensation" for removal of rights as a result of the breakthrough rules (including the voluntary adoption by companies of breakthrough as the result of the optional provisions in article 12, discussed below). This gives rise to issues about quantum and timing.

3.1.1 Compensation – Quantum

First how is this compensation to be assessed? Is it to reflect the private benefits achievable by exercising block-holder power – arguably a price for in-

31 *See* DTI Announcement, clause R24(3). Non constitutional constraints are however specifically addressed in clause R26, which removes restrictions on the transfers of shares to the offeror during the offer period and to any person thereafter (although article 11(2) (offer period) refers to „securities" and to agreements vis-à-vis the offeror and is invoked by article 11(4) (post threshold)).

siders' looting opportunities and not a basis to be recognised in law? It is sometimes argued, as an alternative, that shares with enhanced control rights carry a premium to reflect the benefit to outsiders of such block-holder governance. But it is not clear that these two arguments are really distinct. Special rights holders may indeed be regarded as entitled to a preferential share of the enterprise value at the outsiders' expense to reflect the benefits to outsiders of „blockholder" control. But if the market attaches a premium to special rights shares, this can only be because the market expects cash flow advantages (in the shape of private benefits) to flow from their holding. Whatever the merits of that debate, the bidder's passing of the threshold surely indicates that in the judgement of the members the incumbent management has failed to achieve a competitive performance. This would indicate that the insiders/controllers have failed to secure any advantages to the company as a whole which were envisaged as the quid pro quo for dilution of the outsiders' control. If so, any such implicit bargain to reward block-holders for governance advantages has failed and no compensation is justified, or „equitable" in directive terms. Market valuations may perhaps reflect either of these considerations, private benefits to block-holders or benefits conferred by block-holders on outsiders. Perhaps there is merely a less precise recognition that control confers benefits at the expense of outsiders, which are permissible within the overall flexible framework of discretionary operational control and business judgement. But it should be noted that this is hardly consistent with the overall philosophy of the Directive: a control premium is denied under the mandatory bid rule,[32] which seems inconsistent with recognition of a premium for control blocks.

Whatever the merits of these arguments and their implications for quantifying compensation (if any), compensation is now mandatory for „any loss suffered" under articles 11 and 12. The terms and modalities are to be set by member states.

3.1.2 Compensation – Timing

There appear also to be problems about timing of the fixing of such compensation. Because of the difficulties of quantifying it the member states are likely to set up some mechanism of arbitration, appraisal or adjudication. This will have the additional attraction of avoiding the need to settle quantum issues at the implementation stage. But such processes are likely to be

32 Article 5.

controversial and time-consuming. Are they to take place before the offer can proceed, in which case the delays are likely to kill the viability of the breakthrough mechanism, or after the event?

Article 6(3)(e) indicates that a bidder who wishes to rely on breakthrough must make an offer of compensation in advance. This provision requires the offer document to state, inter alia, „the compensation offered for the rights which might be removed as a result of the breakthrough rule", with particulars of how it is to be paid and the method to be employed in determining it. But it is difficult to understand how this provision for an offer of compensation in the offer document is intended to work.

The legislative objective is that the shareholders whose shares are not acquired should have their rights broken through and it is difficult to follow how the level of compensation to be given to them can be made the subject of a contractual offer. Where an offer is addressed to shareholders whose rights might be broken through, and such shareholders accept the offer, no issue of equitable compensation for them can arise. Moreover, since the directive requires equivalent treatment of shareholders of the same class, it is difficult to see how one set of shareholders with special rights could be awarded compensation for breakthrough while another set achieves merely the offer price for voluntary surrender of their rights.[33]

On the other hand, where such an offer is made the costs of compensating the shareholders whose rights are to be broken through will depend on how many of them accept the offer. General Principle (e) in article 2(1) of the Directive, which corresponds to General Principle 3 in the City Code, requires that the offeror should be sure that he has access to the finances needed to complete the offer. How can this be achieved with no certainty as to the cost of breakthrough? Although the offer of compensation is required in the offer document, this may not be accepted. Some form of ex post adjudication or appraisal will still be required to achieve an equitable measure of compensation. Indeed what that measure is may depend in part on the extent to which shareholders with special rights, and perhaps others who are not shareholders, have accepted the offer in the offer document.

33 Article 3(1)(a) – equivalent treatment. Article 6(3)(e) appears also to require the offer document to offer the compensation not only to shareholders but also to other holders of rights to be broken through. Is the offer document to be addressed to them?

3.1.3 Compensation and Class Rights

As we shall see below, member states are free to opt out of the breakthrough rule, but if they do companies are to be given the option to opt back in, so as to subject themselves voluntarily to the regime. This is to be done by resolution in general meeting in accordance with the law applicable to amendment of the articles of association.[34] Many, but not all of the necessary changes, which will be required to remove special rights which are to be overridden by the adoption of the breakthrough regime, will be rights attaching to a class of shares. Variations of companies' articles in most systems require special majorities of the class affected to authorise such alterations of their rights.

So in the case of such rights, if the member state in question adopts the optional approach to breakthrough, the problems of compensation can, arguably, be solved in advance by consent. Special resolutions of meetings of the classes affected will be required and if these are carried then there is no longer a case for equitable compensation in respect of the rights waived or modified. The UK Government proposes to adopt this route.[35] It is an elegant solution, but open to objection on two possible scores. The first objection is that the directive is intended to facilitate mergers by creating favourable conditions for bidders and the imposition of an additional resolution over and above the standard resolution required for altering the articles is an impermissible additional impediment. The second objection is that the directive requires that all rights holders should be allowed equitable compensation and the solution proposed may not be equitable for the minority dissentients in the class meetings. These arguments deserve consideration,[36] but they are not persuasive. First, the reference in article 12 to the rules for varying the articles must include all the relevant rules, including special rules in class rights cases. And second a qualified majority acceptance of whatever terms have been set for the variation of rights may legitimately be regarded as providing an indication of the equitability of those terms, satisfying the directive test of equitable compensation for all. General company law provisions protect minorities from unfair treatment at the hands of the majority.

However unfortunately even if this conclusion is correct, this solution to the problem both of quantum and of timing of compensation for loss of rights

34 Article 12(2) 2nd.

35 *See* DTI Announcement 2005, above, explanatory notes, 16, 17. Companies Act 1985 ss. 125–129.

36 Not least because if they are correct some rights holders have individual rights and some only class rights, see below.

through breakthrough is incomplete. It does not deal with rights which are not class rights of shareholders. Parties to agreements with rights restricting the transfer of shares will not necessarily be shareholders and their rights are normal contractual ones, rather than rights under the articles. They are not therefore protected by the class rights provisions. For this reason the UK Government proposal includes special provisions allowing the holders of such rights to apply to the court for compensation for the breakthrough of their rights.[37] Unfortunately a scheme providing for the consent of such rights holders, similar to the regime for class rights holders, does not look consistent with the directive.[38]

The implementation of the provisions for compensation for breakthrough looks likely to present formidable problems for the member states, particularly for those which do not opt out of article 11. As we shall see below, all member states have an inescapable obligation to make such provision as a result of the provisions of article 12 on options.

3.2 Jurisdiction

The Directive rules on jurisdiction may also raise issues in the breakthrough context.

Article 4(2) provides, to simplify somewhat, that where a company is formed[39] in one member state, but only listed in another or others, the member state of listing is to have jurisdiction in such matters as the bid price, bid procedure, the offer document and disclosure of the bid. But the state of formation is to have jurisdiction on employee matters and „company law" matters, such as the definition of control and the conditions under which frustrating board action is to be allowed. In such dual jurisdiction cases who is to have authority for setting and regulating the breakthrough process?

37 Ibid., clause R26(5). Quaere whether this provision needs to extend further to cover contractual rights as against the company for the appointment or dismissal of directors. These too need not be contained in articles nor be conferred on shareholders.

38 There is a case for directive amendment if only for consistent treatment of rights holders. After 5 years the Commission is to review the operation of the Directive and make proposals for revision – article 20. Compare the facility under a Companies Act 1985 section 425 scheme of arrangement.

39 Strictly speaking „has its registered office" there, which may raise complications for countries which apply the „real seat" doctrine, problems beyond the scope of this paper.

As to compensation, the answer appears to be the place of listing, because this relates to the price. Moreover, as we have seen, the compensation must be disclosed in the offer document – a matter for the state of listing. But as to whether the threshold is achieved and what restrictions are to be treated as broken through and the effects of this at the various stages in the process, there seems to be more difficulty. Is each of these a „matter relating to company law" under article 4(2)(e)? Arguably the issue is analogous to the percentage of voting rights required for control for mandatory bid purposes, or the conditions under which management may take action to frustrate the bid, and is therefore a matter for the law of the target company's incorporation.[40] If this is correct then particularly close co-operation between the authorities concerned will be required in such cases.[41] The UK government in draft clauses implementing the Directive recently published treats compensation matters as a matter for the law of the registered office, applying the relevant provisions to British registered companies.[42] But when the UK Takeover Panel makes rules about the offer document to implement article 6(3) these will need to extend to companies incorporated elsewhere in the EEA but not listed there and listed in the UK.

3.3 Mandatory Bids

Finally there may be questions on the relationship of the breakthrough rule with Article 5, which requires a mandatory bid on the acquisition of control. If breakthrough would apply if a bid were to be made, should the potential for breakthrough change the threshold for determining control on the ground that if the target is subject to the rule acquisition of control is easier? Since the Directive is silent on this it is presumably for member states to resolve. The short and simple answer appears to be that a company is subject to the manda-

40 Whether reciprocity action is available to the target and under what conditions is apparently a matter for the member state of the registered office, but the circumstances in which it can be invoked and its relationship with the board's duties under general principle (c) in Article 2(1) are less clear – see article 12 and the discussion below.

41 Such co-operation is required under article 4(4).

42 *See* DTI Announcement July 2005, above, Clause R26(5), providing compensation for loss resulting from the overriding of agreements restricting the transfer of shares relating to British registered companies. Other restrictions are dealt with under the British opt-out regime by class protection rights at the company opt-in stage – see above.

tory bid rule because it is in a position to exercise control now, without the need to acquire more shares or exercise breakthrough powers in consequence. So the fact that breakthrough might become possible in relation to the target should be treated as irrelevant. It may also not be possible to say with certainty whether, if a bid were to be made, the breakthrough rule would apply, as this may depend on a company's use of optionality.

4. Operating the Directive: Optionality

The preceding section examined some aspects of the breakthrough regime in article 11 of the Directive and its relationship with the neutrality or „no frustration" rule in article 9.

However the effect of these provisions is complicated by the compromise solution on neutrality and breakthrough adopted in the Directive. This was designed to meet the opposition in the European Parliament and in some member states on a number of grounds. The respectable argument was that the directive imposed neutrality but could only achieve a „level playing field" for operation of neutrality through a breakthrough provision which was incomplete and interfered with property rights. The less respectable argument, which undoubtedly had a role to play, was that the directive neutrality regime, even in its modified form, would allow national structures of control and political and economic influence to be broken down by cross-frontier bids.

The solution was to confer both member state and company options on the application of both neutrality and breakthrough. This solution was so far reaching that it met all these arguments.

This part of the chapter examines some aspects of how those options are likely to play out. The ground rules for the use of the options will be identified first.

The section then turns to the likely outcomes from a UK perspective[43] –

- First in terms of the choice by the UK government on whether to opt out of article 9 (neutrality), or 11 (breakthrough), or both.

43 The reader who regards this as parochial may draw comfort from the fact that it makes for simplicity, by excluding many permutations.

- Next the implications of such choice for the decisions of companies under the likely UK regime will be examined.
- Finally the likely use by the UK government of the reciprocity option (Article 12) and the consequences for British companies, first as targets and then as bidders, will be assessed.

4.1 Neutrality/Breakthrough Options – Ground Rules

There are 3 basic ground rules for the exercise of the options open in respect of neutrality and breakthrough, which can be appreciated from Table 1 below which sets out a route map of the possible options for any company subject to the Directive.

Table 1: 13th Directive Optionality – A Road Map

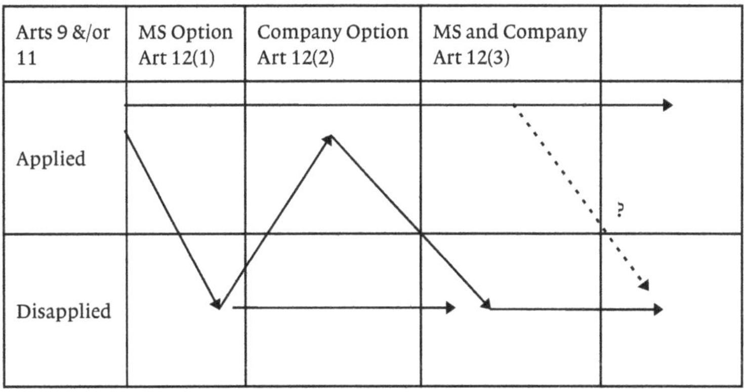

With acknowledgements to Professor *Zimmer*.[44]

The rules can be explained as follows –

(i) Member states may opt out of Articles 9 (neutrality) and/or 11 (breakthrough) (hereafter for simplicity „9 and/or 11") – Article 12(1). If a member state retains 9 and/or 11, companies incorporated in that state are bound by it/them, and have no options (probably however subject to their being permit-

44 This Table is a slightly modified version of a Table offered by Profesor *Zimmer* at a BIICL conference on the 13th Directive in 2005.

ted by the relevant member state under ground rule (iii) below to opt out when faced with a bid from a company which does not apply the same articles – the „reciprocity power“, see below).

(ii) In relation to an article which a member state opts out of in this way, it must allow its companies to opt back in. This decision is reversible by the company and is to be taken by the shareholders in general meeting by enhanced majority – article 12(2). It was argued that even though companies might be permitted by member states to adopt the less open position of rejecting neutrality and/or breakthrough they should be given the opportunity to choose, or be thrust by market forces into, a more liberal or open stance.

(iii) Member states clearly have an option to allow any company opting back in again under article 12(2) in this way, to decide to opt out again in certain circumstances, (the reciprocity power already mentioned which is provided for by article 12(3)). Key rules for those circumstances are – there must be a bid by a company (or an associate of such a company) which does not apply the „same“ articles, as a consequence of the optional arrangements. This decision (the reciprocity opt-out) may be taken by a company board but it must have been authorised by the general meeting to do so no more than 18 months before the bid was announced.[45]

Tiresome, but potentially important, questions of interpretation arise on the scope of this reciprocity power.

There is no doubt from the text that it may be conferred on target companies which have been exempted from 9 and/or 11 by the relevant member state implementing provision under article 12(1) but have chosen to opt back in under article 12(2) (ie companies voluntarily subject to 9 and/or 11). But it is more doubtful whether article 12(3) also allows member states to enable a company to exercise this reciprocity power where 9 and/or 11 apply to it involuntarily. This will be because the company has not opted back in under article 12(2), but because the member state has not opted out of those articles under article 12(1) in the first place.[46]

The relevant texts are the substantial provision in article 12(3) and the explanatory words in the preamble, paragraph (21).

Article 12(3) allows member states to exempt „*companies which apply* Articles 9(2) and (3) and/or 11 from applying Articles 9(2) and (3) and or 11 if they be-

45 Article 12(3) and (5), read with preamble, paragraph (21).
46 *See* the dotted line in the Table.

come subject to *an offer launched by a company which does not apply the same articles* as they do ...". Paragraph (21) of the preamble expands this by stating „Without prejudice to international agreements .... Member States should be allowed not to require *companies which apply these provisions in accordance with the optional arrangements* to apply them when they become subject to an offer launched by a company *which does not apply the same provisions as a consequence of the use of these optional arrangements*" [emphasis added].

The natural meaning of these texts, read together, seems on a first impression to be that they enable member states to confer the reciprocity power *only on companies which have opted back in under article 12* (ie which „apply these provisions in accordance with the optional arrangements") and that the reciprocity power is only exercisable against bidding companies to which the same articles do not apply as a result of the use of the same opting arrangements (ie they have decided not to opt back in under article 12(2), or conceivably have done so but then reversed that decision).

However this strict interpretation is very arguably absurd, at least in relation to target companies.

As for such targets, why should the position of a target company be different where it is a subject to article 9 and/or 11 by operation of member state law, as opposed to where it has exercised its own option to adopt 9 and/or 11? And why should the decision by a member state to apply 9 and/or 11 to all its companies preclude it from conferring on them a power which it could confer if it did not take that arguably stricter and more desirable position? This would be an incentive for member states to opt out of those articles. Only then could companies secure the benefit of reciprocity by voluntarily adopting them.

This argument from the merits can be accommodated in the texts in two steps. First on the substantive provision in article 12(3), it is reasonably arguable that target companies which are subject to 9 and/or 11 involuntarily (ie because member states have not opted out) nevertheless do „apply" those articles. The language of article 12(1), which allows member states „not to require companies ... to *apply*" 9 and/or 11, confirms this use of the word. Such companies therefore fall within article 12(3) consistently with the use of language in the directive text.

As for the preamble provision, it can then be argued that the language should not be read as restricting this effect, ie such a target company is a company which applies 9 and/or 11 „in accordance with the optional arrangements" in the sense that the member state has failed to exercise the option to opt out of them. This is admittedly a somewhat more stretched use of language, particularly bearing in mind that the article 12 regime is an exception and reciprocity an exception to the exception, normally requiring strict construction.[47]

To my mind however the argument on the merits supported by this textual analysis is on balance reasonably convincing. This view of the scope of article 12(3) – the „liberal view" – (allowing the benefits of reciprocity to be conferred on companies which are subject to 9 and/or 11 involuntarily as a result of a member state decision not to opt out) is the preferable one. The rest of this paper adopts that view but, because the conclusion cannot be claimed as certain, at appropriate points it refers to the implications of the stricter view.[48] (The two views are referred to below as the „liberal" and the „strict" view.)

4.2 UK Government Options on Articles 9 and 11

Adopting the British perspective, how will the UK exercise the options? As to Article 9, the UK was always very unlikely to contemplate an opt-out from neutrality. This would require a complete rewrite of the City Code, with the discarding of the fundamental General Principle 7 on board neutrality, and undermine the common law Proper Purpose doctrine which provides that directors are not to use their powers for purposes which subvert the overall control over the ownership of the company, which lies with shareholders.[49] It would even call into question the basic loyalty duty which requires directors to act in the best interest of the company, by which is meant that of the mem-

47 Some assistance might be gained from the similar (though not identical) language used in the preamble to describe the offeror company against which reciprocity can be invoked. This is described there as a company which „does not apply the same provisions as a consequence of the use of these optional arrangements". Unfortunately however the attractive a contrario argument, that companies which *do* apply such provisions involuntarily must be immune from reciprocity and are therefore cannot be companies which „do not apply the same provisions as a consequence of the use of these optional arrangements" does not run. All offeror companies which fail to apply 9 and/or 11 will do so voluntarily by use of the optional arrangements, in the sense that they will have failed to opt back in.

48 This „more liberal" view is taken by J Simon, above, OPA: Divine Surprise ou Faux Semblant?, EUREDIA 2003/3, 329, 340 (with slight hesitation) and S Maul and A Kouloridas, the Takeover bids Directive, (2004) 5 German Law Journal No 4, at [12] (without discussion).

49 *Hogg v Cramphorn* [1967] Ch 254, *Howard Smith v Ampol* [1974] AC 821 PC.

bers as a whole. The UK Government has now announced its intention to opt into article 9 and takeover rules implementing that decision as part of the implementation of the Directive are expected to be announced shortly.[50]

But the position is very different for article 11. As we have seen above, there are powerful objections to applying the breakthrough regime to British listed companies. These objections are based on 3 main consideration –

First there are cases where breakthrough will override arguably wholly legitimate property rights. These fall into three main classes.

First a small minority of listed companies entrench blockholder, often family holding, structures through equity shares with differentiated voting rights. Many of these have reached the point where an increasingly diffuse, perhaps second or third generation, family holding may allow bidders to acquire sufficient of the family shares to achieve the threshold (however it is to be defined – see above). Typically these companies are of minor economic and political importance, (for example family owned breweries which are fast disappearing) but some are significant. For example, one is a major media group – Daily Mail and General Trust plc. (But note that the Daily Mail share structure is a two class one, of voting and non-voting shares. The discussion above suggests that probably, because the absence of a vote is not a breakthrough restriction, Daily Mail is immune from article 11.) Newly listed companies may well wish to retain family holding structures or existing control structures of this kind and to outlaw them might deter legitimate new entry to the listed market. It is uncertain how many UK companies may be in this position.

A second class of such companies involves structures designed to protect a particular company ethos inherent in the value of the company. An example is Reuters plc, another major listed media and technology company, whose share structure includes a voting trust designed to prevent damaging changes

50 *See* Implementation of the Directive on Takeover Bids – A Consultative Document, DTI, London, January 2005 URN 05/511, 3.6 and DTI Announcement 2005, above, draft clauses R24. I have argued elsewhere – see note 16 above – that there is one possible counter-argument – that a UK opt-out of article 9 would allow companies to opt back in under article 12(2), thus giving such companies the advantage of invoking the reciprocity power to opt out again under article 12(3), when faced with a bidder not applying „the same" Articles. But this depended on the stricter view of article 12(3), rejected above. In any event this argument never seemed likely to have any weight in the UK. UK companies are already subject to this alleged handicap and the objections to enabling them to empower their boards to engage in such tactics are overwhelming. There are also major objections in principle to the reciprocity power and the UK appears firmly to have decided not invoke it – see below.

of control or company policy. The Reuters structure resembles state golden share provisions but the interest designed to be protected – editorial independence – is not such as could be protected by a member state golden share. The exemption for state special rights under article 11(6) very arguably extends to such provisions. However without activation of that article, which is not currently intended by the UK government,[51] the Reuters structure would apparently in its present form be broken by the directive breakthrough mechanism if Reuters were to opt in.[52]

The third class of such companies are the so-called „double headed" companies. These are enterprises usually formed from companies incorporated in two jurisdictions and bound together by articles provisions designed to ensure an indissoluble link of management and ownership. This would for example prevent control of one company being acquired without control of the other. Typical such mechanisms require common board membership and that shares in both companies are held in the same hands. This involves special rights of board appointment and dismissal and restrictions on transfers of shares (for example requiring that acquisition of shares in one company must be accompanied by acquisition of shares in the other or that directors must be appointed to both boards). These restrictions would clearly be subject to breakthrough, allowing one company to be taken over without the other, destroying the dual character of the enterprise.[53]

A second group of objections to adopting article 11 centre on the uncertainties and inconsistencies of the restriction and threshold components of the rule and the obscurity and apparent unworkability of the compensation regime, discussed above.

Thirdly, related to these considerations, if the limits of the restrictions broken through have been correctly identified above, then adoption of article 11 will provide a powerful incentive to companies to adopt those defensive structures

51 *See* the DTI Announcement July 2005, above, and draft clauses.

52 It involves a ceiling on shareholdings of 15% in the articles and a special share with enhanced voting powers enabling override of resolutions proposed by anyone controlling Reuters or which threaten its editorial independence see <http://about.reuters.com/aboutus/overview/ independence.asp>. The government proposes to opt out of article 11 see below. But the failure to invoke article 11(6) prevents Reuters from opting in without changing its constitution (assuming that the Reuters provisions' justification by reference to editorial independence renders them consistent with community law).

53 *See* for example the account of Unilever's structure in F Barca and M Becht, The Control of Corporate Europe, Oxford 2001, 35.

which escape the provision – mainly non-voting and time-lapse voting shares and possibly non share equity rights. In this way they can retain disproportionate voting structures while gaining the benefits of technical article 11 conformity – closed company wolves in open company sheep's clothing so to speak.

While UK institutional investors favour article 11, as was clear from the Government's consultation, even if the UK opts out of article 11 companies are nevertheless free to opt into it under art 12(2) and institutional investors are free to exercise their influence to bring this about.

It may be objected that this very right to opt back in means that the difficulties identified with article 11 will have to be addressed anyway. This is true. However the problems will be smaller in practical effect if they need only be addressed for companies which opt back in.

The UK government has now announced that it proposes to opt out of article 11, citing many of the arguments above together with fears that imposing one share: one vote structures on companies may lead them to seek listing outside the EU or in an EU state which had opted out.[54]

4.3 UK Company opt-ins to article 11

If the UK government does not opt out of article 9, but does of article 11, as currently proposed, it must provide for companies to opt to reapply article 11, see article 12(2). Provision will therefore have to be made in any event to address all the problems of the breakthrough regime set out above.

Will UK companies opt for „reapplying“[55] Art 11 in this way?

For the typical one share/one vote company this will make no difference to their current vulnerability to bids, but may enhance their powers as bidders, because of consequent immunity to reciprocal action, see below. Even if the UK decides not to exercise the option to confer reciprocity powers on UK

54 *See* the DTI 2004 consultation document note 48 above, 3.7–3.9.

55 There is a minor awkwardness in speaking of companies which already comply with the one share one vote open structure embodied in the breakthrough conditions as „opting in“ to article 11. They are already „in“. This problem is resolved in the UK draft clauses by providing that such companies may pass a resolution to opt in. See clause R24 referred to above. There is no doubt that this is legitimate under the Directive

companies, such immunity will still be an advantage. Although it will in that case make no difference to UK bidders for UK targets, the immunity will be available against target companies in other member states. Few such open structured UK companies are likely to be deterred from opting in by the concern that they might wish at some later stage to change their constitution into a more „closed“, or disproportionate form. Even if they were they are reasonably free by special resolution to opt out again.[56] Such companies will therefore very probably opt in under article 12(2). They have nothing of significance to lose and an immunity against reciprocal defensive measures in some cases to gain. What those cases are is discussed below.

There will also be a number of UK companies which are not one share/one vote companies but which have share structures which are not vulnerable to breakthrough, particularly those which rely on non-voting shares to achieve restricted control, such as Daily Mail and General Trust plc. These companies too will have nothing to lose by opting back in to article 11. Moreover they will have something to gain, because by doing so they will render themselves immune to reciprocity measures under article 12(3) by any company for which they may choose to make a bid. They thus become „wolves in sheep's clothing“ as already described. This is a particularly outrageous effect of the limits on the restrictions subject to breakthrough which is likely to deter many community companies from opting back in under article 12(2). The reciprocity regime is very far from achieving „equality of arms“.

For other companies the decision will be more balanced. It will be possible to opt in in a way which retains existing control structures for general purposes, leaving the company open only in relation to successful (i.e. threshold achieving) bidders. The decision to reverse the „reapplication“ of article 11 (opting out again), must be in general meeting by qualified majority but the closed structures may operate in relation to this decision.[57] Evidently existing control structures will operate in such meetings.

56 Article 12(2). The proposed UK clauses will however require that this is not done for 12 months to prevent abuse by short term opting in and out to achieve tactical advantage during bids, see DTI Announcement 2005, above, clause R25(6) and explanatory notes, 16.

57 Art 12(2). The UK clauses allow a company to opt in to article 11 either by altering the company's constitution to remove the restrictions entirely or by adopting measures which ensure that they only operate consistently with article 11 – see clause R24(3)(a)(i) and (ii).

However it seems unlikely that the decision to opt back in to article 11 will be attractive to UK blockholders and holders of special rights who are rendered vulnerable by article 11.

4.4 UK Government Option on Reciprocity

If, as is now very likely, the UK finally decides to apply article 9 but to opt out of article 11, the next question is whether to allow companies which are subject to either article (in the first case whether they like it or not, but in the second because they have opted back in) the benefit of the reciprocity power under article 12(3).

4.4.1 Application of Article 9 to the UK Target

We have assumed that the UK will subject all UK registered companies to Article 9 neutrality. Will a UK company ever be able to opt *out of* Article 9?

The answer to this question depends in part on whether the liberal or strict view is taken of article 12(3), discussed above. On the strict view the UK could not enable UK companies to disapply article 9 when faced with a bidder who does not apply the same articles because such companies are not „applying the article in accordance with the optional arrangements“.[58]

But even if the liberal view is correct, it has always been very unlikely that the UK will exercise the option to allow UK companies to opt out of article 9 neutrality in reciprocity cases for the same reasons (discussed above) as it seems likely that it will not opt out of the article under article 12(1). (If these arguments are not enough there are also objections in principle to allowing company boards to exercise reciprocity powers, which are discussed in the context of article 11, below.)

The UK government has also now announced that it does not intend to allow reciprocity in relation to article 9 (or indeed 11, but the arguments on this are perhaps more open and are discussed separately below).[59] It will therefore be assumed below that UK companies will not be free to opt out of article 9.

58 Preamble (21), 3rd sentence – discussed above.

59 *See* DTI Consultation Document 2004, note 48 above.

4.4.2 Application of article 11 to the UK Target

Will the UK exercise its power under art 12(3) to allow companies which have opted back into article 11 to engage in reciprocity? What are the merits of such reciprocity in principle? Vulnerability to breakthrough creates a stronger discipline on management and controlling shareholders by strengthening the hand of outsiders. Is there any case for allowing this discipline to be diluted where the bidder is not subject to the same discipline?

There are a number of arguments against doing so –

First, the bidder's structure is normally irrelevant to offeree shareholders. There may be an argument that in a share for share offer the offerees stand to be locked into a company with a less open structure than their own. But. so long as they are properly informed, as they should be under article 10, they can express their wishes on this by not accepting and/or demanding a higher price.

Second, the reciprocity power is to be exercised by the board, though on the basis of a shareholder authority.[60] To confer such a power on a board in a bid seems inconsistent with the neutrality principle and raises all the dangers of conflict of interest which led the UK, and more recently the EU, to adopt the shareholder decision model.

Third, the resolution conferring the power can be achieved on the basis of pre-breakthrough majorities. It will be likely to be exploited to achieve the special interests of those benefiting from disproportionate restrictions.

But the most important objections are more general and fundamental ones. The purpose which the power serves raises fundamental issues of legal principle and economic policy at both national and community law level.

At national level the main argument in favour of the provision appears to be that it is somehow legitimate for directors of a target company to inhibit a commercial transaction which would otherwise properly proceed, because the constitution of a bidder is objectionable, in the sense that the bidder would not be open to a similar bid itself. This is a mercantilist, or international trade policy, argument about the conditions of international establishment and the risks of the companies from one member state (or perhaps a third country, but

60 The authority must have been conferred a maximum of 18 months before the bid announcement (creating a recurring shareholder discipline), but an ordinary resolution is sufficient for community purposes – article 12(5).

as to this see below) taking over those from another without the possibility of reciprocal vulnerability. There is a fear of „one way traffic" in corporate control with „national assets" being „stolen". This general policy argument is likely to be completely irrelevant to the merits of the bid, and not a matter which should be of concern to the target board. Indeed such a consideration is ruled out by the directive itself, which, by the overriding principle in article 3(1)(c), requires the target board „to act in the interests of the company as a whole". Making target boards the instruments of such international policy objectives is wholly inappropriate so far as the interests they are constituted to serve are concerned.

Moreover at the level of community law (these objections to allowing company boards to sacrifice the interests of their shareholders on the altar of national interest apart) the adoption by a member state of this mechanism is contrary to well recognised treaty principles on freedom of establishment and free movement of capital. The reciprocity power as it operates for cross-frontier bids is a restriction on freedom of establishment and free movement of capital which requires to be justified in accordance with the „rule of reason". General economic objectives, such as the desire to achieve equality in the conditions of establishment between one state and another cannot justify member state action of this kind. „... economic grounds can never serve as justification for obstacles prohibited by the Treaty".[61]

There are also difficulties with the detail of the reciprocity option which suggest that it is unattractive, see below.

On the other hand allowing companies to opt back out again for reciprocity reasons may be something of an incentive to their opting in.

The merits of the option for the member state and for companies also depend on its practical effect, which is discussed in detail below.

However, on balance and on the basis of the argument so far, it has always seemed unlikely that the UK would exercise the member state option in favour of allowing a UK target, which has chosen to opt back in to article 11, the reciprocity power to disapply the provision when faced by a bidder which does not apply the same articles as the UK target does. The UK government has now announced that it does not intend to allow reciprocity to UK company targets in such cases, on anti-protectionist grounds and for reasons of sim-

61 *See* in particular the Golden Share cases, eg Commission v Portugal ECJ C-367/98, esp. at 52 and now Commission v Italy C-174/04.

plicity.[62] However this decision is perhaps the one most likely to come under pressure as the UK legislation progresses and is also the form of reciprocity likely to be most attractive to other member state governments. It therefore seems worthwhile to examine the implications of allowing such reciprocity.

4.5 Reciprocity Options at Company Level

If the UK were to make the option available for article 11 would it be used? This depends on the benefits of the option for UK companies as targets. Reciprocity is also relevant at company level for UK companies as bidders because (regardless of the UK government's final decision) the threat of the invocation of reciprocity against them may affect their decisions on whether to opt back in to article 11. The issues are similar and can be conveniently dealt with sequentially, beginning with UK targets.

4.5.1 Reciprocity: Issues for UK Targets

If the UK decides to apply article 9 (and not to allow reciprocity in relation to it), but to opt out of article 11, as suggested, and (contrary to the UK government's current intention) to allow reciprocity in relation to article 11 under art 12(3), in what circumstances (if any) will UK companies as targets be able to disapply article 11 against a bidder?

It should first be noted for the sake of completeness that (obviously) if the UK target company does not reverse the application of the opt-out from Article 11 conferred by the UK under article 12(1), its exemption from article 11 is clearly always available.

But if it opts *back into* article 11 under article 12(2), in what circumstances could it opt back out again („reciprocate") under Article 12(3), if the UK were to allow this by conferring the reciprocity power in all the relevant circumstances under that article?

To repeat, we are assuming a UK target company which is involuntarily subject to article 9 and is not permitted to disapply that article in any circumstances, but which is voluntarily subject to article 11 as a result of having

62 DTI Consultation Document 2004, at note 48 above, 28. The document also argues that the provision ought not to operate against third country company bidders for fear of retaliation and in the interests of international trade. However the provision is probably not applicable against third country companies anyway – see below.

opted back in under article 12(2). That is to say it applies both articles – 9 mandatorily and 11 voluntarily.

Article 12(3), taken with preamble paragraph (21), provides that the target may opt back in again where the bidder does not apply the „same articles“ as it does, as a consequence of the use of the relevant optional arrangements.

The implications of these words and the various permutations for bidders and targets may be best understood by reference to the following table, taken with the explanatory text which follows. The Table sets out the complete matrix of possibilities for bidders and targets together in applying article 9 but not 11, 11 but not 9, both articles, or neither.

Table 2: 13th Directive – Can a target opt out under article 12(3), and if so how?

Bidder applies / Target applies	Both 9 and 11[63]	9 only[64]	11 only[65]	Neither 9 nor 11[66]
Both 9 and 11 – ie can target disapply either or both?	No – same	Yes, but only 11, or also 9?	Yes, but only 9 or also 11?	Yes – both 9 and 11
9 only – ie can target disapply 9?	No? but not same	No – same	Yes? Not same (but bidder applies 11)	Yes – not same
11 only – ie can target disapply 11?	No? but not same	Yes? Not same (but bidder applies 9)	No – same	Yes – not same
Neither 9 nor 11 – ie nothing to disapply.	N/A	N/A	N/A	N/A

63 Does it make a difference whether bidder applies both by virtue of reapplication of them under art.12(2), or compulsorily, as a result of application of the „normal“ rule – ie because the MS has never disapplied them under art 12(1)? See Preamble para (21) „when they [sc targets] become the subject of offers launched by companies which do not apply the same provisions, as a consequence of the use of those optional arrangements“.

64 Same issue as in note 1.

65 Same issue as in note 1.

66 Same issue as in note 1.

Reverting to the position of UK companies as targets, there are 7 cases,[67] ie where such a bidder is subject to –

(i) both Articles 9 and 11 (ie as a mandatory requirement under the home law) – Here there can be no reciprocation (the bidder is subject to the same articles as the target).[68]

(ii) Article 9 (so mandatory), but not 11 – Here reciprocation is allowed, because the articles the bidder applies are not the same as those applied by the target and the bidder has done this by use of an option (ie an option not to opt back into article 11).

(iii) Article 11(so mandatory), but not 9 – This seems a doubtful case. On the one hand the articles applied by the bidder are not „the same" as those applied by the target. On the other hand the target by opting out of article 11 will make itself exempt from an article which does apply to the bidder. This might be thought anomalous. (And it might be argued that the bidder applies „the same" article.) However, very arguably, it makes sense to allow a company subject to neutrality, targeted by a company which is immune from neutrality, to block breakthrough even though the bidder is subject to breakthrough. (This conclusion is supported by the detailed text – the provision applies where the bidder does not apply „the same articles [plural]".)

(iv) Both articles 9 and 11 (as a result of the bidding company having opted back in under article 12(2)) – No reciprocation is allowed (the articles applied by bidder and target are the same)

(v) Neither article (by a decision to opt out of both) – Yes, reciprocation is permissible. The bidder is subject to different provisions by company option.

(vi) Article 9, but not 11 (by bidder's option in both cases) – Yes, for the same reason.

67 If one was completely satisfied with the liberal view, above, on the availability of article 12(3) to companies involuntarily bound by 9 and/or 11 there would only be 4 cases where reciprocity could arise. These are where the bidding company is bound – in whatever way, (i) by both 9 and 11, (ii) by 9, but not 11, (iii) by 11, but not 9, and (iv) by neither. (There are 7 cases and not 8 above because being bound by one or both may be voluntary or involuntary, but being bound by neither will always be voluntary). However it seems useful to extract all 7 cases in order to illustrate the different effect of the strict view.

68 On a very strict interpretation of article 12(3) the bidder does not „apply the same provisions as a consequence of the use of those optional arrangements" see Preamble 21, but see the discussion above.

(vii) Article 11, but not 9 (by bidder's option in both cases) – Arguably again yes; compare case (iii).[69]

In sum, if this analysis is correct, the UK target may opt out of Article 11 in all cases, except where the bidder is bound, by member state law or company option, into both articles 9 and 11. This is (probably) true *even where the bidder is subject to Article 11*.

This analysis does not seem to affect the merits for the UK of denying the reciprocity option to UK companies, unless the policy merits of allowing opt out of 11 where a bidder applies 11 (but not 9) are disputed while the legal analysis is accepted.

Nor does it seem to affect the merits of the UK decision to apply article 9 but not 11. Those UK companies which opt back into article 11 will (probably) not be subject to reciprocity as bidders, see below. There is no need for the UK to immunise British companies against reciprocity by opting into art 11.

4.5.2 Reciprocity against Third Country, Unlisted and Unincorporated Bidders

The power to engage in reciprocal action under article 12 arises for member state companies where the offer is by a company which „does not apply the same articles as they do" (Article 12(3)) „by the use of these optional arrangements" (Preamble paragraph (21)) (or the offer is by a seventh directive subsidiary of such a company).

Whatever the ambiguity of these words, they apparently exclude offers by individuals, companies not listed within the community (wherever incorporated), which are not subsidiaries of community listed companies (such subsidiaries are expressly within article 12(3)) and, remarkably, third country companies, because these do not fail to apply the 9 and/or 11 „by use of the optional arrangements". They are in that position irrespective of any option under article 12 of the directive, which simply does not apply to them.[70] It ap-

69 The first three possible cases involve the member state imposing article 9 and/or 11 and companies not opting into the articles not imposed. Cases (iv), to (vii) are cases where the member state leaves the company free to opt back into 9 and/or 11 as a result of disapplying both.

70 Article 12(1) applies to companies referred to in article 1(1) (i.e. governed by the law of a member state with securities admitted to listing on a community regulated market) with registered office within a member state. Articles 9 and 11 themselves only apply to such companies (article 9 via the definition of offeree company, take-

plies only to companies listed within the community with registered offices within the territories of the member states.

The effect in relation to third country companies is particularly surprising as the preamble says that the provision is „without prejudice to international agreements", words apparently intended to ensure that where companies from third countries are entitled to national treatment in connection with takeover bids their rights are not affected. Moreover one of the main preoccupations of those arguing for a level playing field was the alleged immunity of third country, particularly US, companies to contested bids as the result of a lack of board neutrality.[71]

is third country point was never likely to influence the UK's decision to apply article 9, since the position described already exists. But one might expect many member states to opt out of articles 9 and 11 to take care of the point. Company boards too, concerned at the prospect of vulnerability to third country takeovers may be unlikely to propose to their general meetings that they should resolve to reapply these articles. If this is indeed the effect of the Directive it is particularly unfortunate.

A final point in this connection is that if this argument is correct the effect of the article 12 reciprocity power is to discriminate against community bidders in favour of third country bidders.[72] This may be a further argument for regarding the Directive as treating 3rd country and community company bidders not applying the articles alike .

over bid and article 1(1), article 11 explicitly). A possible contrary argument is that third country companies are always open to reciprocity because all such companies (whether or not subject to their own national neutrality/breakthrough provisions) are not such companies as apply the same articles „as a consequence of the use of those optional arrangements", because they could not make such use. This displacement of a negative might be regarded as a minor violence to an obscure text. The travaux are ambiguous – see the European Parliament proceedings, referred to below.

71 The European Parliament recognised this problem. See the Report of 8 December 2003, FINAL A5 0469/2003, at pp. 80–82 and 91–92, where the Committee on Industrial, External Trade, etc matters proposed a special reciprocity article (new Article 17a) addressing bids from third country companies. However this article was not adopted in the final agreed text.

72 Very arguably unlawful under article 12 (discrimination on grounds of nationality) of the Treaty Establishing the European Community.

4.5.3 Reciprocity: Issues for UK Bidders

Now consider the vulnerability of a UK registered company bidding for an EU target where the UK has exercised (as indeed it is now expected to do) the member state option to apply article 9 and not article 11. This offeror will be unaffected for this purpose by whether the UK allows reciprocal action under article 12(3), since this decision does not affect the vulnerability of UK bidders to reciprocal action by the target. However the vulnerability of the UK bidder to possible reciprocal action (assuming such action is permitted by the target's member state) will depend (under the „same articles" test) on whether it retains its opted out status from Article 11 under article 12(2), or opts back in. What difference will it make in practice? Let us consider first the position where the UK company retains the opt-out from article 11.

4.5.3.1 If the UK bidder retains its opt-out from Article 11

On this first scenario the 6 cases can be considered[73] – ie where the Target is:

(i) bound by both articles 9 and 11 (by mandatory Member State law) – On the „liberal" view reciprocation is possible since the articles applied are not the same; it may even be possible for the target to repudiate *both articles 9 and 11*, if the governing member state law allows this, since no limitation is imposed by article 12(3) on the scope of the action allowed;[74] arguably the text is defective; or perhaps the directive is to be interpreted as only allowing opting out of an article, where that same article is not applied; but the argument has been made for allowing opting out of both articles in similar cases involving a UK target, above.

(ii) bound by Article 11 only (mandatory), but opted out of 9

– On the liberal view the target may opt out of 11 because the articles applied by the bidder are not the same. On the strict view there can be no retaliation. On any view the target keeps the benefit of the disapplication of article 9;

(iii) bound by article 9 only (mandatory), but opted out of 11

73 If we were wholly satisfied that the liberal view applied we would need to consider only 3 cases. The missing seventh case, as compared with the analysis of the position of UK companies as targets, is the case where neither article applies. Obviously the question of reciprocal action cannot arise where the target is already opted out of both articles.

74 On the strict interpretation of article 12(3) however no reciprocation is possible because the target's status is not the company's option.

– no reciprocation is possible on article 9 (whether on a strict or a liberal view, since the articles applied are the same), but of course the target keeps the benefit on 11

(iv) opted into both – Yes reciprocation is possible on any view. The target can certainly opt out of article 11, and apparently also 9 (the offeror satisfies the „not the same" test). This is perhaps a surprising result, but see (i), above.

(v) opted into 9, not 11 – No reciprocation by the target is permitted – (The articles applied are the same.)

(vi) opted into 11, not 9 – Yes. The target may take reciprocal action and opt out of 11 (the articles applied are not the same; the bidder operates by use of the company option).

4.5.3.2 If the UK bidder opts back into Article 11

On the second scenario, where the UK bidder has opted back in to article 11, one can consider the same 6 cases- ie where Target is:

(i) bound by both articles (mandatory) – No reciprocation is allowed as the articles applied are the same (This on the liberal view produces a different result for the UK bidder than his position on retaining the opt-out, but the same on the strict view)

(ii) bound by 11 only (mandatory) – On the liberal view the target is free to retaliate on 11 because the articles applied are not the same, but this is an absurd result because the bidder is bound more strictly than the target; on the strict view the target is not free to retaliate on 11 which applies to him as a result of a member state option; on any view he remains exempt from 9 (here again whether the result is the same for the bidder depends on whether one adopts the liberal view)

(iii) bound by 9 only (mandatory) – on the liberal view similarly the target is free to retaliate on article 9, but not so on the strict one, and remains exempt from 11 (here again whether the result is the same for the bidder depends on whether one adopts the liberal view).

(iv) opted into both – No retaliation (same articles applied) (with a different result for the bidder from that on the first scenario).

(v) opted into 9, not 11 – Arguably the target can „reciprocate" by opting out of article 9 although it applies to the UK bidder. The articles applied are not

„the same" because the bidder applies both; but this is perverse; the bidder does apply what the target applies, and more.

(vi) opted into 11, not 9 – Arguably similarly the target can „reciprocate" by opting out of article 11, for similar reasons. The articles applied are not the same because the bidder applies both. The same comment applies as for the previous case.

Arguably cases (ii), (iii), (v) and (vi) produce a perverse result. The target is allowed to retaliate because there is a mismatch between the provisions applied but this is because of an exemption of the target not enjoyed by the bidder.[75] Case (v), for example seems particularly outrageous – the UK bidder is worse off after opting into 11 than he would be if he had remained opted out! Compare case (v) in the first scenario above.

4.6 Should UK Companies Opt back in to block Reciprocal Action?

One would expect that where the UK bidder has been exempted from, but opted back into, article 11 and is bound by 9 there would be no case where reciprocation would be allowed. This result can be achieved by adopting a purposive construction of the „not the same" provision to the effect that it only allows reciprocation where the restrictions applied by the bidder are both not the same as the target's restrictions and the result is the target being subject to a restriction to which the bidder is not subject. On that basis one would conclude that the case for the UK company opting into art 11 on reciprocity grounds will depend on the merits of being immune from reciprocity in cases (iv) and (vi) and, if one takes the liberal view, cases (i) and (ii). Whether this is likely to happen seems to depend on the facts, but it seems entirely possible, indeed probable , given that, as indicated above, most UK companies have little if anything to lose by opting into 11.

75 It may be asked why the converse case where the UK company is the target does not raise similar problems. I believe the answer is that the UK company will always be bound by art 9 on our scenario. It will never be in a position where it applies one of the articles by not opting out and disapplies another as a result of opting out and not having opted back in. So it can never be a target within cases (v) or (vi).

4.7 Reversibility of Article 12(2) opt-ins: Tactical Considerations

As noted above, under article 12(2) the option which member states must give to companies to reapply articles 9(2) and (3) and/or 11 is reversible. There are serious dangers that companies will be tempted to make tactical use of this decision. For bidders this allows temporary immunisation from reciprocal action by opting into both, or one, of these articles again, bearing in mind that in due course they can reverse the position. For targets it seems to allow them to immunise themselves from the consequences of opting back in by reversing their article 11(2) option. But both decisions have to be taken by a qualified majority in the general meeting; so they are relatively „sticky" and are likely to take place in the full glare of publicity. The UK government proposes to deal with the risks of tactical opting out by requiring a 12 month interval after an opt in before this can be done.[76] There is no equivalent interval to deal with tactical opting in by bidders.

4.8 Conclusions on Reciprocity

The member state reciprocity option looks deeply unattractive. Its merits for companies and it legality at company and community level look very questionable. It raises apparently difficult and complex questions as to the effect in particular cases, which will complicate and add expense to control transactions. The UK has managed without it hitherto and is now very unlikely to exercise the reciprocity power. In the new environment UK companies may choose to subject themselves to breakthrough even though the UK rejects it. It may therefore be argued that they should be allowed the means to mitigate the consequences of doing so. But that argument seems unlikely on balance to change the calculus.

If reciprocity is to be allowed a simple and rational scheme could be argued for as follows:

- where a bidder does not apply article 9 and/or article 11 then a target which does apply article 9 and/or 11 may opt out of either such article, or, as the case may be, both.

[76] DTI July 2005 Announcement, above, clause R25(6).

- The case for allowing a target to opt out of an article only if that same article is not applied by the bidder, needs to be considered carefully. While omitting such a restriction may be regarded as unreasonable in that it allows targets to opt out of articles applied by bidders, since articles 9 and 11 will bear differently on different kinds of company it makes some sense to allow a target to remove both if either is not adopted by the bidder. On the other hand this argument should not be taken too far.
- Certainly where the bidder applies both articles targets should not be allowed to opt back out of either or both.

This regime, while arguably not strictly required by the Directive, is not inconsistent with it. Member States are explicitly entitled to apply the reciprocity regime under conditions determined by national law. They should do so in this sense, if at all.

But the case for this approach rests on the legitimacy of allowing target company boards to seek to achieve a kind of equality of arms with companies making public offers to their shareholders. As explained, these arguments have no merit. If member states wish to restrict the free movement of capital and establishment for this purpose this is a matter for member state action, not one to be entrusted to company boards at the expense of shareholders. For this reason it is hoped and expected that the UK at least will maintain its intention not to exercise its option under article 12(3) to confer reciprocity powers on UK registered companies even in relation to breakthrough. Indeed the policy arguments against any member state applying the reciprocity regime at all are very strong and its legality in community law is in the highest degree dubious.

5. Afterword

This chapter has examined the interplay of the European Neutrality and breakthrough rules from a UK perspective. It now seems very likely that the UK government will retain the neutrality principle in its absolute form, with no room for UK companies to escape it. The position on breakthrough is different. Companies will remain free to adopt „one share: one vote“ constitutions or not as they please, although for market reasons and the need to reduce the cost of capital the process of alignment of all UK listed companies on that model can be expected to continue.

Whatever their constitutions, all UK listed companies will in future have the right under EU law as implemented in the UK to adopt such open structures to apply when they are involved in takeovers as targets. The effects of doing so are regrettably unclear, both in terms of the implications for their own governance, and in terms of their position as bidders for companies in other member states. The prospects of UK companies being permitted to engage in „reciprocal" action on this front (by reapplying restrictions on voting and ownership rights when faced with a bidder with a closed constitution from a closed member state regime) now look remote. The implications of this possibility have however been examined above. Such examination may have helped to illustrate the implications of the alternative approach both for the UK and more widely within the EU. It is to be hoped that it is academic.

Implementing the European Takeover Directive in Italy: Requirements and Options

Guido Ferrarini

Gliederung

1. Introduction

In this paper, I analyse the main issues concerning the European Takeover Directive's implementation in Italy. First of all, I consider those aspects of Italian law – such as the regulation of mandatory bids, squeeze-outs and sell-outs – which do not fully comply with the Directive, and I examine how they should be modified. Moreover, I consider those provisions of the Directive that are optional for Member States, such as those on pre-bid and post-bid defences, and ask whether they should be adopted in Italy. In the absence of official plans for the Directive's implementation, I try to predict which solutions will prevail by looking at the course Italian law has followed since the adoption in 1998 of the Consolidated Financial Services Act (CFSA), which incorporated the core rules on takeovers (more specific rules are included in the Regulation on Issuers adopted by Consob under the CFSA).

Both the CFSA and the Consob Regulation were largely inspired by an earlier draft of the Directive. As a result, the European core principles, such as the principle of equal treatment of target shareholders and that of sufficient time for evaluating information (see Article 3(1) of the Directive), were incorporated into Italian law well before the Directive's adoption. The CFSA was also inspired, to a large extent, by the City Code on Takeovers and Mergers, which concurrently exercised a substantial influence on the formation of the Directive's provisions, including those on frustrating actions (Article 9 of the Directive). However, reference to the City Code was limited to substantive rules. Rather than importing the UK self-regulatory structure, the CFSA conferred regulatory and supervisory powers over the whole area of takeovers on Consob. It is also worth noting that Consob's acts are subject to judicial review by the Administrative Courts. As a result, jurisdiction over takeovers is, to a large extent, entrusted to the Rome Administrative Tribunal (*T.A.R. Lazio*), in the first instance, and to the Council of State (*Consiglio di Stato*), for appelate review. There is no need to emphasize that administrative judges are not the best equipped people to deal with the financial and legal complexities of takeovers, although they do skilfully scrutinize whether Consob has complied with due process requirements.

Furthermore, the CFSA introduced a regulation of pre-bid defences which, to some extent, anticipated the "breakthrough" rule subsequently included in Article 11 of the Directive. In addition, the recent company law reform has forbidden listed companies from imposing voting caps.[1] Therefore, as I further argue below, the Directive's implementation should not lead to any radical changes in the Italian regime concerning pre-bid defences.

2. Mandatory Bids and Partial Bids

2.1 Mandatory bids are foreseen by Article 106 (1) CFSA, which states that: "Any person who, as a result of purchases for a consideration, comes to own a shareholding exceeding the threshold of thirty per cent, shall make a public offer to buy all the shares listed on Italian regulated markets giving the right to vote on the matters specified in Article 105." This provision was clearly inspired by a similar rule in the City Code.[2] However, the mandatory bid price is calculated in terms different from those contemplated by the City Code. Article 106 (2) CFSA requires the bid price to be "no lower than the arithmetic mean of the weighted average market price in the last twelve months and the highest price agreed in the same period by the offeror for the purchase of

1 *See*, for an introduction, *Ferrarini/Giudici/Stella-Richter* 'Company Law Reform in Italy: Real Progress? 2005, 69 RabelsZ 658.

2 *See* Section F ("The Mandatory Offer and its Terms"), Rule 9.1 ("When it is required and who is primarily responsible for making it"), The City Code on Takeovers and Mergers.

shares of the same class." This rule is aimed at making mandatory bids less costly than would be the case under the City Code, which makes reference to the highest price paid by the offeror.[3] The "discount" on the bid price provided for by the CFSA was intended to enhance contests for corporate control by making the cost of bids more affordable to acquirers. At the same time, minority investors are protected by the reference to the average market price, which should offer a "floor" to the bid price, at least in the case of rising (or stable) markets. The main problem with the Italian solution is that it creates incentives for strategic behaviour by the bidders, who will select the time for their acquisitions so as to minimize the mandatory bid price.

The Directive follows the City Code model by requiring the mandatory bid price to be "the highest price paid for the same securities by the offeror, or by persons acting in concert with him/her, over a period, to be determined by Member States, of not less than 6 months and not more than 12 months before the bid ..." (Article 5 (4)). This "equitable price" can be adjusted by the supervisory authorities either upwards or downwards in special circumstances that have to be clearly defined in advance, e.g. in order to enable a firm in difficulty to be rescued (in which case, the bid price will be set at a lower level than that arrived at by applying the general rule).

Italian law will have to be modified accordingly. On the one hand, the European concept of equitable price should be adopted; on the other, Consob will likely be empowered to adjust the mandatory bid price in special circumstances. It may also happen that either the Italian legislator or Consob will interpret one of these circumstances ("where the highest price was set by agreement between the purchaser and a seller": Article 5 (4) 2nd alinea) as allowing for the criteria currently in force to be applied in most cases, especially considering that the Directive refers to "the average market value over a particular period" as one of the criteria that supervisory authorities may apply in similar circumstances. However, such an approach would in practice frustrate the Directive's equitable price concept, as defined in general by Article 5 (4) first alinea, with reference to the highest price paid by the bidder or by persons acting in concert with the same.

2.2 The CFSA followed the City Code approach also with respect to partial (voluntary) bids. Article 107 (1) provides that " the obligation to make a public offer ... shall not arise where the shareholding is owned as a result of a public offer to buy or exchange at least sixty per cent of the shares listed on Italian

3 *See* Rule 9.5 ("Consideration to be offered").

regulated markets giving the right to vote. ..." Some additional conditions must be satisfied for the rule to apply, including approval of the partial offer by the target shareholders through a referendum, similarly to what is foreseen under the City Code. The rationale for this regime is easily explained. On the one hand, the sale of corporate control is enhanced to the extent that the offeror may avoid the cost of a full acquisition; on the other, investors in the target are protected by the requirement that they express their consent to a partial bid in advance.

Can a similar regime be maintained when implementing the Directive? Under Article 5 of the Directive, the mandatory bid must be addressed to all holders of the relevant securities for all their holdings (para. 1); however, where control has been acquired following a voluntary bid to all the holders of the relevant securities, the obligation to launch a bid no longer applies (para. 2). In other words, mandatory bids are defined as full-acquisition bids and can be replaced only by voluntary bids directed to purchase all relevant securities. Consequently, there appears to be no room for voluntary/partial bids leading to the acquisition of control in the target, and the relevant provisions of the CFSA (as well as that of the City Code) will have to be removed. However, partial bids should still be permitted, provided that they are not directed to the acquisition of control.

3. Squeeze-out and Sell-out

3.1 Squeeze-out rights are foreseen under Article 111 CFSA. Any bidder owning more than 98% of the shares with voting rights in a company, as a result of a public offer to buy all the shares with voting rights, is entitled to acquire the remaining shares within four months of the close of the offer (para. 1). The purchase price is set by an expert appointed by the President of the court, taking into account, *inter alia*, the offer price and the market price during the last six months (para. 2).

The Directive includes a regime that is in part different and, in any case, more specific (Article 15) than the existing Italian rule. First, squeeze-out rights belong either to a bidder who holds securities representing not less than 90% of the voting rights in the target or to a bidder who, following acceptance of the bid, has acquired or has firmly contracted to acquire securities representing not less than 90% of the target's capital carrying voting rights and 90% of the voting rights comprised in the bid. However, Member States may set a higher threshold that may not be higher than 95% of the capital carrying voting rights and 95% of the voting rights. Second, the squeeze-out right must be exercised within three months after the end of the specified acceptance period of the bid. Third, the purchase price must be fair and take the same form as the consideration offered in the bid, or be in cash. It is further specified that "following a voluntary bid ... the consideration offered in the bid shall be presumed to be fair where, through acceptance of the bid, the offeror has acquired securities representing not less than 90% of the capital carrying voting rights comprised in the bid."

Italian law will have to be adapted to the requirements just described, which however does not imply any profound changes except for the threshold, which should be lowered to at most 95% and possibly to 90%, the former being the likely choice given the resistance already expressed to squeeze-out rights in the existing provisions of the CFSA (a 98% threshold).

3.2 Sell-out rights are regulated under Article 108 CFSA: any person who comes to own more than 90% of the shares with voting rights must make a public offer to buy the remaining shares unless he/she restores, within 120 days, a free float sufficient to ensure regular trading. Consob sets the sell-out purchase price. Few changes are required for the Directive's implementation. First, the Directive does not make provision for the free-float's restoration, so the Italian provision allowing such restoration will have to be deleted. Second, the Directive specifies that the price should be fair, a requirement which is, however, already implicit in the mandate to Consob to fix the bid price.

4. Frustrating Actions

4.1 The City Code approach is also tracked by Article 104(1) CFSA, which requires that target shareholders approve any frustrating action: "Unless authorized by the ordinary shareholders' meeting or by the extraordinary shareholders' meeting for matters within the scope of its authority, Italian companies whose shares that are subject of an offer are listed on regulated markets in Italy or other EU countries shall refrain from taking action that may hinder the achievement of the objectives of the offer."[4] This provision applies a rule of board neutrality to pre-bid defences. It is not clear, however,

[4] *See* Rule 21 ("Restrictions on frustrating Action").

at what point in time the rule begins to apply. In Consob's opinion, the relevant time is when the offer is first communicated to the market.[5] However, in the case of *INA v. Generali,* both the *TAR Lazio* and the *Consiglio di Stato* (affirming the first instance judgement)[6] held that the passivity rule only applies to the board of the target when an offer is pending, i.e., after a formal communication of the intention to launch a bid and delivery of the relevant 'offer document' has been made to Consob under Article 102 (1). As some time could elapse between the date when the bid is made known to the public and the date when a formal communication is sent to Consob, the target board may have sufficient time to adopt defensive measures before being subject to the neutrality rule.

This solution is clearly unsatisfactory and could frustrate the neutrality rule.[7] However, the Directive's implementation should solve this problem, as Article 6 (1) clearly states that a decision to launch a bid must be made public without delay, while Article 9 (2) specifies that the passivity rule applies from the moment that the board of the offeree company receives the information referred to in Article 6 (1) until the result of the bid is made public or the bid elapses. The Italian legislator should also consider whether to make the passivity rule applicable at an earlier stage, for example, as soon as the board of the offeree company becomes aware that a bid is imminent (as allowed by Article 9 (2), third sentence).

4.2 Article 12 (1) of the Directive allows Member States to waive application of Article 9 for companies that have their registered offices in the State's territory. However, it is safe to predict that Italian law will keep the board neutrality rule, except for amending it as suggested. Moreover, Article 12 (3) allows Member States to exempt companies from applying Article 9 if they become the subject of an offer launched by a company that does not apply such provision.

Assuming that State A adopts Article 9 while State B does not, target company X, registered in State A, is entitled to an exemption from the neutrality rule to adopt defensive measures against bidding company Y, registered in State B. It is difficult to predict whether Italy will exercise this "reciprocity" option. It is my belief that it should not. The board passivity rule protects

5 *See* Communication No. DIS/9901382, 27-2-1999, concerning the takeover of Telecom Italia.

6 *See Consiglio di Stato,* decree 29-10-1999, No. 1984/99 and *TAR Lazio,* decree 21-10-1999, No. 2964/99 (2000) Banca borsa titoli di credito, II, 130.

7 *See G. Ferrarini* 'A chi la difesa della società bersaglio?' (2000) 2 Mercato, concorrenza, regole 140.

shareholders against managerial entrenchment: it is difficult to understand why this rule should not apply if the bidder's shareholders do not enjoy the same protection. Clearly, the passivity rule and the reciprocity rule stand on different grounds: the former protects investors in publicly traded corporations; the latter reflects a nationalistic approach to market integration by trying to protect certain interests (unions, politicians, competitors).

5. Pre-bid Defences

5.1 The Italian treatment of pre-bid defences does not appear to diverge substantially from that included in Article 11 of the Directive, including the well known "breakthrough" rule. Several takeover barriers are either forbidden or substantially limited in their scope or effectiveness.

(i) *Voting rights*. Multiple voting shares have been forbidden in Italy for more than sixty years (Article 2351 (4) Civil Code). Voting caps are also now forbidden for listed companies (Article 2351 (3)), with the exception of formerly State-owned companies, for which voting caps are allowed by the 1994 Privatizations Law if the company's charter still includes such rights although it is now publicly traded. The Italian Government appears to believe that the relevant provisions of the Privatizations Law still have force as *lex specialis* with respect to the voting caps' prohibition included in the Civil Code.

The issuance of non-voting shares is permitted for stock corporations in general (Article 2351 (2) Civil Code). However, in the case of listed companies, non-voting shares must be issued as "savings shares" (*azioni di risparmio*) and are subject to the relevant CFSA provisions, including the requirement that they confer preferential rights on shareholders. Limited voting shares are also allowed, such as (a) shares with voting rights limited to the extraordinary general meeting (these shares usually confer preferential rights on their holders), (b) shares with voting rights limited to the appointment of directors, and (c) shares with voting rights subject to the occurrence of specific conditions, including the launching of a takeover bid (provided that the triggering of voting rights is subject to the shareholders' approval required for defensive measures). The sum of non-voting and limited voting shares must not exceed half of the legal capital.

(ii) *Share transfer restrictions*. Clauses requiring board approval of share transfers are generally permitted (see Article 2355-*bis* (2), stating conditions for the validity of similar clauses). However, their non-inclusion in a company's charter is a condition for the listing of shares (which must be freely transferable) at the Italian Exchange. Moreover, third party approval of share transfers is permitted also for listed companies when required by law, as in the case of "golden shares" included in the charters of formerly State-owned companies.

(iii) *Shareholder agreements.* These agreements are no longer effective as a pre-bid defence. Article 123 (3) CFSA includes a "mini-breakthrough" rule under which shareholders are entitled to back out of voting pacts, blocking agreements and similar arrangements when a takeover bid aimed at gaining at least 60 per cent of the votes is in place. Withdrawal from the relevant agreements is ineffective if the share transfer to the bidder does not take place (e.g., because the bid does not go through). This right was exercised several times by parties to shareholder agreements, allowing takeover bids to be successfully completed.

5.2 Therefore, the impact of Article 11 of the Directive on Italian law – assuming its adoption, which is however optional under Article 12 (1) – would be quite limited. First of all, multiple voting shares and voting caps are already forbidden. To the extent that voting caps are still included in the charters of privatized companies, the Italian Government would likely invoke the exemption foreseen by Article 11 (7), arguing that voting caps are part of the "golden share" mechanism.

Moreover, non-voting shares issued by listed companies as saving shares carry preferential rights, so that the Directive's "breakthrough" would not apply to them (Article 11 (6)). Also, limited voting shares would be covered only to the extent that they did not confer preferential rights upon their holders (a case presently unknown in Italian practice). To the extent that voting restrictions may be included in shareholder agreements, application of the European breakthrough rule would allow the parties to these agreements freedom to vote on defensive measures, including in the case foreseen by Article 11 (4). However, the benefit of such a provision is unclear, save for allowing shareholders bound by a voting pact to vote against defensive measures even if the other members of the pact were in favour of the same.

Share transfer restrictions may not be included in the charters of Italian listed companies, as listed shares must be freely transferable. Such restrictions may be included in shareholder agreements; however, shareholders can back-out of these agreements, which means that a provision like Article 11 (2) would serve no useful purpose in Italy.

5.3 In conclusion, Italy should opt-out of Article 11 of the Directive, as allowed by Article 12 (1). Firstly, under Italian law, pre-bid defences (at least those concerning voting rights and share transfers) are limited in scope, while a "mini-breakthrough" rule already applies to shareholder agreements (other defences, like pyramidal groups, are not covered by the Directive). Secondly, the European "breakthrough" rule would also apply to cases for which the rationale is unclear: for example, voting restrictions included in shareholders' agreements would not apply in the first general meeting convened by the bidder holding 75 per cent or more of the voting rights.

Thirdly, "equitable compensation" should be provided under national law for any loss suffered by the holders of the rights subject to "breakthrough", as required by Article 11 (5), which is a provision that is extremely difficult to implement in practice. Fourthly, the question of reciprocity would also arise under Article 12 (3) of the Directive. However, introducing a similar condition into Italian law would substantially reduce its regulatory bite with respect to some important pre-bid defences. For example, the Italian "mini-breakthrough" applies to shareholder agreements unconditionally. If the European "breakthrough" were adopted under a condition of reciprocity, voting agreements would be a valid defence against most EU companies, assuming that most Member States will not adopt Article 11 of the Directive. As a result, implementing the European breakthrough and reciprocity rules would make Italian listed companies less subject to corporate control transactions than they currently are, which is an outcome that I find unlikely and totally inconsistent with the path followed by Italian law since adoption of the CFSA.

Die Implementierung der 13. (Übernahme-)Richtlinie: Umsetzungspflichten und Umsetzungsoptionen aus der Sicht des deutschen Rechts*

*Andreas Fuchs***

Gliederung

* Leicht überarbeitete und ergänzte Fassung des Vortrags vom 9. November 2005. Die Vortragsform wurde beibehalten. Der Fußnotenapparat beschränkt sich auf ein Minimum.

** Prof. Dr. iur., LL.M. (University of Michigan, Ann Arbor), Universität Osnabrück, Geschäftsführender Direktor des Instituts für Handels- und Wirtschaftsrecht.

I. Einführung

Mit der Verabschiedung der europäischen Übernahmerichtlinie am 21. April 2004 ist ein fast 30 Jahre währendes Ringen um einen einheitlichen Rechtsrahmen für öffentliche Übernahmeangebote in Europa vorerst mit einem Kompromiss zu Ende gegangen. Das Ergebnis war für viele enttäuschend, insbesondere auch für die Kommission. Als großer Wurf kann die europäische Übernahmerichtlinie (im folgenden: ÜRL) in der Tat nicht bezeichnet werden. Das lange Jahre primär verfolgte Ziel eines Abbaus von nationalen Übernahmehindernissen und der Verwirklichung gleicher Ausgangsbedingungen für Übernahmeangebote im Sinne eines *level playing field* konnte letztlich nicht verwirklicht werden. Nach dem zweistufigen Optionsmodell bei dem Vereitelungsverbot (Art. 9 ÜRL) und der Durchbrechungsregel (Art. 11 ÜRL) ist es wahrscheinlich, dass sich europaweit zwei Gruppen von Gesellschaften herausbilden: kapitalmarktoffene Unternehmen, die auf Abwehrmaßnahmen verzichten, und solche, die daran festhalten und dafür möglicherweise Kursabschläge und Imageverluste erleiden müssen. Zudem wird es auch wegen der begrenzten Wirkung der Durchbruchsregel weiterhin ein buntes Mosaik nationaler Abwehrhürden geben.

Für den deutschen Gesetzgeber, der bekanntlich im Jahre 2002 mit dem WpÜG vorangeprescht war, ohne die Verabschiedung der Richtlinie abzuwarten, stellt sich nun die Frage, welche Strategie er bei der Umsetzung der Richtlinienvorgaben wählen soll. Vor allem zwei Grundkonzepte kommen in

Betracht: Zum einen könnte er sich für die weitgehende Beibehaltung der bisherigen Regeln im WpÜG entscheiden und die Umsetzung strikt auf die obligatorischen Vorgaben der Richtlinie beschränken; zum anderen könnte der deutsche Gesetzgeber die notwendige Umsetzung der ÜRL aber auch zum Anlass nehmen, das gesamte Übernahmerecht auf den Prüfstand zu stellen. Die ÜRL lässt Raum für beide Wege, da sie im Wesentlichen nur die Einhaltung von Mindeststandards vorschreibt und die konkrete Ausgestaltung der Einzelheiten den Mitgliedstaaten überlässt.

Eine Überprüfung sämtlicher Vorschriften des WpÜG auf ihre sachliche Berechtigung und Bewährung in einer knapp vierjährigen Anwendungspraxis erscheint allerdings eher unwahrscheinlich. Im BMF neigt man offenbar dazu, so wenig wie möglich am gegenwärtigen Rechtszustand zu ändern, so dass damit zu rechnen ist, dass sich die Reform des WpÜG weitgehend auf die Umsetzung der zwingenden Vorgaben der Richtlinie und die Ausübung einiger Wahlrechte beschränken wird.[1] Dementsprechend werde ich mich im Folgenden schwerpunktmäßig nur mit den Punkten befassen, bei denen eine Umsetzungspflicht besteht, und dabei ggf. alternative Umsetzungsmöglichkeiten und nahe liegende zusätzliche Wahlmöglichkeiten aufzeigen. Die sich ebenfalls aufdrängende Frage nach weiterem Reformbedarf muss dagegen ausgeblendet bleiben. Das hat im wesentlichen zwei Gründe: Zum einen hängt es nicht zuletzt vom wirtschaftspolitischen Standpunkt des Betrachters ab, welche sonstigen Änderungen des WpÜG vielleicht wünschenswert wären. Eine umfassende Analyse und Begründung der normativen Anforderungen, denen ein (mehr oder weniger) „optimales" Übernahmerecht genügen müsste, ist im Rahmen dieses Vortrags angesichts der engen zeitlichen Vorgaben nicht darstellbar. Zum anderen wird Herr Zschocke in seinem folgenden Referat noch über die Erwartungen der Praxis an die Überarbeitung des Übernahmerechts sprechen und dabei sicher auf die eine oder andere sonstige

1 So jetzt in der Tat der Referentenentwurf vom 19. 12. 2005 „Entwurf eines Gesetzes zur Umsetzung der Richtlinie 2004/25/EG des Europäischen Parlaments und des Rates vom 21. April 2004 betreffend Übernahmeangebote (Übernahmerichtlinie-Umsetzungsgesetz)", noch unveröffentlicht, Begründung A.I. S. 1 (Umsetzung der Richtlinie „Eins zu Eins"; mit Ausnahme der Veröffentlichungsvorschriften, bei denen eine Veröffentlichung im Elektronischen Bundesanzeiger ermöglicht wird, sollen die gegenwärtigen übernahmerechtlichen Regelungen überall dort unverändert bestehen bleiben, wo dies möglich ist). Eine eingehende Berücksichtigung des RefE bei den einzelnen umzusetzenden Vorschriften war im Rahmen der Drucklegung dieses Beitrags leider nicht mehr möglich. Lediglich zu einzelnen Punkten konnten noch kurze Hinweise in den Fußnoten aufgenommen werden.

rechtspolitisch wünschenswerte Änderung des WpÜG eingehen, die zur Umsetzung der Richtlinie nicht unbedingt erforderlich ist.

Leitlinie bei der Reform des Übernahmerechts sollte für den deutschen Gesetzgeber jedenfalls sein, Unternehmensübernahmen auch weiterhin weder gezielt zu fördern noch zu behindern, sondern sich darauf zu konzentrieren, einen verlässlichen und neutralen Ordnungsrahmen bereit zu stellen, der für ein faires und effizientes Übernahmeverfahren sorgt, mögliche Funktionsdefizite des Marktprozesses kompensiert und, soweit erforderlich, einen ausreichenden Individualschutz der Betroffenen gewährleistet.

II. Allgemeine Regelungen

1. Anwendungsbereich des WpÜG und Aufsichtszuständigkeiten der BaFin

a) Gegenwärtige Rechtslage

Das WpÜG erfasst derzeit *öffentliche Angebote* zum Erwerb von Wertpapieren *börsennotierter* Zielgesellschaften, die ihren satzungsmäßigen Sitz im Inland, also Deutschland, haben *und* deren Wertpapiere an einem geregelten Markt im Sinne der Wertpapierdienstleistungsrichtlinie in einem Staat des Europäischen Wirtschaftsraums zugelassen sind. Die Zuständigkeit der BaFin erstreckt sich auf alle Angebote, die nach den Vorschriften des WpÜG abzugeben sind. Das Gesetz unterscheidet dabei zwischen einfachen *Angeboten*, die sich nur auf den Erwerb oder Tausch eines Teils der Aktien des Zielunternehmens beziehen (Abschnitt 3, §§ 10ff. WpÜG), *Übernahmeangeboten*, die auf den Erwerb der Kontrolle der Zielgesellschaft gerichtet sind (Abschnitt 4, §§ 29ff. WpÜG),[2] und *Pflichtangeboten* (Abschnitt 5, §§ 35ff. WpÜG), die – nach anderweitiger Kontrollerlangung über die Zielgesellschaft – den Erwerb aller

2 Der unbestimmte Rechtsbegriff der Erlangung der Kontrolle über das Zielunternehmen wird durch eine unwiderlegliche gesetzliche Vermutung konkretisiert: Nach § 29 Abs. 2 WpÜG ist Kontrolle das Halten von mindestens 30 Prozent der Stimmrechte an der Zielgesellschaft. Das schließt nicht aus, im Einzelfall aufgrund besonderer Umstände auch unterhalb dieser Schwelle einen Kontrollerwerb anzunehmen. Die allgemeinen Vorschriften über kontrollneutrale öffentliche Angebote zum Erwerb von Wertpapieren sind nach §§ 34, 39 WpÜG im Grundsatz auch auf Übernahme- und Pflichtangebote anwendbar, soweit für diese keine abweichenden Sonderregelungen bestehen.

noch ausstehenden Aktien der Zielgesellschaft zum Gegenstand haben müssen.

Der Anwendungsbereich der Richtlinie ist demgegenüber teils enger, teils weiter. Die Richtlinie erfasst alle öffentlichen *Übernahmeangebote*, die sich auf den Erwerb von *Stimmrechtsaktien* einer dem Recht eines *Mitgliedstaats* unterliegenden Gesellschaft richten, deren Aktien jedenfalls *zum Teil* zum Handel auf einem *geregelten Markt in einem oder mehreren Mitgliedstaaten zugelassen* sind (Art. 1 Abs. 1 i.V.m. Art. 2 Abs. 1 ÜRL). Im Gegensatz zur ÜRL bezieht sich also das WpÜG weitergehend auch auf stimmrechtslose Vorzugsaktien, auf nicht auf den Kontrollerwerb gerichtete Teilangebote sowie auf Aktien, die zum Handel (nur) in einem Staat des EWR zugelassen sind. Ein Anpassungserfordernis besteht insofern aber nicht, da der Anwendungsbereich des WpÜG über den der ÜRL hinausgehen kann. Daher dürfte es auch nicht zu der an sich wünschenswerten Klarstellung durch den deutschen Gesetzgeber kommen, ob das WpÜG tatsächlich – wie von der BaFin und der wohl herrschenden Lehre bejaht, von Teilen der Literatur aber bestritten[3] – auf öffentliche Angebote zum Erwerb eigener Aktien anwendbar ist.[4]

b) Notwendige Anpassungen

Dringender Anpassungsbedarf ergibt sich aber in den Fällen, in denen der Anwendungsbereich der ÜRL weiter ist als der des WpÜG. Das ist der Fall im Hinblick auf Zielgesellschaften, die dem Recht eines anderen Mitgliedstaats unterliegen, also keinen Sitz in Deutschland haben, deren Anteile aber auf einem inländischen geregelten Markt notiert sind. Der Begriff der Zielgesellschaft in § 2 Abs. 3 WpÜG ist also grundsätzlich auf solche EU-Gesellschaften zu erstrecken, die im Inland notiert sind.

Zusätzlich verkompliziert wird die Sache dadurch, dass die ÜRL eine Parallelisierung von materieller Regelungskompetenz und Aufsichtszuständigkeit anstrebt und dabei sowohl für das anwendbare Recht (Regelungskompetenz) als auch für die Aufsichtszuständigkeiten zwischen primär gesellschaftsrechtlichen und primär kapitalmarktrechtlichen Fragen differenziert. Dadurch soll bei grenzüberschreitenden Sachverhalten einerseits eine einheitli-

[3] Vgl. zum Meinungsstand nur MünchKomm AktG/*Wackerbarth* Band 9/1, 2. Aufl. 2004, § 2 WpÜG Rn. 23 ff. m. w. N.

[4] Entgegen *Seibt/Heiser* ZGR 2005, 200, 203 ist die Anwendung der ÜRL auf den Erwerb eigener Aktien nicht offen, sondern eindeutig zu verneinen, da die ÜRL nur auf den Erwerb der Kontrolle gerichtete Übernahmeangebote sowie Pflichtangebote nach anderweitiger Kontrollerlangung erfasst.

che kollisionsrechtliche Anknüpfung, andererseits eine eindeutige Allokation der Aufsichtszuständigkeiten zwischen den Behörden verschiedener Mitgliedstaaten ohne Überschneidungen erreicht werden.

Das Gesellschaftsstatut bestimmt sich nach dem Satzungssitz. Das ist zwar in der ÜRL nicht ausdrücklich geregelt, dafür spricht aber die Entwicklung der EuGH-Rechtsprechung mit den Urteilen „Centros", „Überseering" und „Inspire Art".[5] Der deutsche Gesetzgeber ist mithin berufen zur Regelung der primär gesellschaftsrechtlichen Fragen des Übernahmerechts für Aktiengesellschaften mit Satzungssitz im Inland. Gleiches gilt im Übrigen für Vorschriften zur Unterrichtung der Arbeitnehmer (vgl. Art. 4 Abs. 2 lit. e) ÜRL).[6] Als gesellschaftsrechtlich sieht die ÜRL insbesondere die Festlegung des die Kontrolle begründenden Stimmrechtsanteils an, Vorschriften über die Befreiung vom Pflichtangebot sowie die Bedingungen für die Zulässigkeit von Abwehrmaßnahmen der Zielgesellschaft (vgl. Art. 4 Abs. 2 lit. e) ÜRL). Als kapitalmarktrechtlich werden dagegen Fragen im Zusammenhang mit der angebotenen Gegenleistung und dem Angebotsverfahren qualifiziert. Die Anknüpfung erfolgt insoweit nach dem Recht des Mitgliedstaats der zuständigen Aufsichtsbehörde.

Daraus ergibt sich folgendes: Unverändert bleibt die Zuständigkeit der BaFin gemäß § 4 WpÜG für Angebote an Gesellschaften mit Sitz im Inland, deren Wertpapiere zum Handel auf einem geregelten Markt in Deutschland zugelassen sind[7] (Art. 4 Abs. 2 lit. a) ÜRL). Im Übrigen sind die Aufsichtszuständigkeiten der BaFin nach Art. 4 Abs. 2 lit. b) und c) ÜRL zu *erstrecken* auf:[8]

- *EU-Gesellschaften*, deren Wertpapiere *nur in Deutschland* zum Handel auf einem geregelten Markt *zugelassen* sind (Art. 4 Abs. 2 lit. b) UAbs. 1 ÜRL);
- EU-Gesellschaften, deren Wertpapiere *in mehreren Mitgliedstaaten* zum Handel auf einem geregelten Markt *zugelassen* sind, aber *zuerst in Deutschland* zugelassen wurden (Art. 4 Abs. 2 lit. b) UAbs. 2 ÜRL);
- Gesellschaften, deren Wertpapiere *zeitgleich in mehreren Mitgliedstaaten* zum Handel auf einem geregelten Markt zugelassen werden, sofern sich die *Ge-*

[5] EuGH, ZIP 1999, 438 (Centros); EuGH, Slg. 2002, I-9919 = ZIP 2002, 2037 (Überseering); EuGH, Urt. v. 30. 9. 2003 – Rs. C 167/01, AG 2003, 680 (Inspire Art).

[6] Im Einzelnen: Art. 6 Abs. 1 Satz 3, Abs. 2 UAbs. 1 Satz 3, Art. 8 Abs. 2, Art. 9 Abs. 5 Satz 2 ÜRL.

[7] *Maul/Muffat-Jeandet* AG 2004, 221, 228.

[8] Vgl. *Hopt/Mülbert/Kumpan* AG 2005, 109, 110; *Maul/Muffat-Jeandet* AG 2004, 221, 228 f.; *Seibt/Heiser* ZGR 2005, 200, 204 ff.

sellschaft für die BaFin als Aufsichtsbehörde *entscheidet*; in diesem Fall ist eine Mitteilung an die betroffenen geregelten Märkte und deren Aufsichtsstellen vorzusehen (Art. 4 Abs. 2 lit. c) UAbs. 1 ÜRL);

- Gesellschaften, deren Wertpapiere *zeitgleich vor Umsetzung der Richtlinie* (Art. 21 Abs. 1 ÜRL) *in mehreren Mitgliedstaaten* zum Handel auf einem geregelten Markt *zugelassen* wurden, sofern die betroffenen Aufsichtsstellen der Mitgliedstaaten die BaFin als Aufsichtsbehörde gemeinsam festgelegt haben, oder wenn keine Aufsichtsstelle benannt wurde und sich die Zielgesellschaft für die BaFin als Aufsichtsstelle entscheidet (Art. 4 Abs. 2 lit. c) UAbs. 2 ÜRL). Die Entscheidungen über die Festlegung einer Aufsichtsbehörde sind zu veröffentlichen (Art. 4 Abs. 2 lit. d) ÜRL).

Auf der anderen Seite ist die *Aufsichtszuständigkeit der BaFin einzuschränken bei deutschen Gesellschaften*, deren Wertpapiere *nur in anderen Mitgliedstaaten* zum Handel auf einem geregelten Markt *zugelassen* sind. Hier bleibt die BaFin nur für die gesellschaftsrechtlichen Fragen zuständig (also insbesondere Kontrollschwelle, Ausnahmen vom Pflichtangebot, Abwehrmaßnahmen sowie die Unterrichtung der Arbeitnehmer), während sich die primär kapitalmarktrechtlichen Fragen des Angebotsverfahrens und der Höhe der Gegenleistung (bei Pflichtangeboten) nach dem Marktrecht des Handelsstaates richten und von dessen Aufsichtsbehörde überwacht werden (Art. 4 Abs. 2 lit. e) S. 2 ÜRL).[9]

Festzuhalten bleibt, dass es zu einer derart *gespaltenen Rechtsanwendung* zwischen dem Recht des Sitzmitgliedstaats und des Börsenhandelsmitgliedstaats nur kommt, wenn beides auseinander fällt. Die Zulassung der Aktien zu einem geregelten Markt im Sitzmitgliedstaat führt dagegen immer zur Anwendung von dessen Recht und Überwachungszuständigkeit, selbst wenn vorher oder gleichzeitig eine Zulassung auch in anderen Mitgliedstaaten bestanden hat. Bei einer bloßen „Zweitzulassung" der stimmberechtigten Wertpapiere ausländischer Gesellschaften in Deutschland bedeutet dies, dass sich die Regelungsbefugnis des deutschen Gesetzgebers darauf beschränkt, eine Übersetzung der Angebotsunterlage sowie eine Reihe von Zusatzangaben verlangen zu können (Art. 6 Abs. 2 UAbs. 2 Satz 2 ÜRL).[10]

9 *Krause* BB 2004, 113, 117; *Seibt/Heiser* ZGR 2005, 200, 204.

10 *Hopt/Mülbert/Kumpan* AG 2005, 109. Vgl. auch die instruktive tabellenförmige Übersicht bei *Seibt/Heiser* ZGR 2005, 200, 206.

2. Die Bedeutung der allgemeinen Grundsätze des Übernahmerechts

Nach Art. 3 Abs. 1 ÜRL stellen die Mitgliedstaaten zur Umsetzung der Richtlinie sicher, dass die dort in lit. a) bis f) aufgelisteten allgemeinen Grundsätze beachtet werden. Die Richtlinie bedient sich insoweit einer ähnlichen Regelungstechnik wie der Londoner *City Code on Takeovers and Mergers* (City Code),[11] der auch inhaltlich erheblichen Einfluss auf die Ausgestaltung der europäischen wie der deutschen Übernahmeregelung entfaltet hat. In der Literatur geht man allerdings im Zusammenhang mit der Umsetzung der ÜRL meist gar nicht auf die allgemeinen Grundsätze des Art. 3 Abs. 1 ÜRL ein. Das mag seinen Grund darin haben, dass man diesen Grundsätzen eine eigenständige, rechtlich relevante Bedeutung abspricht oder jedenfalls wegen der vergleichbaren Regelungen in § 3 WpÜG von vornherein keinen Umsetzungsbedarf sieht. Ob diese unausgesprochenen Annahmen zutreffen, bedarf jedoch genauerer Analyse.

Gegen die pauschale Einordnung der allgemeinen Prinzipien als unverbindliche Programmsätze spricht schon, dass einzelne Grundsätze teilweise sehr detaillierte Vorgaben enthalten (z.B. Art. 3 Abs. 1 lit. b) zweiter Halbsatz ÜRL, wonach das Leitungs- bzw. Verwaltungsorgan der Zielgesellschaft bei der Beratung der Inhaber von Wertpapieren auf die Auswirkungen der Durchführung des Angebots auf die Beschäftigung, die Beschäftigungsbedingungen und die Standorte der Gesellschaft eingehen muss). Hinzu kommt, dass die verschiedenen Grundsätze teilweise in einem Spannungsverhältnis zueinander stehen mit der Folge, dass die Überbetonung eines Grundsatzes die Einhaltung eines anderen Grundsatzes gefährden könnte: So müssen z.B. die Inhaber von Wertpapieren der Zielgesellschaft einerseits über genügend Zeit und ausreichende Informationen verfügen, um in ausreichender Kenntnis der Sachlage über das Angebot entscheiden zu können, Art. 3 Abs. 1 lit. b) Halbsatz 1 ÜRL. Andererseits gilt es, eine durch das Angebot ausgelöste Behinderung der Geschäftstätigkeit der Zielgesellschaft über einen angemessenen Zeitraum hinaus zu vermeiden. Daher dürfen z.B. Annahme- oder sonstige Entscheidungsfristen auch nicht beliebig ausgedehnt werden. Die ÜRL

11 Die 38 Einzelregelungen (rules) und 10 allgemeinen Prinzipien (general principles) dieses auf einer freiwilligen Selbstregulierung beruhenden Verhaltenskodex lassen sich vier übergreifenden Regulierungszielen zuordnen: Gleichbehandlung der Aktionäre, Gewährleistung eines hinreichenden Informationsflusses, Verbot der Irreführung des Kapitalmarkts sowie das Gebot zum Handeln im Interesse der Anteilseigner.

schreibt zwar in Art. 7 vor, dass die Annahmefrist nicht weniger als zwei und nicht länger als zehn Wochen ab der Bekanntmachung der Angebotsunterlage betragen darf. Weiter heißt es jedoch: „Sofern der allgemeine Grundsatz nach Artikel 3 Absatz 1 Buchstabe f) eingehalten wird, können die Mitgliedstaaten vorsehen, dass die Frist von zehn Wochen unter der Bedingung verlängert werden kann, dass der Bieter seine Absicht zur Schließung des Angebots mindestens zwei Wochen vorher bekannt gibt." Weitere Abweichungen von der strikten Annahmefrist sind nach Art. 7 Abs. 2 ÜRL möglich. Diese müssen ebenfalls im Lichte des allgemeinen Beschleunigungsgebots bzw. Behinderungsverbots gesehen und ggf. ausgefüllt werden. Das zeigt auch Art. 4 Abs. 5 ÜRL, der den Erlass nationaler Ausnahmevorschriften bzw. die Gewährung von Befreiungen durch nationale Aufsichtsbehörden nur unter der Voraussetzung erlaubt, dass die in Art. 3 Abs. 1 festgelegten allgemeinen Grundsätze eingehalten werden. Daraus erhellt sich die normative Bedeutung dieser Grundsätze.

Die fünf in § 3 WpÜG bereits kodifizierten übernahmerechtlichen Grundsätze der Gleichbehandlung, der Transparenz, des Handelns im Interesse der Zielgesellschaft, der raschen Durchführung des Übernahmeverfahrens und der Vermeidung von Marktverzerrungen stimmen allerdings – zusammen mit ergänzenden konkreten Vorschriften des WpÜG – mit den Grundsätzen nach Art. 3 Abs. 1 ÜRL so weitgehend überein, dass kein relevanter Anpassungsbedarf mehr besteht (vgl. die Gegenüberstellung in Tabelle 1).

Tabelle 1

Vergleich Art. 3 ÜRL – § 3 WpÜG

Art. 3 Abs. 1 lit. a)	**Gattungsbezogene Gleichbehandlung** Schutz bei Kontrollerwerb (Pflichtangebot)	**Gattungsbezogene Gleichbehandlung** (–) als allg. Grds., aber konkrete Regeln	§ 3 Abs. 1 WpÜG §§ 35 ff. WpÜG
Art. 3 Abs. 1 lit. b)	**Transparenz** (genügend Zeit und ausreichende Information für sachgerechte Entscheidung über Angebot	**Transparenz**	§ 3 Abs. 2 WpÜG

	Beratung über Auswirkung des Angebots insbes. auf die Beschäftigung = Stellungnahmepflicht)	(–) als allg. Grds., aber konkrete Regel	§ 27 WpÜG
Art. 3 Abs. 1 lit. c)	Verpflichtung des Leitungsorgans der Zielgesellschaft auf ein **Handeln im Interesse der gesamten Gesellschaft** **Vereitelungsverbot**	Handeln im Interesse der Zielgesellschaft Kein allg. Grds., sondern konkrete Regel, jedoch mit weitreichenden Ausnahmetatbeständen	§ 3 Abs. 3 WpÜG § 33 Abs. 1 Satz 1 WpÜG Ausnahmen gemäß § 33 Abs. 1 Satz 2, Abs. 2 WpÜG
Art. 3 Abs. 1 lit. d)	**Verbot von Marktverzerrungen**	**Verbot von Marktverzerrungen**	§ 3 Abs. 5 WpÜG
Art. 3 Abs. 1 lit. e)	**Sicherstellung der Finanzierung des Angebots durch den Bieter**	Kein allg. Grds., sondern konkrete Regel	§ 13 Abs. 1 Satz 1 WpÜG
Art. 3 Abs. 1 lit. f)	**Verbot der Behinderung der Zielgesellschaft über einen angemessenen Zeitraum hinaus**	**Verbot der Behinderung der Zielgesellschaf über einen angemessenen Zeitraum hinaus**	§ 3 Abs. 4 WpÜG

Die allgemeinen Grundsätze stellen zwar keine konkreten Handlungsanweisungen für den Einzelfall dar. Diese finden sich vielmehr grundsätzlich in anderen Vorschriften des WpÜG, die ausdrücklich spezifische Pflichten der Gesellschaft und ihrer zuständigen Organe begründen. Die vom Gesetzgeber aufgestellten Grundsätze wirken aber als *verbindliche Leitlinien* auf die Auslegung der konkreten Gesetzesvorgaben zurück und geben den Beteiligten eine Abwägungshilfe, die insbesondere durch den Vorstand im Rahmen der Ausübung seines unternehmerischen Ermessens bei der Unternehmensleitung heranzuziehen ist.[12] Denn sie enthalten *grundlegende Wertungen*, die auf die Auslegung einzelner Rechtsvorschriften ausstrahlen können, z. B. bei der Bestimmung der Reichweite der spezielleren Pflichten oder bei der Schließung etwaiger Lücken. Dagegen ist die isolierte Verletzung der allgemeinen Grundsätze in aller Regel nicht geeignet, für sich genommen etwa einen Schadensersatzanspruch der betroffenen Wertpapierinhaber zu begründen. Ausnahmsweise können sie aber im Zusammenwirken mit anderen Vorschriften durchaus zur Quelle eigenständiger Verpflichtungen werden. So kann dem Transparenzgebot, dem wegen der eingehenden Regelung spezieller Informationspflichten im WpÜG grundsätzlich nur deklaratorische Bedeutung zukommt, im Zusammenspiel mit dem Gleichbehandlungsgebot z. B. unmittelbar eine Pflicht zur unverzüglichen Veröffentlichung von entscheidungsrelevanten Informationen zu entnehmen sein, die zuvor einzelnen Wertpapierinhabern zugänglich gemacht wurden.[13]

Für die ÜRL fragt sich, ob der Grundsatz nach Art. 3 Abs. 1 lit. c), wonach das Leitungs- und Verwaltungsorgan einer Zielgesellschaft im Interesse der gesamten Gesellschaft handeln muss und den Inhabern von Wertpapieren nicht die Möglichkeit vorenthalten darf, das Angebot selbst zu beurteilen, im Zusammenspiel mit der nur auf Art. 9 Abs. 2 und 3 ÜRL begrenzten *Opt-out*-Möglichkeit mittelbar dazu führt, die Zulässigkeit von Abwehrmaßnahmen durch das Leitungs- bzw. Verwaltungsorgan der Zielgesellschaft spürbar zu begrenzen. Da der Erlass der ÜRL in Kenntnis der bestehenden nationalen Übernahmeregelungen erfolgte, lässt sich aus dem Grundsatz des „Vorenthaltungsverbots" nach Art. 3 Abs. 1 lit. c) ÜRL aber wohl nur der Schluss ziehen, dass eine *weitere Ausdehnung* von Abwehrmaßnahmen, mit der sich ein Mitgliedstaat noch weiter von dem mit Art. 9 ÜRL angestrebten Zustand entfernen würde, nicht gestattet ist. Dagegen besteht keine Notwendigkeit, auch im Falle des *opt-out* bereits existierende Vorschriften wie den § 33 Abs. 2 WpÜG abzuschaffen, der entgegen dem Regelungsanliegen der ÜRL Vorratsermächtigungen der Hauptversammlung zu präventiven Abwehrmaßnahmen gestattet.[14]

12 Für eine ermessensleitende Funktion auch *Baums/Hecker* in Baums/Thoma, WpÜG, § 3 Rn. 3.

13 Vgl. näher *Fuchs* in Fleischer (Hrsg.), Handbuch des Vorstandsrechts (im Druck), § 22 Rn. 16 ff., 21 aE, 24.

14 Dementsprechend ist im RefE die Beibehaltung des § 33 Abs. 2 WpÜG vorgesehen. Für Unvereinbarkeit des § 33 Abs. 2 WpÜG mit der Richtlinie auch im Rahmen eines *opt-out* aber *Glade/Haak/Hellich* Der Konzern 2004, 515, 520 f. unter Berufung auf

3. Erhöhte Transparenzanforderungen nach Art. 10 ÜRL

Zur Stärkung des freien Wertpapierhandels und der freien Stimmrechtsausübung sieht die ÜRL in Art. 10 vor, dass die Abwehrstrukturen und -mechanismen einer Gesellschaft, durch die Übernahmen be- oder verhindert werden könnten, offen gelegt und regelmäßig der Hauptversammlung im Lagebericht mitgeteilt werden müssen (vgl. a. Erwägungsgrund 18). Das gilt unabhängig davon, ob ein Übernahmeangebot vorliegt oder zu erwarten ist. Denn die erhöhte Transparenz soll potentielle Bieter generell in die Lage versetzen, sich bereits im Vorfeld ein umfassendes Bild über mögliche Zielgesellschaften, insbesondere ihre Struktur und etwaige Übernahmehindernisse, zu machen.

Art. 10 Abs. 1 ÜRL enthält insoweit gewissermaßen einen „11-Punkte-Plan" zur Offenlegung der für ein Übernahmeangebot besonders relevanten Verhältnisse einer potentiellen Zielgesellschaft.[15] Die einzelnen Punkte werden vom Gesetzgeber auszulegen sein,[16] als diskussionswürdig und teilweise problematisch werden in der Literatur insbesondere die Einzelheiten hinsichtlich der Erfassung von Konsortialvereinbarungen und Stimmbindungsverträgen (vgl. Art. 10 Abs. 1 lit. g) ÜRL), Change-of-Control-Klauseln (Art. 10 Abs. 1 lit. j) ÜRL) sowie Abfindungsklauseln (Art. 10 Abs. 1 lit. k) ÜRL) angesehen.[17] Darauf kann hier nicht näher eingegangen werden.

Als Form der Offenlegung (dazu Art. 10 Abs. 2 ÜRL) wird zutreffend eine erweiterte Berichterstattung im Rahmen des (Konzern-)Lageberichts vorgeschlagen, die durch Anfügung jeweils eines weiteren Absatzes 4 bei den §§ 289, 315 HGB umzusetzen sei;[18] die Vorlagepflicht des Art. 10 Abs. 3 ÜRL ergibt sich dann aus dem unveränderten § 175 Abs. 2 AktG.

Art. 9 Abs. 2 Unterabs. 1 ÜRL, der eine Ermächtigung des Vorstands zu Abwehrmaßnahmen nur innerhalb der Angebotsdauer erlaube; unentschieden *Hopt/Mülbert/Kumpan* AG 2005, 109, 111f.

15 *Glade/Haak/Hellich* Der Konzern 2004, 455, 459.

16 *Wiesner* ZIP 2004, 343, 347.

17 Vgl. *Glade/Haak/Hellich* Der Konzern 2004, 455, 460ff.; *Maul/Muffat-Jeandet* AG 2004, 306, 308f.; *Seibt/Heiser* ZGR 2005, 200, 236ff.; *Hopt/Mülbert/Kumpan* AG 2005, 109, 118f.

18 So jetzt in der Tat Art. 2 Nr. 1–2 RefE (oben Fn. 1).

III. Die Pflichten des Bieters im Angebotsverfahren (Umsetzung von Art. 6–8 ÜRL)

1. Überblick

Die Regelung des Angebotsverfahrens in den §§ 10ff. WpÜG entspricht bereits weitgehend den europarechtlichen Anforderungen. Zur Umsetzung der Art. 6 bis 8 ÜRL sind nur wenige Ergänzungen zum einen wegen des erweiterten Anwendungsbereichs dieser marktbezogenen Vorschriften auch auf ausländische Gesellschaften mit inländischer „Erstzulassung“, zum anderen wegen einzelner weitergehender Informationsanforderungen geboten. So sollten die bisher inhaltlich wie terminologisch allein auf deutsche Gesellschaften zugeschnittenen Vorschriften in den §§ 10ff. WpÜG offener formuliert werden, so dass sie auch die Besonderheiten der ggf. anwendbaren anderen europäischen Gesellschaftsrechtsordnungen berücksichtigen.[19] Das gilt insbesondere für die nach Art. 6 Abs. 3 lit. e) ÜRL gebotenen Angaben über die zu zahlende Entschädigung bei Anwendung der Durchgriffsklausel.[20] Für ausländische Zielgesellschaften mit inländischer „Zweitzulassung“ kann der deutsche Gesetzgebers dagegen nur eine Pflicht zur Übersetzung der Informationen in die deutsche Sprache sowie zu bestimmten ergänzenden Angaben einführen, die für den deutschen Markt spezifisch sind und sich auf steuerliche Fragen oder Förmlichkeiten bei der Annahme des Angebots bzw. Erhalt der fälligen Gegenleistung beziehen (Art. 6 Abs. 2 UAbs. 2 S. 2 ÜRL).[21] Im Übrigen ist die von der zuständigen ausländischen Aufsichtsstelle erfolgte Billigung der Angebotsunterlage auch für die BAFin bindend.[22]

19 Vgl. *Hopt/Mülbert/Kumpan* AG 2005, 109, 111; *Mülbert* NZG 2004, 633, 640. Der RefE (Fn. 1) enthält in Art. 1 Nr. 1 (= § 1 Abs. 4 WpÜG-E) eine Ermächtigungsgrundlage für das Bundesministerium der Finanzen, nähere Bestimmungen über den Umfang der Anwendung von Vorschriften des WpÜG in diesen Fällen per Rechtsverordnung zu treffen; vgl. auch Art. 5 mit dem Entwurf einer „WpÜG-Anwendbarkeitsverordnung“.

20 Der RefE (Fn. 1) begnügt sich mit der lapidaren Feststellung, dass der Bieter „zur Entschädigung in Geld verpflichtet ist“, § 33b Abs. 4 WpÜG-E.

21 *Hopt/Mülbert/Kumpan* AG 2005, 109, 111; *Mülbert* NZG 2004, 633, 640.

22 Die Anerkennung im Inland ohne zusätzliches Billigungsverfahren stellt der RefE in § 11a WpÜG-E „Europäischer Pass“ klar.

2. Information über die Entscheidung zur Abgabe eines Angebotes

Bzgl. der Information über die Entscheidung zur Abgabe eines Angebotes enthält § 10 WpÜG weitgehend dem Art. 6 Abs. 1 ÜRL entsprechende Vorschriften.[23] Durch die Anpassung des Anwendungsbereichs in § 1 WpÜG werden davon insbesondere auch ausländische Zielgesellschaften mit inländischer Erstzulassung erfasst.[24] Allerdings besteht bei § 10 Abs. 3 WpÜG Anpassungsbedarf bzgl. der Art und Weise der Bekanntmachung (vgl. Art. 8 ÜRL).[25] Außerdem ist eine Unterrichtungspflicht des Bieters gegenüber dessen Arbeitnehmern (Art. 6 Abs. 1 S. 3 ÜRL) einzufügen.[26]

3. Veröffentlichung und Inhalt der Angebotsunterlage

Die §§ 11ff. WpÜG über die Veröffentlichung der Angebotsunterlage sind in einer Reihe von Einzelpunkten ergänzungsbedürftig.[27] Zusätzlich anzugeben sind

- die gem. Art. 2 Abs. 1 lit. d) ÜRL gemeinsam mit der Zielgesellschaft handelnden Personen (Art. 6 Abs. 3 lit. m) ÜRL)
- der Gerichtsstand für Streitigkeiten zwischen Bieter und annehmenden Aktionären (Art. 6 Abs. 3 lit. n ÜRL)[28]
- die gem. Art. 11 Abs. 4 zu gewährende Entschädigung (Art. 6 Abs. 3 lit. e) ÜRL); für inländische Gesellschaften ist das aber nur relevant, sofern sie sich gem. Art. 12 Abs. 2 ÜRL für die Anwendung des Art. 11 ÜRL entscheiden und aufgrund des § 5 Abs. 1 EGAktG noch Übernahmehindernisse i.S.v. Art. 11 ÜRL bestehen.

23 *Maul/Muffat-Jeandet* AG 2004, 221, 232; *Mülbert* NZG 2004, 633, 639.

24 *Mülbert* NZG 2004, 633, 640.

25 *Hopt/Mülbert/Kumpan* AG 2005, 109, 110. Der RefE (Fn. 1) sieht eine Bekanntgabe im Internet vor.

26 *Kindler/Horstmann* DStR 2004, 866, 872; *Maul* NZG 2005, 151, 156; *Mülbert* NZG 2004, 633, 640. Dem trägt der RefE (Fn. 1) mit der Einfügung eines neuen § 10 Abs. 5 WpÜG Rechnung (Mitteilung an den Betriebsrat oder, falls ein solcher nicht besteht, unmittelbar den Arbeitnehmern unverzüglich nach der Veröffentlichung).

27 *Hopt/Mülbert/Kumpan* AG 2005, 109, 110f.; *Maul/Muffat-Jeandet* AG 2004, 221, 233, 234; *Mülbert* NZG 2004, 633, 639f.

28 *Kindler/Horstmann* DStR 2004, 866, 871 (entweder in § 2 Nr. 2 WpÜG-AV, oder in § 11 II 3 Nr. 5 WpÜG).

Ferner ist die Art und Weise der Veröffentlichung der Angebotsunterlage nach § 14 Abs. 3 WpÜG wegen Art. 8 Abs. 2 ÜRL so anzupassen, dass sie zumindest in den Mitgliedstaaten, in denen die Wertpapiere zu einem geregelten Markt zugelassen sind, sowie den Arbeitnehmern bzw. ihren Vertretern ohne weiteres und umgehend zur Verfügung stehen. Einzuführen ist ferner eine eigene Unterrichtungspflicht des Bieters gegenüber dessen Arbeitnehmern gem. Art. 6 Abs. 2 UAbs. 1 S. 3 ÜRL.[29]

Die Regelungen des § 16 WpÜG über die Annahmefrist stehen im Einklang mit den Vorgaben der ÜRL in Art. 7 (nicht weniger als zwei, nicht mehr als zehn Wochen ab Veröffentlichung der Angebotsunterlage). Auch die weitergehenden Regelungen nach §§ 16 Abs. 2 und 3, 21 Abs. 5, 22 Abs. 2 WpÜG, die jeweils zu einer Verlängerung der Annahmefrist führen, sind gemäß Art. 7 Abs. 1 S. 2 ÜRL zulässig.[30]

4. Begriff der Kontrolle und Zurechnung von Stimmrechten

Durch den Verweis des Art. 5 Abs. 3 ÜRL auf das nationale Recht bleiben die Regelungen der §§ 29 Abs. 2, 30 Abs. 1 WpÜG – auch bzgl. der nur mittelbaren Kontrolle – unberührt.[31] Allerdings wird unabhängig von der ÜRL eine Loslösung des § 29 Abs. 2 WpÜG von § 9 WpÜG-AV und eine Anknüpfung an § 17 Abs. 1 WpÜG vorgeschlagen.[32]

Bei der Zurechnung von Stimmrechten gem. § 30 Abs. 2 WpÜG wird eine volle Bezugnahme auf den anzupassenden § 2 Abs. 5 WpÜG[33] hinsichtlich der gemeinsam handelnden Personen vorgeschlagen.[34] Die von der BaFin und Teilen des Schrifttums vertretene enge Interpretation des § 30 Abs. 2 S. 1 WpÜG (Koordinierung der Stimmrechtsausübung, keine Erfassung des Par-

29 Der RefE (Fn. 1) sieht in § 14 Abs. 3 Satz 1 Nr. 2 WpÜG-E die Veröffentlichung im Elektronischen Bundesanzeiger und in dem neuen § 14 Abs. 4 WpÜG-E die Übermittlung der Angebotsunterlage an den Betriebsrat oder, sofern ein solcher nicht besteht, unmittelbar an die Arbeitnehmer vor.

30 Vgl. *Maul/Muffat-Jeandet* AG 2004, 221, 234; *Mülbert* NZG 2004, 633, 639; *Seibt/Heiser* ZGR 2005, 200, 211f.

31 *Mülbert* NZG 2004, 633, 636.

32 *Hopt/Mülbert/Kumpan* AG 2005, 109, 111; *Habersack* ZHR 166 (2002), 619, 622f.

33 *Hopt/Mülbert/Kumpan* AG 2005, 109, 110; *Maul/Muffat-Jeandet* AG 2004, 221, 230.

34 *Hopt/Mülbert/Kumpan* AG 2005, 109, 111. Der RefE (Fn. 1) lässt jedoch § 30 Abs. 2 WpÜG unverändert und erweitert lediglich die Definition in § 2 Abs. 5 WpÜG-E.

allelerwerbs) ist mit den Vorgaben in Art. 2 Abs. 1 lit. d) ÜRL nicht vereinbar, dürfte aber durch die Anpassung dieser Vorschrift an § 2 Abs. 5 WpÜG ausgeräumt werden.[35] Auch eine bisher zum Teil erwogene Beschränkung auf rechtliche Vereinbarungen[36] ist mit der weiten Fassung des Art. 2 Abs. 1 lit. d) ÜRL nicht vereinbar.[37] Im Übrigen stellt Art. 5 Abs. 1 ÜRL nur eine Mindestvorgabe zur Zurechnung von Stimmrechtsanteilen dar, so dass strengere nationale Regelungen möglich bleiben.[38] Dies gilt aufgrund des Art. 3 Abs. 2 lit. b) ÜRL etwa für die Unzulässigkeit von Teilangeboten gem. § 32 WpÜG.[39]

5. Anpassungsbedarf bei der Mindestpreisregel?

Einige sehen in der Regelung des § 31 WpÜG einen Widerspruch zur Richtlinienkonzeption bezüglich freiwilliger Angebote und wollen ihn daher streichen.[40] Andere halten diese Regelung unter Verweis auf Art. 3 Abs. 2 lit. b) ÜRL dagegen für zulässig.[41] Auch wenn sich der Anwendungsbereich der umzusetzenden Preisregel des Art. 5 Abs. 5 Unterabsatz 3 ÜRL auf Pflichtangebote beschränkt, ist der Gesetzgeber nicht gehindert, eine damit übereinstimmende Mindestpreisregel auch für freiwillige Übernahmeangebote vorzusehen.[42] Dagegen mag es in der Sache durchaus bedenkenswerte Einwände geben,[43] doch sollte die ÜRL insoweit nicht für eine aus anderen Gründen vielleicht als wünschenswert angesehene Gesetzesänderung instrumentalisiert werden.

35 *Hopt/Mülbert/Kumpan* AG 2005, 109, 111; *Mülbert* NZG 2004, 633, 636f.; vgl. auch *Seibt/Heiser* ZGR 2005, 200, 250.

36 *Seibt/Heiser* ZGR 2005, 200, 216.

37 *Hopt/Mülbert/Kumpan* AG 2005, 109, 111.

38 *Mülbert* NZG 2004, 633, 637.

39 *Kindler/Horstmann* DStR 2004, 866, 871; *Maul/Muffat-Jeandet* AG 2004, 221, 225; *Mülbert* NZG 2004, 633, 640.

40 *Hopt/Mülbert/Kumpan* AG 2005, 109, 111; *Mülbert* NZG 2004, 633, 640f.

41 *Kindler/Horstmann* DStR 2004, 866, 872; *Seibt/Heiser* ZIP 2002, 2193, 2195; *Wiesner* ZIP 2004, 343, 347 Fn. 32.

42 Die im RefE (Fn. 1) vorgesehene Neufassung des § 31 Abs. 3 WpÜG-E gibt die Trennung der Tatbestände des Vor- und Parallelerwerbs auf und legt zur Berechnung des einschlägigen Schwellenwertes nunmehr eine einzige Referenzperiode fest, die sechs Monate vor der Veröffentlichung zur Abgabe eines Angebots beginnt und mit Ablauf der Annahmefrist endet.

43 Vgl. z.B. MünchKomm AktG/*Wackerbarth* § 31 WpÜG Rn. 6ff. m.w.N., der allerdings mit seiner These einer drastischen teleologischen Reduktion des § 31 WpÜG auf Pflichtangebote jedenfalls *de lege lata* zu weit geht.

IV. Das übernahmerechtliche Vereitelungsverbot

1. Ausgangslage und Alternativen für die Umsetzung des zweistufigen Optionsmodells

Die Richtlinie enthält in Art. 9 Abs. 2 und 3 ein strenges Vereitelungsverbot für die Geschäftsleitung der Zielgesellschaft, das nur zwei eng begrenzte Ausnahmen kennt: die Suche nach konkurrierenden Angeboten und Maßnahmen im normalen Geschäftsbetrieb der Gesellschaft. Im übrigen bedarf der Vorstand nach Bekanntgabe der Entscheidung zur Unterbreitung eines Übernahmeangebots für alle Maßnahmen, durch die das Angebot objektiv vereitelt werden könnte, der innerhalb der Angebotsfrist zu diesem Zweck erteilten Zustimmung oder Ermächtigung der Hauptversammlung. Präventive Vorratsbeschlüsse sind also unzulässig.

Von dieser harten Neutralitätspflicht können die Mitgliedstaaten jedoch im Rahmen eines zweistufigen Optionsmodells nach Art. 12 ÜRL abweichen. Dieses Herzstück des Brüsseler Kompromisses stellt es den Mitgliedstaaten frei, die Art. 9 Abs. 2 und 3 (ebenso wie die sog. Durchgriffsregel nach Art. 11, nach der bestimmte Übernahmehindernisse während der Annahmefrist für unwirksam erklärt werden) nicht zur Anwendung zu bringen. Entscheiden sie sich auf der ersten Stufe nach Art. 12 Abs. 1 ÜRL für ein solches generelles *opt-out*, gilt das zunächst für alle Emittenten des betreffenden Landes. Die Mitgliedstaaten müssen aber den Gesellschaften mit Sitz in ihrem Hoheitsgebiet die Möglichkeit eröffnen, sich individuell, freiwillig und widerruflich durch Beschluss der Hauptversammlung mit satzungsändernder Mehrheit den Beschränkungen der Richtlinie zu unterwerfen (Art. 12 Abs. 2 UAbs. 1). Das Votum für ein derartiges individuelles *opt-in* ist den Aufsichtsbehörden des Sitzstaates und der Mitgliedstaaten, in denen die Wertpapiere der Gesellschaft zum Handel an einem geregelten Markt zugelassen sind, mitzuteilen (Art. 12 Abs. 2 UAbs. 2 Satz 2 ÜRL). Diese Entscheidung, die gewissermaßen zur Qualifikation als kapitalmarktorientiertes Unternehmen führt, kann später durch gegenteiligen Hauptversammlungsbeschluss wieder rückgängig gemacht werden. Darüber hinaus können die Mitgliedstaaten Unternehmen der kapitalmarktoffenen Klasse gestatten, sich gegen einen Angriff durch Gesellschaften aus der geschützten Klasse, die nicht der Neutralitätspflicht der und/oder der Durchbruchsregel unterliegen, zu verteidigen. Dazu bedarf es eines entsprechenden Hauptversammlungsbeschlusses, der als Vorratsbeschluss, allerdings frühestens 18 Monate vor Bekanntgabe des Angebots, ergehen darf (Art. 12 Abs. 3 und 5 ÜRL), sog. Reziprozitätsregel.

Daraus folgt: Sofern Deutschland von seinem *opt-out*-Recht Gebrauch macht, womit zu rechnen ist,[44] bleibt für die Gesellschaften, die keine *opt-in*-Beschlüsse fassen, insoweit alles beim Alten. Das in § 33 Abs. 1 Satz 1 WpÜG enthaltene Vereitelungsverbot entspricht ohnehin den europarechtlichen Anforderungen. Die weiten Ausnahmetatbestände des § 33 Abs. 1 Satz 2 und Abs. 2 WpÜG gehen zwar erheblich über die von der ÜRL generell erlaubte Einschränkung der Neutralitätspflicht hinaus, können aber bei einem *opt-out* Deutschlands unverändert bestehen bleiben. Allerdings ist darauf hinzuweisen, dass die Ausnahmen nur von der übernahmerechtlichen Neutralitätspflicht entbinden, nicht dagegen von allgemeinen aktienrechtlichen Beschränkungen für Abwehrmaßnahmen. Daher sind deutsche Gesellschaften weit weniger gegen feindliche Übernahmen abgeschirmt, als vielfach angenommen wird.

Dennoch gibt es erheblichen Änderungsbedarf im WpÜG, weil der deutsche Gesetzgeber die gesetzlichen Voraussetzungen schaffen muss für die Gesellschaften, die einen *opt-in*-Beschluss fassen wollen. Man könnte zunächst daran denken, die Ausnahmen in § 33 Abs. 1 Satz 2 und Abs. 2 jeweils oder insgesamt zur Disposition der Hauptversammlung zu stellen. Besser erscheint es jedoch, in einem neuen § 33a WpÜG das Rechtsregime, das im Falle eines *opt-in*-Beschlusses gelten soll, einheitlich zu regeln.[45] Zudem dürfen die Gesellschaften nach zutreffender, wenngleich nicht unumstrittener Interpretation der ÜRL nicht nur auf einzelne Ausnahmetatbestände verzichten, sondern müssen sich zwischen den Alternativen der strikten Neutralitätspflicht im Umfang der Richtlinie einerseits und dem Regime des bisherigen (oder ggf. modifizierten) § 33 WpÜG andererseits entscheiden.[46] Das Votum für die freiwillige Anwendung der europarechtlichen Neutralitätspflicht kann immer nur „ganz oder gar nicht" erfolgen. Dafür spricht, dass andernfalls die Markttransparenz schwer beeinträchtigt und der Harmonisierungszweck völlig verfehlt würde, weil dann selbst Unternehmen, die demselben Gesellschaftsstatut unterliegen, je nach individueller Entscheidung über unterschiedlich weit reichende Abwehrmöglichkeiten verfügen würden. Gleiches

44 So jetzt in der Tat der RefE (Fn. 1), der § 33 WpÜG unverändert lässt und lediglich die Möglichkeit einer individuellen Unterstellung unter ein „Europäisches Verhinderungsverbot" (§ 33 a WpÜG-E) und/oder eine „Europäische Durchgriffsregel" (§ 33 b WpÜG-E) sowie die Option zur Anwendung einer Reziprozitätsregel („Vorbehalt der Gegenseitigkeit, § 33c WpÜG-E) schafft. Erforderlich ist jeweils der Beschluss einer entsprechenden Satzungsbestimmung der Zielgesellschaft.

45 So jetzt auch der RefE (Fn. 1), vgl. vorherige Fn.

46 So insbes. *Glade/Haak/Hellich* Der Konzern 2004, 517; *Krause* BB 2004, 113, 114; **a. A.** *Seibt/Heiser* ZGR 2005, 200, 233.

gilt im Übrigen für die Anwendung der Durchbruchsregeln nach Art. 11 ÜRL, nach denen bestimmte Übernahmehindernisse durch Veräußerungs- und Stimmrechtsbeschränkungen überwunden werden können. Auch hier kann es nur ein „entweder – oder", aber keine individuelle, maßgeschneiderte Zusammenstellung der anwendbaren Tatbestände geben.

Fraglich ist, ob das zweistufige Optionsmodell der ÜRL mit der Möglichkeit eines generellen *opt-out* durch den jeweiligen Mitgliedstaat und eines individuellen *opt-in* durch einzelne Gesellschaften auch andersherum implementiert werden könnte. Die Alternative, dass ein Mitgliedstaat sich für ein generelles *opt-in* entscheidet, seinen Gesellschaften aber die Möglichkeit zu einem individuellen *opt-out* einräumt, ist in der ÜRL nicht (zumindest nicht explizit) vorgesehen.[47] Für eine solche Möglichkeit könnte sprechen, dass der Mitgliedstaat damit einerseits eine mildere Alternative gegenüber der ihm ebenfalls möglichen strikten Einführung des übernahmerechtlichen Vereitelungsverbots wählen, andererseits aber einen höheren Schutzstandard zugunsten der Aktionäre der Zielgesellschaft als bei einem generellen „opt-out" verwirklichen würde. Auch wenn sich ein solches Modell wohl noch mit dem Wortlaut des Art. 12 Abs. 1 ÜRL vereinbaren ließe, da die Gestattung eines individuellen *opt-out* ebenfalls eine Form der nicht zwingenden Anwendung der Neutralitätspflicht bzw. Durchbruchsregel ist, widerspräche sie jedoch eindeutig dem Wortlaut des Art. 12 Abs. 2 ÜRL. Diese Vorschrift bezieht sich unzweideutig allein auf die Einräumung der widerruflichen Wahlmöglichkeit im Sinne eines *„opt-in"* und verlangt zudem entsprechende Mitteilungen an die betroffenen Aufsichtsbehörden. Vor diesem Hintergrund und der Tendenz der ÜRL zu einer eindeutigen und klaren Zuweisung der Aufsichtszuständigkeiten an die einzelnen Behörden der Mitgliedstaaten erscheint die *Umkehrung des Regel-Ausnahmeverhältnisses* bei Einführung einer individuellen *opt-out*-Möglichkeit (statt des im Text der ÜRL vorgesehenen individuellen *opt-in*) *bedenklich*. Dass der deutsche Gesetzgeber diesen unsicheren Weg beschreiten könnte, dürfte aber ohnehin unwahrscheinlich sein.

2. Reformbedarf im Falle eines *„opt-in"*

Die Einrichtung eines mit den Vorgaben des Art. 9 ÜRL in vollem Umfang kompatiblen Regelungsregimes setzt folgende Änderungen gegenüber der derzeitigen Regelung in § 33 WpÜG voraus:

47 Dennoch für diese Möglichkeit *Seibt/Heiser* ZGR 2005, 200, 231.

Zunächst ist die Ausnahme des § 33 Abs. 1 S. 2 *Fall 3* WpÜG (Zulässigkeit von Abwehrmaßnahmen mit Zustimmung des Aufsichtsrates) zu streichen.[48] § 33 Abs. 1 S. 2 *Fall 2* WpÜG (Suche nach einem konkurrierenden Angebot) kann dagegen unverändert bestehen bleiben, da sie Art. 9 Abs. 2 UAbs. 1 entspricht.[49]

Streitig ist der Änderungsbedarf im *Fall 1* des § 33 Abs. 1 S. 2 WpÜG, der Handlungen erlaubt, die auch ein ordentlicher und gewissenhafter Geschäftsleiter einer Gesellschaft, die nicht von einem Übernahmeangebot betroffen ist, vorgenommen hätte. Manche sehen aufgrund des mit Art. 9 Abs. 3 ÜRL übereinstimmenden Regelungszwecks keinen Anpassungsbedarf;[50] nach überwiegender Meinung erfasst die Richtlinie mit dem Abstellen auf den „normalen Geschäftsbetrieb der Gesellschaft" aber nur eine Teilmenge des § 33 Abs. 1 S. 2 Fall 1 WpÜG. Da die Auslegung sowohl der deutschen Vorschrift als auch des Art. 9 Abs. 3 ÜRL umstritten ist,[51] besteht insoweit Unklarheit über die Umsetzungspflicht.[52]

Der hypothetische Vergleich mit dem nicht von einem Übernahmeangebot betroffenen ordentlichen Geschäftsleiter im WpÜG soll klarstellen, dass es dem Vorstand gestattet ist, das *Tagesgeschäft* weiterzuführen und den schon vor Veröffentlichung der Entscheidung zur Abgabe eines Angebots begründeten Rechtspflichten nachzukommen. Andernfalls würde die Zielgesellschaft während der Angebotsphase unangemessen in ihrer Geschäftstätigkeit behindert oder gar gelähmt. Nach der Gesetzesbegründung sind auch weitergehende Maßnahmen gedeckt wie die *Weiterverfolgung einer bereits eingeschlagenen Unternehmensstrategie*. Dahinter kann sich auch der Verkauf von Unternehmensteilen, der Erwerb fremder Unternehmen oder die Eingehung neuer vertraglicher sowie sonstiger Verpflichtungen verbergen, solange die Maßnahme sich in die vorgezeichnete Unternehmensstrategie einfügt.

48 *Hopt/Mülbert/Kumpan* AG 2005, 109, 112; *Glade/Haak/Hellich* Der Konzern 2004, 515, 520; vgl. *Maul* NZG 2005, 151, 153; *Seibt/Heiser* ZGR 2005, 200, 223; *Wiesner* ZIP 2004, 343, 349.

49 Vgl. den Gesetzesvorschlag von *Hopt/Mülbert/Kumpan* AG 2005, 109, 112; s. a. *Krause* BB 2004, 113, 114.

50 *Kindler/Horstmann* DStR 2004, 866, 872; *Wiesner* ZIP 2004, 343, 347 Fn. 33.

51 Für wörtliche Auslegung des Art. 9 Abs. 3 ÜRL z. B. *Glade/Haak/Hellich* Der Konzern 2004, 515, 520; anders *Krause* BB 2004, 113, 114 (Erfassung auch des „angebahnten, aber noch nicht Vertragsschluss besiegelten" Verkaufs eines wesentlichen Unternehmensteils als Maßnahme des normalen Geschäftsbetriebs).

52 *Glade/Haak/Hellich* Der Konzern 2004, 515, 520; *Hopt/Mülbert/Kumpan* AG 2005, 109, 112; *Krause* BB 2004, 113, 114.

Die Handlungsmöglichkeiten des Vorstands erstrecken sich danach *auch* auf *außergewöhnliche Maßnahmen*, welche den Erfolg des Übernahmeangebots erschweren oder gar verhindern können. Zur Verhinderung einer leichten Umgehung des Vereitelungsverbots werden in Teilen der Literatur strenge Anforderungen an den Konkretisierungsgrad der Unternehmensstrategie gestellt. Zum Zeitpunkt der Veröffentlichung der Entscheidung zur Abgabe eines Übernahmeangebots müsse die verfolgte Unternehmensstrategie der Zielgesellschaft bereits ausreichend verfestigt, inhaltlich weitgehend ausgereift und publiziert oder zumindest unternehmensintern ausreichend dokumentiert sein. Für weitergehende Einschränkungen des unternehmerischen Ermessens des Vorstands, wie sie in Teilen der Literatur unter Hinweis auf einen Interessenkonflikt in Übernahmesituationen gefordert werden, besteht dagegen kein Anlass. Denn die Freistellung vom Vereitelungsverbot gilt insoweit nur für Handlungen, die bereits vor der Bekanntgabe der Übernahmeabsicht angelegt waren, also zu einem Zeitpunkt, in dem noch kein Interessenkonflikt bestand.

Die in Art. 9 Abs. 3 ÜRL enthaltene Regelung ist dagegen offenbar enger. Danach bedürfen Entscheidungen, die vor der Bekanntgabe des Übernahmeangebots gefasst, aber weder teilweise noch vollständig umgesetzt worden sind, der Zustimmung oder Bestätigung durch die Hauptversammlung der Zielgesellschaft, wenn diese *Entscheidungen außerhalb des normalen Geschäftsverlaufs* gefasst wurden und ihre Umsetzung dazu führen könnte, dass das Angebot vereitelt wird. Daraus wird teilweise gefolgert, dass Vorstand und Aufsichtsrat allein derartige Maßnahmen nicht durchführen dürften, die über das Tagesgeschäft wesentlich hinausgingen und den Erfolg des Übernahmeangebots erheblich gefährden könnten; dazu gehöre insbesondere auch die Weiterverfolgung einer bereits eingeschlagenen, aber neuartigen und für den Bieter nachteiligen Unternehmensstrategie.[53] Insoweit wird allerdings teilweise auch eine einschränkende richtlinienkonforme Auslegung des § 33 Abs. 1 Satz 2 Fall 3 WpÜG für ausreichend gehalten.[54]

Unter dem Blickwinkel des allgemeinen Grundsatzes nach Art. 3 Abs. 1 lit. f), dass eine Zielgesellschaft in ihrer Geschäftstätigkeit nicht über einen angemessenen Zeitraum hinaus durch ein Angebot behindert werden darf, ist Art. 9 Abs. 3 ÜRL jedoch so auszulegen, dass jedenfalls die bereits begonnene *teilweise Umsetzung* einer Entscheidung, die vor Abgabe des Übernahmeange-

53 *Seibt/Heiser* ZGR 2005, 200, 223.

54 *Seibt/Heiser* ZGR 2005, 200, 223; für ausdrückliche Beschränkung auf Geschäfte des normalen Geschäftsbetriebs *Hopt/Mülbert/Kumpan* AG 2005, 109, 112.

bots getroffen wurde, keiner (erneuten) Bestätigung durch die Hauptversammlung bedarf, selbst wenn die Entscheidung außerhalb des normalen Geschäftsbetriebs liegt. Nach dem Wortlaut, gerade auch in der englischen Fassung, scheint auf den ersten Blick sogar eine noch weitergehende Interpretation möglich, die auf jegliche Ausführungshandlung der vor Angebotsabgabe außerhalb des normalen Geschäftsbetriebs getroffenen Entscheidung verzichtet.[55] Bei einem Verzicht auf jeglichen Ansatz zur Implementierung würden allerdings Abgrenzungsschwierigkeiten zu unzulässigen Vorratsermächtigungen auftreten. In der Sache dürfte daher letztlich ein weitgehender Gleichklang zwischen Art. 9 Abs. 3 ÜRL und § 33 Abs. 1 Satz 2 *Fall 1* WpÜG bestehen, so dass insoweit im Ergebnis kein ausdrücklicher Anpassungsbedarf besteht.[56] Aus Gründen der Rechtsklarheit dürfte sich der deutsche Gesetzgeber aber wohl für eine eigenständige, am Wortlaut des Art. 9 ÜRL orientierte Vorschrift zur Umsetzung des europäischen Verhinderungsverbots entscheiden.[57]

Die in § 33 Abs. 2 WpÜG vorgesehenen Vorratsbeschlüsse vor Abgabe eines Übernahmeangebots[58] können im Rahmen eines richtlinienkompatiblen Regelungsregimes keinen Bestand haben.[59] Praktische Relevanz hat diese Aus-

55 „As regards decisions taken before the beginning of the period referred to in the second subparagraph of paragraph 2 *and not yet partly or fully implemented*, the general meeting of the shareholders shall approve or confirm any decision which does not form part of the normal course of the company's business ...." (Hervorhebung hinzugefügt).

56 Ebenso im Ergebnis *Krause* BB 2004, 113, 114; wohl auch *Kindler/Horstmann* DStR 2004, 866, 872.

57 So jetzt RefE (Fn. 1) mit § 33a WpÜG-E; vgl. insbesondere § 33a Abs. 2 Nr. 3 WpÜG-E, der sämtliche Handlungen außerhalb des normalen Geschäftsbetriebs zur Umsetzung von vor der Angebotsabgabe getroffenen Entscheidungen erfasst, sofern diese „noch nicht vollständig umgesetzt wurden". Letzteres ist nach dem Vorstehenden so zu interpretieren, dass mit der Ausführung der Entscheidung zumindest ansatzweise begonnen worden sein muss.

58 Nach § 33 Abs. 2 WpÜG kann der Vorstand Handlungen zur Verhinderung von Übernahmen ergreifen, die auf einer im Voraus erteilten Ermächtigung der Hauptversammlung beruhen. Ein derartiger Vorratsbeschluss, der die zulässigen Maßnahmen nur der Art nach bestimmen muss, erfordert eine Mehrheit und kann für die Dauer von 18 Monaten beschlossen werden. Die Ausnutzung der Vorratsermächtigung muss im Unternehmensinteresse liegen und ist an die Einwilligung des Aufsichtsrats (§ 33 Abs. 2 S. 4 WpÜG) gebunden. Problematisch ist, dass die Hauptversammlung ihre Zustimmung in aller Regel ohne Kenntnis des konkreten Übernahmeangebots erteilt.

59 *Glade/Haak/Hellich* Der Konzern 2004, 515, 519ff.; *Maul* NZG 2005, 151, 153; *Seibt/Heiser* ZGR 2005, 200, 223; *Wiesner* ZIP 2004, 343, 349.

nahme im deutschen Recht freilich bisher nicht erlangt. Das dürfte zum einen daran liegen, dass die anderen Ausnahmevorschriften ohnehin schon sehr weitreichende Möglichkeiten zu Verteidigungshandlungen bieten. Zum anderen haftet den aktienrechtlich üblichen Ermächtigungen – beispielsweise dem genehmigten Kapital nach § 202 AktG oder der Ermächtigung zum Erwerb eigener Aktien nach § 71 Abs. 1 Nr. 8 AktG – nicht der Makel einer Vorbereitung von Abwehrmaßnahmen an, deren stigmatisierende Wirkung im Kapitalmarkt offenbar gefürchtet wird. Schließlich bleibt immer die Möglichkeit, *ad hoc* eine Hauptversammlung zur Beschlussfassung über etwaige Abwehrmaßnahmen einzuberufen. Dies wird durch verschiedene Regelungen in § 16 WpÜG erleichtert.

Als zusätzliche Umsetzungsmaßnahme vorgeschlagen wird teilweise die explizite Anerkennung der in Art. 9 Abs. 2 UAbs. 1 ÜRL vorgesehenen Autorisierung von Abwehrmaßnahmen durch die Hauptversammlung während der Dauer des Übernahmeangebots.[60] Zudem könnte klargestellt werden, dass Adressat der sog. Neutralitätspflicht des § 33 Abs. 1 S. 1 WpÜG nicht nur der Vorstand, sondern nach Art. 9 Abs. 6 ÜRL auch der Aufsichtsrat ist.[61] In der Literatur wird dies zum großen Teil bereits *de lege lata* anerkannt, soweit es um die Kontrolltätigkeit des Aufsichtsrats außerhalb des § 33 Abs. 1 Satz 2 Fall 3 WpÜG geht.[62] Beide Änderungen erscheinen zwar zweckmäßig, aber nicht unbedingt erforderlich.

3. Reformbedarf im Falle eines „*opt-out*"

Entscheidet sich der deutsche Gesetzgeber erwartungsgemäß für ein „*opt-out*", kann er zwar den gegenwärtigen § 33 WpÜG unverändert lassen, muss daneben aber zusätzlich das soeben skizzierte europarechtskonforme Regelungsregime schaffen, um den deutschen Aktiengesellschaften die Möglichkeit für ein individuelles „*opt-in*" zu verschaffen. Dies könnte in einem neuen

60 *Hopt/Mülbert/Kumpan* AG 2005, 109, 112. Vom RefE (Fn. 1) aufgenommen in § 33a Abs. 2 Nr. 1 WpÜG-E („Handlungen, zu denen die Hauptversammlung den Vorstand oder Aufsichtsrat nach Veröffentlichung der Entscheidung zur Abgabe eines Angebots ermächtigt hat").

61 *Maul/Muffat-Jeandet* AG 2004, 306, 310 f.; nach bisheriger Rechtslage war streitig, ob der Aufsichtsrat erfasst wird, s. dazu *Ehricke/Ekkenga/Oechsler* WpÜG, § 33 Rn. 24; *Grunewald* in: Baums/Thoma, WpÜG, § 33 Rn. 16; dies bejahend und daher Änderungsbedarf verneinend: *Seibt/Heiser* ZGR 2005, 200, 223 f.

62 *Seibt/Heiser* ZGR 2005, 200, 223 f. m. w. N.

§ 33a WpÜG geschehen,[63] dessen Anwendung von einem freiwilligen und widerruflichen Hauptversammlungsbeschluss mit satzungsändernder Mehrheit (also grds. einfacher Stimmen- und -Kapitalmehrheit nach §§ 133 Abs.1, 179 Abs. 3 AktG) abhängig zu machen ist.[64]

Weitergehend wird die Einführung einer Pflicht der Unternehmen zur regelmäßigen Mitteilung über die Einhaltung der Neutralitätspflicht und der Durchbrechungsregel vorgeschlagen.[65]

4. Gewährleistung von „Waffengleichheit" – die Befreiungsmöglichkeit nach Art. 12 Abs. 3 ÜRL

Das zweistufige Optionsmodell führt zu erheblichen Unterschieden zwischen verschiedenen Gesellschaften in ihren Verteidigungsmöglichkeiten gegen Übernahmeangebote. Um zu verhindern, dass Gesellschaften, die von der Anwendung des Vereitelungsverbots nach ihrem nationalen Recht befreit sind, einen Wettbewerbsvorteil gegenüber Unternehmen erlangen, die einem strengeren Neutralitätsgebot unterliegen, sieht die ÜRL in Art. 12 Abs. 3 eine Art Gegenseitigkeitsregel vor: die Möglichkeit zu einer selektiven Befreiung von der Anwendung des strikten Vereitelungsverbots gegenüber solchen Bietergesellschaften, die selbst nicht diesem strengen Neutralitätsgebot unterliegen. Entscheidet sich der deutsche Gesetzgeber zur Implementierung einer solchen weiteren Ausnahme, muss er eine Rechtsgrundlage für einen Vorratsbeschluss der Hauptversammlung schaffen, durch den Vorstand und Aufsichtsrat zur Ergreifung von Abwehrmaßnahmen ermächtigt werden. Diese Ermächtigung muss nach Art. 12 Abs. 5 ÜRL alle 18 Monate erneuert werden. Die Struktur des erforderlichen Ermächtigungsbeschlusses stimmt mit der gegenwärtig in § 33 Abs. 2 WpÜG vorgesehenen generellen Möglichkeit zu Vorratsbeschlüssen der Hauptversammlung überein, so dass sich ein Verweis auf diese Norm anbietet im Rahmen der Vorschrift, die das Rechtsregime für

63 *Glade/Haak/Hellich* Der Konzern 2004, 515, 517; *Hopt/Mülbert/Kumpan* AG 2005, 109, 113; *Kindler/ Horstmann* DStR 2004, 866, 871f.; *Krause* BB 2004, 113, 114f.; *Maul/ Muffat-Jeandet* AG 2004, 306, 310; *Seibt/Heiser* ZGR 2005, 200, 231f. Dem ist der RefE (Fn. 1) gefolgt.

64 Für einfache Stimmenmehrheit ohne Begründung *Hopt/Mülbert/Kumpan* AG 2005, 109, 112.

65 Vgl. *Glade/Haak/Hellich* Der Konzern 2004, 515, 517; *Hopt/Mülbert/Kumpan* AG 2005, 109, 113.

Gesellschaften nach einem individuellen *„opt-in"* regelt.[66] Die ÜRL schreibt in Art. 12 Abs. 5 zwar kein konkretes Mehrheitserfordernis vor, doch sollte der deutsche Gesetzgeber auch insoweit bei dem schon in § 33 Abs. 2 WpÜG eingeführten qualifizieren Mehrheitserfordernis für den Vorratsbeschluss der Hauptversammlung bleiben.

Fraglich ist, ob sich der Anwendungsbereich der Gegenseitigkeitsregel auf börsennotierte Bietergesellschaften mit Satzungssitz innerhalb der EU beschränkt.[67] Der Wortlaut von Art. 12 Abs. 3 ÜRL ist insoweit offen (Gesellschaften, die Art. 9 Abs. 2 und 3 und/oder Art. 11 anwenden, gegenüber einer Gesellschaft, die ihrerseits dieselben Artikel nicht anwendet). Andererseits haben Bietergesellschaften aus Drittstaaten gar nicht die Möglichkeit, sich freiwillig dem europäischen Vereitelungsverbot und der Durchbrechungsregel zu unterwerfen. Daher könnte man in einer Anwendung auf Gesellschaften aus Drittstaaten, insbes. USA, eine Diskriminierung dieser Gesellschaften sehen, die etwa gegen das GATS (General Agreement on Trade and Services) verstoßen könnte. Erwägungsgrund 21 der ÜRL deutet dies etwas kryptisch an („Unbeschadet internationaler Übereinkünfte, bei denen die Europäische Gemeinschaft Vertragspartei ist") und bezieht sich bei der Gegenseitigkeitsregel ausdrücklich nur auf „Gesellschaften, die ihrerseits die gleichen Bestimmungen als Folge des Einsatzes dieser freiwilligen Regelungen nicht anwenden".

Würde man dieser Auslegung folgen, bliebe es bei dem vielfach kritisierten Wettbewerbsnachteil der europäischen Gesellschaften insbesondere gegenüber US-Unternehmen. Da für die Regelung von Abwehrmaßnahmen gegen Bieter aus Drittstaaten kein Angleichungs- oder sonstiges eigenes Regelungsinteresse der EU erkennbar ist, sollte diese Frage im Ergebnis der Entscheidung der Mitgliedstaaten überlassen bleiben.[68] Der Wortlaut des Art. 12 Abs. 3 ÜRL lässt – wie schon gesagt – diese Interpretation zu und verweist im

66 Der RefE (Fn. 1) sieht in § 33c Abs. 1 und Abs. 2 WpÜG-E jeweils einen eigenständigen Gegenseitigkeitsvorbehalt für das „Europäische Verhinderungsverbot" (§ 33a WpÜG-E) und die „Europäische Durchgriffsregel" (§ 33b WpÜG-E) vor. Die Gültigkeitsdauer des Hauptversammlungsbeschlusses wird in Abs. 3 für beide Fälle auf höchstens 18 Monate begrenzt.

67 Dafür *Seibt/Heister* ZGR 2005, 200, 234f.

68 Dieser Sicht folgt auch der RefE (Fn. 1), der in § 33c Abs. 1 und Abs. 2 WpÜG-E allein auf die inhaltliche Gleichwertigkeit der auf andere Gesellschaften anwendbaren Regeln mit dem Verhinderungsverbot bzw. der Durchgriffsregel abstellt, so dass auch Unternehmen aus Drittstaaten erfasst sind, so ausdrücklich RefE (Fn. 1), Begründung, S. 21.

übrigen auch ausdrücklich auf die „nach nationalem Recht festgelegten Bedingungen“.

V. Die Durchbrechungsregel: Inhalt und Anwendungsbereich

Die in Art. 11 ÜRL enthaltene Durchbrechungs- oder Durchgriffsregelung besagt, dass bestimmte Beschränkungen der Übertragbarkeit von Aktien der Zielgesellschaft und der Ausübung von Stimmrechten, die den Bieter an der Kontrollerlangung hindern können, für gewisse Zeiträume *dem Bieter gegenüber nicht gelten* und somit in ihrer Wirksamkeit (partiell) durchbrochen werden. Dazu gehören zum einen dingliche (in der Satzung enthaltene) sowie schuldrechtliche (auf Vereinbarungen mit der Gesellschaft oder zwischen Aktionären beruhende) *Übertragungsbeschränkungen*; diese gelten dem Bieter gegenüber während der Annahmefrist nicht. Zum anderen entfalten dingliche oder vertragliche *Beschränkungen des Stimmrechts* während der Laufzeit des Übernahmeangebots keine Wirkung in Hauptversammlungen der Zielgesellschaft, die über Abwehrmaßnahmen beschließen. Für deutsche Aktiengesellschaften hat diese Regelung allerdings keine praktische Bedeutung, da Mehrstimmrechte mit Wirkung zum 1. 6. 2003 ohnehin zwingend abgeschafft sind (Art. 5 Abs. 1 EGAktG) und Höchststimmrechte bei börsennotierten Gesellschaften unzulässig sind (§ 134 Abs. 1 Satz 2 AktG). Direkt auf gesetzlicher Regelung beruhende Höchststimmrechte wie bei VW sowie generelle Sonderrechte auf gesetzlicher Basis (sog. *„golden shares“*) werden von Art. 11 ÜRL nicht erfasst.

Die Durchgriffsregel gilt dagegen auch für Übertragungs- und Stimmrechtsbeschränkungen sowie etwaige außerordentliche *Aktionärsrechte auf Ernennung oder Abberufung von Mitgliedern des Leitungs- bzw. Verwaltungsorgans* (z.B. Entsendungsrechte in den Aufsichtsrat, § 101 Abs. 2 AktG).[69] Diese werden für die erste Hauptversammlung nach Angebotsschluss außer Kraft gesetzt, sofern der Bieter infolge des Angebots über mindestens 75% des stimmberechtigten Kapitals verfügt. Schafft der Bieter derartige Sonderrechte oder Beschränkungen nicht ab, gelten sie fort.

69 Kein Umkehrschluss aus Art. 9 Abs. 6 ÜRL, insoweit Redaktionsversehen, vgl. *Seibt/Heiser* ZGR 2005, 200, 225.

Für die Einführung der Durchbruchsregel gem. Art. 11 ÜRL wird die Schaffung einer neuen Vorschrift im 4. Abschnitt des WpÜG vorgeschlagen.[70] Der Bestandsschutz für Altverträge (schuldrechtliche Vereinbarungen, die vor der Verabschiedung der Richtlinie am 30. 3. 2004 geschlossen worden sind, Art. 11 Abs. 2 UAbs. 2, Abs. 3 UAbs. 2 ÜRL) soll in einer Übergangsvorschrift sichergestellt werden.[71]

Weitergehende Vorschläge in der Literatur richten sich z. B. auf die Erweiterung des zeitlichen Anwendungsbereichs des Art. 11 Abs. 2 ÜRL auf die Übertragung der Wertpapiere nach Angebotsschluss,[72] die Erweiterung des sachlichen Anwendungsbereichs des Art. 11 Abs. 2 ÜRL auf die aufschiebend bedingte Übertragung der Wertpapiere auf die Zielgesellschaft für den Fall eines Übernahmeangebots[73] (Umgehungsschutz) und die Sicherung der Verbindlichkeit von vereinbarten Haltefristen („*lock-ups*") auch für den Erwerber.[74] Ob es dazu kommt, erscheint jedoch fraglich, jedenfalls wenn sich der Gesetzgeber zu einer Umsetzung der Richtlinie nur in dem unbedingt notwendigen Umfang entschließt.

Zwingend ist die Einfügung einer Entschädigungsregel für den erlittenen Rechtsverlust bei der Durchbrechungsregel (Art. 11 Abs. 5). Aus deutscher Perspektive dürfte dies aber allenfalls bei Entsendungsrechten nach § 101 Abs. 2 AktG relevant werden. Mangels Existenz eines „Marktes für Entsendungsrechte" wirft die Bemessung einer Entschädigungssumme größte Schwierigkeiten auf.[75] Bei der Durchbrechung einer Anteilsvinkulierung

70 *Glade/Haak/Hellich* Der Konzern 2004, 515, 524; *Hopt/Mülbert/Kumpan* AG 2005, 109, 113; *Krause*, BB 2004, 113, 115 f.; *Seibt/Heiser* ZGR 2005, 200, 233. Dem folgt der RefE (Fn. 1) mit § 33 b WpÜG-E („Europäische Durchgriffsregel").

71 *Hopt/Mülbert/Kumpan* AG 2005, 109, 113. Vgl. jetzt § 33 b Abs. 1 Satz 2 WpÜG-E (keine Geltung für stimmrechtslose Vorzugsaktien sowie für vor dem 22. 4. 2004 zwischen der Zielgesellschaft und Aktionären oder zwischen Aktionären vereinbarte Übertragungsbeschränkungen und Stimmbindungen).

72 *Glade/Haak/Hellich* Der Konzern 2004, 515, 522; *Hopt/Mülbert/Kumpan* AG 2005, 109, 113; *Krause* BB 2004, 113, 115.

73 *Glade/Haak/Hellich*, Der Konzern 2004 515, 523; *Hopt/Mülbert/Kumpan* AG 2005, 109, 113; *Seibt/Heiser* ZIP 2002, 2193, 2200.

74 *Glade/Haak/Hellich* Der Konzern 2004, 515, 522; *Hopt/Mülbert/Kumpan* AG 2005, 109, 113.

75 *Seibt/Heiser* ZGR 2005, 200, 230. Der RefE (Fn. 1) begnügt sich in § 33 b Abs. 4 WpÜG-E mit der lapidaren Feststellung, dass der Bieter zur Entschädigung in Geld verpflichtet sei, sofern Rechte auf der Grundlage der Durchgriffsregel entzogen werden. Dem Bieter wird durch § 2 Nr. 3 a der WpÜG-AV-E auferlegt, in der Angebotsunterlage die zur Berechnung der Entschädigung angewandten Methoden sowie die Gründe, warum deren Anwendung angemessen ist, anzugeben.

kommt mangels unmittelbaren Rechtsentzugs keine Entschädigungspflicht in Betracht.[76]

Entscheidet sich der Gesetzgeber für die in Art. 12 Abs. 3 ÜRL niedergelegte „Gegenseitigkeitsklausel", ist insoweit ebenfalls die Schaffung eines gesonderten, durch Satzungsbestimmung auszuübenden Vorbehalts erforderlich.[77]

VI. Reformbedarf beim Pflichtangebot

1. Allgemeines

§ 35 Abs. 2 WpÜG steht im Einklang mit Art. 5 Abs. 1 ÜRL, insbesondere soll der Anwendungsbereich nicht auf Erwerbsvorgänge beschränkt bleiben.[78] Zu beachten ist jedoch, dass Einschränkungen bzgl. der Angebotspflicht nicht mehr mittels restriktiver Auslegung gewonnen werden können, sondern eine gesetzliche Regelung erforderlich ist (vgl. Art. 4 Abs. 5 UAbs. 2 i.V.m. Abs. 2 lit. e) ÜRL).[79] Die Ausnahmeregelung des § 35 Abs. 3 steht im Einklang mit Art. 5 Abs. 2 ÜRL und kann daher beibehalten werden.[80]

2. Bestimmung der Gegenleistung

Gem. Art. 5 Abs. 4 ÜRL soll der Vorerwerbszeitraum mindestens 6 und höchstens 12 Monate betragen. Der in § 4 WpÜG-Angebotsverordnung (im folgenden WpÜG-AV) genannte 3-monatige Zeitraum ist daher auf wenigstens 6 Monate zu verlängern.[81] Um Umgehungsgestaltungen zu verhindern, sollte an der strengeren deutschen Regelung, die nicht an die „Zahlung" (Art. 5

76 So *Seibt/Heiser* ZGR 2005, 200, 228 f.

77 *Seibt/Heiser* ZGR 2005, 200, 235 f. Dieser findet sich jetzt in § 33 b Abs. 2 WpÜG-E.

78 *Seibt/Heiser* ZGR 2005, 200, 214 f.

79 *Mülbert* NZG 2004, 633, 641.

80 *Maul/Muffat-Jeandet* AG 2004, 221, 230.

81 *Krause* BB 2004, 113, 116; *Glade/Haak/Hellich* Der Konzern 2004, 455, 457 f.; *Maul/Muffat-Jeandet* AG 2004, 221, 230 f.; *Seibt/Heiser* ZGR 2005, 200, 218; *Wiesner* ZIP 2004, 343, 349.

Abs. 4 ÜRL), sondern an die „Vereinbarung" der Gegenleistung (§ 4 WpÜG-AV) anknüpft, festgehalten werden.[82]

§ 5 WpÜG-AV knüpft außerdem an den durchschnittlichen Börsenkurs an. Dies stellt eine strengere Regelung dar, die aufgrund Art. 3 Abs. 2 ÜRL – auch im Hinblick auf den dreimonatigen Berechnungszeitraum – bestehen bleiben kann.[83]

Demgegenüber fällt die Berücksichtigung ausländischer Börsenkurse (§ 6 WpÜG-AV) nun nicht mehr in die Aufsichts-, und damit auch nicht in die Regelungskompetenz Deutschlands (Art. 4 Abs. 2 lit. b und e ÜRL) und ist daher zu streichen.[84]

Für die *Form* der Gegenleistung enthält § 31 WpÜG eine zwar restriktivere, aber im Einklang mit Art. 5 Abs. 5 ÜRL stehende Regelung,[85] die daher für das Pflichtangebot übernommen werden sollte.[86]

Überlegenswert erscheint es, den Aktionären eine gerichtliche Kontrollmöglichkeit zu eröffnen (etwa im Rahmen des KapMuG), in der die Anforderungen insbesondere an die Gegenleistung überprüft werden können.[87]

3. Befugnisse der BAFin

Gem. Art. 5 Abs. 4 UAbs. 2 ÜRL kann die BaFin ermächtigt werden, den Preis der Gegenleistung anzupassen. Hierfür müsste eine neue Regelung unter Beachtung des Bestimmtheitsgebotes in Art. 5 Abs. 4 UAbs. 2 S. 1 ÜRL und unter Berücksichtigung der Rechtsprechungsgrundsätze des BVerfG zu Art. 14 GG[88] geschaffen werden, die ggf. die in Art. 5 Abs. 4 UAbs. 2 ÜRL genannten Beispiele aufnimmt. Dabei wird insbesondere die Ermächtigung zur Herabsetzung der Gegenleistung im Sanierungsfall für sinnvoll erachtet.[89] Verein-

82 So *Glade/Haak/Hellich* Der Konzern 2004, 455, 458. Der RefE (Fn. 1) beschränkt sich insoweit in der Tat auf die Änderung des Dreimonatszeitraums auf sechs Monate, vgl. Art. 6 Nr. 3.

83 *Glade/Haak/Hellich* Der Konzern 2004, 455, 458.

84 *Glade/Haak/Hellich* Der Konzern 2004, 455, 458.

85 *Glade/Haak/Hellich* Der Konzern 2004, 455, 459; *Seibt/Heiser* ZGR 2005, 200, 218.

86 *Hopt/Mülbert/Kumpan* AG 2005, 109, 113f.

87 *Hopt/Mülbert/Kumpan* AG 2005, 109, 115; *Seibt/Heiser* ZGR 2005, 200, 219f.

88 Vgl. BVerfGE 100, 289 = ZIP 1999, 1436 – „DAT/Altana", wonach der Börsenkurs als Untergrenze für eine Abfindung angesehen werden muss (1441 f.).

89 *Glade/Haak/Hellich* Der Konzern 2004, 455, 459; *Hopt/Mülbert/Kumpan* AG 2005, 109, 114f.; *Mülbert* NZG 2004, 633, 642; *Seibt/Heiser* ZGR 2005, 200, 219.

zelt wird zusätzlich eine neue Vorschrift vorgeschlagen, mit der die BaFin ermächtigt wird, ein Pflichtangebot auch bei Übernahmeangeboten zu erzwingen.[90]

Die Befreiungsmöglichkeit gem. § 37 WpÜG i.V.m. §§ 8ff. WpÜG-AV erfüllt nicht die Mindestanforderungen des Art. 3 Abs. 2 lit. a) und ist daher zu streichen.[91]

VII. „Squeeze-out" und „Sell-out"

1. Grundlagen

In der Literatur besteht weitgehend Einigkeit darüber, dass neben dem bereits existierenden aktienrechtlichen *„squeeze-out"* in §§ 327a ff. AktG die Schaffung eines besonderen übernahmerechtlichen Ausschlusses von Minderheitsaktionären nach den Vorgaben von Art. 15 ÜRL erforderlich ist. Dieses Recht, das der Bieter innerhalb von drei Monaten nach Ablauf der Annahmefrist für das Übernahmeangebot ausüben muss (Art. 15 Abs. 4 ÜRL), soll ihm nach einer erfolgreichen Übernahme ermöglichen, die verbliebene Minderheit aus einer börsennotierten AG auszuschließen. Gewissermaßen die Kehrseite dazu stellt die Einführung eines bislang im deutschen Recht unbekannten Andienungsrechts für Minderheitsaktionäre („sell-out", Art. 16 ÜRL) im Anschluss an ein Angebot an alle Wertpapierinhaber der Zielgesellschaft (Art. 15 Abs. 1, 16 Abs. 1 ÜRL) dar. Die inhaltliche Ausgestaltung folgt weitgehend den Regeln des *squeeze-outs*, auf die in Art. 16 Abs. 2 und 3 ÜRL verwiesen wird. Beide Regelungskomplexe sollten, so wird vorgeschlagen, in einen neuen Abschnitt des WpÜG nach Abschnitt 5 eingefügt werden.[92]

90 *Hopt/Mülbert/Kumpan* AG 2005, 109, 113; *Habersack* ZHR 166, 2002, 619, 621f.

91 *Glade/Haak/Hellich* Der Konzern 2004, 455, 459; *Hopt/Mülbert/Kumpan* AG 2005, 109, 113; *Mülbert* NZG 2004, 633, 641f.

92 Vgl. *Austmann/Mennicke* NZG 2004, 846, 847, 855; *Hopt/Mülbert/Kumpan* AG 2005, 109, 115, 118; *Kindler/Horstmann* DStR 2004, 866, 873; *Krause* BB 2004, 113, 117f.; *Maul/Muffat-Jeandet* AG 2004, 306, 317; *Seibt/Heiser* ZGR 2005, 200, 240; *Wiesner* ZIP 2004, 343, 349. Nach dem RefE (Fn. 1) soll ein neuer „Abschnitt 5a Ausschluss, Andienungsrecht" mit den §§ 39a–39c in das WpÜG eingefügt werden.

2. Einzelfragen zum übernahmerechtlichen Ausschluss von Minderheitsaktionären

a) Tatbestandliche Anknüpfung

Voraussetzung für die Ausübung des *squeeze-out*-Rechts ist, dass der Bieter im Anschluss an eine Übernahmeangebot mindestens 90% des *stimmberechtigten* Kapitals hält oder durch die Annahme des Angebots erworben hat (bzw. sich vertraglich fest zum Erwerb verpflichtet hat). Da sich bei der zweiten Alternative Anwendungsschwierigkeiten beim stufenweisen Erwerb ergeben, empfiehlt sich eine Umsetzung nur des Tatbestands nach Art. 15 Abs. 2 lit. a) ÜRL (Bieter hält nach dem Übernahmeangebot mindestens 90% des stimmberechtigten Kapitals).[93] Um einen Gleichlauf mit § 327a AktG herzustellen, sollte zugleich die *Schwelle auf 95% erhöht werden.*[94] Nicht erforderlich erscheint dagegen die vereinzelt befürwortete Schaffung der Möglichkeit zu einer ausnahmsweisen Absenkung der Schwelle (sogar unter den 90%-Wert des Art. 15 Abs. 2 ÜRL) durch gerichtliche Entscheidung für den Fall, dass die normale Schwelle nicht erreicht werden kann, weil Aktien (etwa durch Vererbung) verschollen sind.[95]

Problematisch ist, dass die Richtlinie den zu erreichenden Schwellenwert von 90%–95% allein auf das *stimmberechtigte* Kapital bezieht. Das führt dazu, dass bei Unternehmen mit einem erheblichen Anteil an stimmrechtslosen Vorzugsaktien im Extremfall nicht einmal das Halten einer Mehrheit des Gesamtkapitals erforderlich ist, um die übrigen Aktionäre aus der Gesellschaft ausschließen zu können: So würden bei einem Anteil von 50% stimmrechtsloser Vorzugsaktien bereits 45% des Grundkapitals der AG genügen, um den Schwellenwert von 90% des stimmberechtigten Kapitals zu erreichen (bzw. 47,5% bei einem Schwellenwert von 95%). Das erscheint verfassungsrechtlich bedenklich.[96] Der Gesetzgeber sollte daher von der Möglichkeit der Schaffung

93 *Hopt/Mülbert/Kumpan* AG 2005, 109, 115; vgl. auch *Maul* NZG 2005, 151, 157. Auch eine kumulative Umsetzung der lit. a) und b) wird aber als möglich erachtet, *Hopt/Mülbert/Kumpan* AG 2005, 109, 115, 117.

94 *Austmann/Mennicke* NZG 2004, 846, 847 f.; *Hopt/Mülbert/Kumpan* AG 2005, 109, 116; *Kindler/Horstmann* DStR 2004, 866, 873; *Krause* BB 2004, 113, 118; *Maul/Muffat-Jeandet* AG 2004, 306, 316; *Seibt/Heiser* ZGR 2005, 200, 241.

95 So aber der Vorschlag von *Hopt/Mülbert/Kumpan* AG 2005, 109, 116 („überlegenswert").

96 *Austmann/Mennicke* NZG 2004, 846, 848; **a. A.** *Wiesner* ZIP 2004, 343, 348; *Maul/Muffat-Jeandet* AG 2004, 306, 316; vgl. auch *Seibt/Heiser* ZGR 2005, 200, 241 (Beschränkung auf den Erwerb der verbleibenden Stimmrechtsaktien).

eines lediglich *gattungsbezogenen Ausschlussrechts* (Art. 15 Abs. 3 UAbs. 2 ÜRL) Gebrauch machen. Danach beschränkt sich die Ausübung des Ausschlussrechts auf die Gattung, in der der festgelegte Schwellenwert erreicht ist. Zu beachten ist allerdings, dass dann auch § 2 Abs. 2 WpÜG an Art. 2 Abs. 1 lit. e) ÜRL angepasst werden müsste, indem insbesondere zwischen stimmberechtigten und nicht stimmberechtigten Wertpapiergattungen unterschieden wird.[97] Zudem bliebe ein isolierter *squeeze-out* für stimmrechtslose Vorzugsaktien aufgrund des Verweises des Art. 15 Abs. 3 UAbs. 2 ÜRL auf den Schwellenwert für stimmberechtigte Wertpapiere in Art. 15 Abs. 2 ÜRL ausgeschlossen, sofern nicht zugleich die Voraussetzungen für den Ausschluss der stimmberechtigten Minderheitsaktionäre vorliegen.[98] Ist letzteres der Fall, könnte der Gesetzgeber das Recht zum Ausschluss der stimmrechtslosen Vorzugsaktionäre von dem Erreichen des gleichen (oder eines niedrigeren)[99] Schwellenwertes in dieser Gattung abhängig machen.[100]

Die Frist für die Ausübung des Ausschlussrechts durch den Bieter ist auf drei Monate nach Ablauf der Annahmefrist für das Übernahmeangebot begrenzt (Art. 15 Abs. 4). Danach bleibt ein (an keine Frist gebundener) aktienrechtlicher *squeeze-out* nach §§ 327a AktG möglich, sofern dessen Voraussetzungen vorliegen.

b) Notwendigkeit eines Hauptversammlungsbeschlusses?

Überwiegend wird ein Hauptversammlungsbeschluss für das kapitalmarktrechtliche *squeeze-out* abgelehnt und die Übertragung der Wertpapiere durch

97 *Austmann/Mennicke* NZG 2004, 846, 848f.; *Hopt/Mülbert/Kumpan* AG 2005, 109, 110, 115; *Seibt/Heiser* ZGR 2005, 200, 241. Im RefE (Fn. 1) ist eine solche Anpassung des Wertpapierbegriffs nicht vorgesehen; statt dessen wird in § 39a WpÜG-E zwischen stimmberechtigten Aktien und stimmrechtslosen Vorzugsaktien differenziert.

98 *Hopt/Mülbert/Kumpan* AG 2005, 109, 115f.

99 Für deutlich großzügigere Bedingungen beim Ausschluss nicht stimmberechtigter Wertpapiere *Hopt/Mülbert/Kumpan* AG 2005, 109, 116; für Erstreckung des Ausschlussrechts auf stimmrechtslose Vorzugsaktien nur bei Erreichung des Schwellenwertes von mindestens 95% der Aktien auch dieser Gattung dagegen *Seibt/Heiser* ZGR 2005, 200, 241.

100 Der RefE (Fn. 1) beschränkt in § 39a Abs. 1 WpÜG-E den übernahmerechtlichen Ausschluss bei Erreichen des Schwellenwertes von 95% des stimmberechtigten Kapitals bzw. der Stimmrechte zunächst auf die übrigen stimmberechtigten Aktionäre (Satz 1) und macht die auf Antrag mögliche Übertragung der übrigen stimmrechtslosen Vorzugsaktien davon abhängig, dass der Bieter zugleich die Schwelle von 95% des Gesamtkapitals der Gesellschaft erreicht (Satz 2).

Verwaltungsakt der BaFin auf Verlangen des Hauptaktionärs[101] oder durch von der BaFin zu genehmigende Erklärung des Hauptaktionärs[102] vorgeschlagen. Vorzugswürdig erscheint jedoch eine Übertragung durch Gerichtsbeschluss.[103] Dabei ist insbesondere auch zu bestimmen, auf wen die Wertpapiere im Falle gemeinsam handelnder Personen („acting in concert") übergehen sollen.[104] Des Weiteren wird eine Überprüfung des Verlangens des Mehrheitsaktionärs durch die BaFin entsprechend §§ 14, 15 WpÜG vorgeschlagen.[105] Für den Verzicht auf einen Hauptversammlungsbeschluss spricht, dass dieser angesichts der Mehrheitsverhältnisse einerseits lediglich eine Formalität wäre, andererseits ein nicht unerhebliches Anfechtungsrisiko mit sich brächte.

c) Angemessenheit der Abfindung

Für die Bestimmung der Gegenleistung sind einerseits die Vorgaben des Art. 15 Abs. 5 ÜRL, andererseits die Rechtsprechungsgrundsätze des BVerfG zu Art. 14 GG zu beachten.[106] Die Richtlinie verlangt, dass die Abfindung dieselbe Form aufweist wie die Gegenleistung des Angebots oder in Form einer Geldleistung erfolgt, wobei die Mitgliedstaaten anordnen können, dass stets zumindest wahlweise eine Geldleistung angeboten werden muss.[107] Die vom Bieter angebotene Abfindung gilt nach Art. 15 Abs. 5 ÜRL im Falle eines Pflichtangebots stets als angemessen (UAbs. 3), bei freiwilligen Übernahmeangeboten nur dann, wenn eine Annahmequote von mindestens 90% des vom Angebot betroffenen stimmberechtigten Kapitals erreicht worden ist (UAbs. 2). Letzteres unterwirft die Beurteilung der Angemessenheit der gebotenen Abfindung einem Markttest und ist jedenfalls dann unproblematisch, wenn die Regelung in die Form einer widerleglichen Vermutung gekleidet wird.[108] Die

101 *Austmann/Mennicke* NZG 2004, 846, 851 f.; 853; *Hopt/Mülbert/Kumpan* AG 2005, 109, 115.

102 *Seibt/Heiser* ZGR 2005, 200, 247 f.

103 So jetzt auch RefE (Fn. 1) in § 39 a Abs. 1 WpÜG-E.

104 In diesem Sinne ist wohl auch die Andeutung bei *Hopt/Mülbert/Kumpan* AG 2005, 109, 116 zu verstehen.

105 *Hopt/Mülbert/Kumpan* AG 2005, 109, 116, 117.

106 *Austmann/Mennicke* NZG 2004, 846, 850; *Seibt/Heiser* ZGR 2005, 200, 243 f.

107 Nach dem RefE (Fn. 1) beabsichtigt der deutsche Gesetzgeber, von diesem Wahlrecht zugunsten der verbliebenen Aktionäre Gebrauch zu machen, vgl. § 39 a Abs. 3 WpÜG-E.

108 Vgl. *Seibt/Heiser* ZGR 2005, 200, 245; *Hopt/Mülbert/Kumpan* AG 2005, 109, 117; ob Art. 15 Abs. 5 UAbs. 2 ÜRL eine Auslegung als widerlegliche Vermutung zulässt, ist allerdings ungeklärt, vgl. *Seibt/Heiser* ZIP 1002, 2193, 2201; *Mülbert* NZG 2004, 633,

in der Richtlinie vorgesehene Angemessenheitsvermutung beim Pflichtangebot, die sich aus der nur für dieses geltenden verbindlichen Preisregelung (Art. 5 Abs. 4 ÜRL) erklärt, ist für den nationalen Gesetzgeber wohl zunächst verbindlich, aber nicht abschließend.[109]

Fraglich erscheint, ob die gegenwärtig nach §§ 31, 39 WpÜG praktizierte Gleichbehandlung von Übernahme- und Pflichtangeboten bei der Preisbemessung aufrechterhalten werden kann.[110] Wird auch das Pflichtangebot dem Markttest unterworfen, ließe sich dies wohl als zulässige strengere Bestimmung i.S.d. Art. 3 Abs. 2 lit. b) ÜRL ansehen, die zugunsten der Aktionäre zusätzliche Bedingungen für Angebote festlegt. Gleiches gilt für die vorgeschlagene Einführung einer Verzinsungspflicht der Abfindung entsprechend § 327b Abs. 2 AktG.[111]

Zur gerichtlichen Kontrolle der Angemessenheit der Gegenleistung wird in der Literatur meist ein Verfahren nach dem SpruchG oder nach dem KapMuG vorgeschlagen,[112] wobei ersteres bei einem freiwilligen Angebot, letzteres bei einem Pflichtangebot Anwendung finden soll.[113] Diese Vorschläge gehen allerdings davon aus, dass die antragsgemäße Übertragung der Aktien der Minderheitsaktionäre auf den Bieter durch Verwaltungsakt der BaFin erfolgt.[114] Wird aber schon für die Ausübung des übernahmerechtlichen *squeeze-out* ein Gerichtsbeschluss verlangt, wird die Angemessenheit der angebotenen Ab-

634; für unwiderlegliche Vermutung *Austmann/Mennicke* NZG 2004, 846, 851 sowie jetzt RefE (Fn. 1), Begründung, S. 24.

109 So zutreffend *Austmann/Mennicke* NZG 2004 846, 849; **a. A.** *Hopt/Mülbert/Kumpan* AG 2005, 109, 117 („in der Richtlinie zwingend angeordnet"), die allerdings eine Überprüfung der Vereinbarkeit dieser Angemessenheitsvermutung mit der europarechtlichen Eigentumsgarantie anregen. Der RefE (Fn. 1) enthält in § 39a Abs. 3 WpÜG-E nur den Markttest (Annahmequote mindestens 90%), der in gleicher Weise für Übernahme- und Pflichtangebote gilt.

110 Wie hier für Zulässigkeit von Mindestpreisregeln bei freiwilligen Übernahmeangeboten (§ 31 WpÜG) *Kindler/Horstmann* DStR 2004, 866, 872; *Seibt/Heiser* ZIP 2002, 2193, 2195; *Wiesner* ZIP 2004, 343, 347 Fn. 32; dagegen *Mülbert* NZG 2004, 633, 640 f.; *Hopt/Mülbert/Kumpan* AG 2005, 109, 111, die hierin einen Verstoß gegen eine aus Art. 15 Abs. 5 ÜRL abgeleitete Maximalvorgabe der Richtlinie sehen.

111 Vgl. dazu *Austmann/Mennicke* NZG 2004, 846, 851; *Hopt/Mülbert/Kumpan* AG 2005, 109, 116, 117.

112 *Seibt/Heiser* ZGR 2005, 200, 246.

113 So *Hopt/Mülbert/Kumpan* AG 2005, 109, 115, 117 f.; vgl. auch *Kindler/Horstmann* DStR 2004, 866, 873; *Austmann/Mennicke* NZG 2004, 846, 853 (Zulassung eines Ausschlussverlangens des Bieters durch die BaFin).

114 Vgl. außer den in der vorherigen Fn. Genannten *Seibt/Heiser* ZGR 2005, 200, 248 (Freigabe der *squeeze-out*-Erklärung des Hauptaktionärs durch die BaFin).

findung bereits implizit im gerichtlichen Verfahren überprüft (und kann sodann mit Rechtsmitteln angegriffen werden). Ein gesondertes Spruchverfahren entfällt.

3. Das Andienungsrecht für Minderheitsaktionäre („Sell-out")

Spiegelbildlich zum Ausschlussrecht des Bieters ist nach Art. 16 ÜRL den verbliebenen Minderheitsaktionären ein Andienungsrecht zu gewähren. Diese können vom Bieter verlangen, ihre Aktien zu einem angemessenen Preis zu erwerben. Die inhaltliche Ausgestaltung erfolgt nach Art. 16 Abs. 2 ÜRL weitgehend durch die entsprechende Anwendung der Vorschriften über den übernahmerechtlichen *squeeze-out*.

Eine individuelle Ermittlung des Preises für einzelne angediente Aktien ist weder dem Bieter noch dem Aktionär zumutbar. Vielmehr ist es für ein effizientes Verfahren für eine Vielzahl von potentiellen Anspruchstellern erforderlich, einen einheitlichen Erwerbspreis für den Bieter festzulegen. Dies könnte dadurch geschehen, dass der Bieter für den Fall, dass er keinen *squeeze-out* durchführt, verpflichtet wird, selbst eine angemessene Abfindung für angediente Aktien festzulegen und bekannt zu machen.[115] Es dürfte aber auch ausreichen, insoweit auf den Preis des vorausgegangenen Pflichtangebots abzustellen; für freiwillige Übernahmeangebote kann das allerdings nur gelten, wenn auch deren Preis einer Kontrolle unterliegt, wie dies im deutschen Recht nach § 31 WpÜG gewährleistet ist.[116]

Folgt man dem und stellt auf den Preis des vorangegangenen Übernahme- oder Pflichtangebots ab, wirkt das Andienungsrecht letztlich nicht anders als eine Verlängerung der Annahmefrist um drei Monate. Damit stellt sich die Frage nach dem Verhältnis zur „Zaunkönig"-Regel des § 16 Abs. 2 WpÜG. Eine bloße Ausdehnung dieser weiteren Annahmefrist von zwei Wochen auf drei Monate wäre nicht sachgerecht,[117] da sie die Ungewissheit über den Ausgang des Übernahmeverfahrens (bei Fehlen einer vom Bieter festgelegten Mindesterwerbsschwelle) erheblich verlängern und damit gegen das Be-

115 So der Vorschlag von *Seibt/Heiser* ZGR 2005, 200, 249 (mit zusätzlicher Überprüfung des angebotenen Erwerbspreises durch die BaFin).

116 Ohne diese Einschränkung generell für Abstellen auf den Preis des vorangegangenen öffentlichen Angebots *Austmann/Mennicke* NZG 2004, 846, 855; ähnlich *Hopt/Mülbert/Kumpan* AG 2005, 109, 118 („gilt als angemessen").

117 Ebenso *Austmann/Mennicke* NZG 2004, 846, 855.

schleunigungsgebot verstoßen würde. Aber auch ein Verzicht auf die „Zaunkönig"-Regel wegen der Einführung des Andienungsrechts kommt nicht in Betracht, da die beiden Möglichkeiten zur Veräußerung der Aktien nach Ablauf der ursprünglichen Annahmefrist bei ganz unterschiedlichen Schwellenwerten und sonstigen Voraussetzungen eingreifen. Das Andienungsrecht ist deshalb neben der fortbestehenden „Zaunkönig"-Regel einzuführen.

Die spiegelbildliche Schaffung eines Andienungsrechts für Minderheitsaktionäre gewissermaßen als Ausgleich dafür, dass der Bieter ein befristetes übernahmerechtliches Ausschlussrecht erhält, wirft die Frage auf, ob nicht auch dem allgemeinen aktienrechtlichen *squeeze-out*-Recht nach §§ 327a ff. AktG ein entsprechendes Andienungsrecht des Minderheitsaktionärs entgegengesetzt werden sollte. Denn dieser befindet sich insoweit in einer misslichen Lage, als er unter dem Damoklesschwert eines vom Hauptaktionär zu einem frei gewählten Zeitpunkt durchführbaren Ausschluss leben muss. Mit einem Andienungsrecht, das ggf. auf einen bestimmten Zeitkorridor nach Erlangung einer „*squeeze-out*-fähigen" Mehrheitsposition durch den Hauptaktionär zu beschränken ist, könnte dem Minderheitsaktionär ein Initiativrecht zum Ausscheiden aus der Gesellschaft gewährt werden, das den Gefahren einer strategischen Ausnutzung „günstiger" Kapitalmarktsituationen durch den Hauptaktionär für ein Herausdrängen der Minderheit aus der Gesellschaft „unter Wert" entgegenwirken und damit das Anlegervertrauen stärken könnte. Die Einführung eines solchen zusätzlichen Schutzinstruments für die Minderheitsaktionäre steht zwar in keinem direkten Zusammenhang zur Umsetzung der ÜRL, könnte aber aus diesem Anlass oder im Zuge einer späteren Aktiengesetznovelle (ggf. zusammen mit einer Reform der §§ 327a ff. AktG) erfolgen.

VIII. Fazit und Ausblick

Der reduzierte Regulierungsansatz der ÜRL mit ihrem zweistufigen Optionsmodell war für viele insofern eine Enttäuschung, als er nicht das erhoffte *level playing field* für Übernahmen in Europa gebracht hat. Auf der anderen Seite werden wichtige Bereiche des Übernahmerechts durchaus harmonisiert. Das gilt insbesondere für das Verfahren, die Grundprinzipien, das Pflichtangebot, die Gegenleistung sowie die umfangreichen Transparenzgebote. Zudem wird ein europaweiter Mechanismus für die Kooperation der nationalen Aufsichtsbehörden geschaffen und durch die Vereinheitlichung des Kollisionsrechts verhindert, dass Doppelzuständigkeiten oder Anwendungslücken entstehen. Schließlich wohnt dem gefundenen Modell ein *dynamischer Aspekt* inne, der durchaus Anlass zur Hoffnung für die Zukunft gibt: Sofern die Märkte den Weg in die kapitalmarktoffene Klasse durch entsprechende Kurszuschläge für die betreffenden Unternehmen belohnen, dürfte es Nachahmer geben. Dies könnte zumindest *de facto*, später vielleicht auch *de iure* zu einer Vereinheitlichung und marktorientierten Weiterentwicklung der Rahmenbedingungen für öffentliche Übernahmeangebote in Europa führen.

Auch wenn die Richtlinie also weniger an Vereinheitlichung bringt als erhofft, legt sie dennoch zumindest die *Basis für einen Prozess*, der auf einen Abbau von Übernahmehindernissen und auf eine Harmonisierung der Regulierung von Übernahmen in Europa hinführen kann.[118] Das zweistufige Optionsmodell in den Artikeln 9, 11 und 12 ÜRL mit dem Ineinandergreifen von Wahlrechten der Mitgliedstaaten einerseits und der einzelnen Unternehmen in ihnen andererseits hinsichtlich der Zulassung von Verteidigungsmaßnahmen gegen Übernahmen und der Durchbrechung von Übernahmehindernissen könnte – im Zusammenwirken mit den verstärkten Transparenzanforderungen bezüglich Übernahmebeschränkungen – auf längere Sicht eine *kapitalmarktinduzierte Harmonisierung* der in der Praxis tatsächlich angewandten Regeln für Übernahmeangebote bewirken.

118 Vgl. auch Erwägungsgrund 29 („Prozess hin zu einer fairen und ausgewogenen Harmonisierung der Bestimmungen für Übernahmeangebote in der Europäischen Union“).

II. Praxis

Erwartungen der Praxis an die Überarbeitung des Übernahmerechts

Christian Zschocke

Gliederung

1. Der Drittschutz ist zu verbessern
2. Die Voraussetzungen für das *acting in concert* sollten präzisiert werden
3. Die Praxis der BaFin bei Sanierungsübernahmen sollte beibehalten werden
4. Die Regeln zum Mindestpreis haben sich bewährt
5. Kaufangebot und gesellschaftsrechtliche Abfindung: ein unabgestimmtes Verhältnis
6. Der übernahmerechtliche Squeeze out und das neue Andienungsrecht
7. Zusammenfassung

Die Richtlinie 2004/25/EG des Europäischen Parlaments und des Rates vom 21. April 2004 betreffend Übernahmeangebote (Übernahmerichtlinie) bestimmt in Art. 21, dass die Mitgliedsstaaten ihr nationales Recht bis 20. Mai 2006 an die Übernahmerichtlinie anzupassen haben.[1] Dies bietet eine erste Gelegenheit, das deutsche Wertpapiererwerbs- und Übernahmegesetz („WpÜG") sowie die zu dessen Durchführung erlassenen Verordnungen im Hinblick auf die bislang gemachten praktischen Erfahrungen zu überprüfen.

In der Literatur hat diesbezüglich eine Diskussion über die Vorgaben der Übernahmerichtlinie und den anstehenden Reformbedarf eingesetzt.[2] Die Vorlage eines Referentenentwurfes wird für Ende 2005 erwartet.

Große Änderungen des WpÜG sind indessen nicht zu erwarten. Dies liegt zum einen daran, dass der deutsche Gesetzgeber das WpÜG bereits im Hinblick auf die zu erwartende Übernahmerichtlinie ausgerichtet hat und bestimmte Kernelemente (z. B. die Gleichbehandlungs- und Informationsregeln

1 Die nationalen Umsetzungsverfahren sind auch außerhalb Deutschlands weit überwiegend bislang noch nicht abgeschlossen.

2 *Hopt/Mülbert/Kumpan* Reformbedarf im Übernahmerecht, AG 2005, S. 109 ff. (111); vgl. auch *Maul/Muffat-Jeandet* Die EU-Übernahmerichtlinie – Inhalt und Umsetzung in nationales Recht, AG 2004, S. 221 ff., S. 306 ff.

sowie das Pflichtangebot) bereits ins deutsche Recht eingeführt hat. Darüber hinaus hat sich das WpÜG grundsätzlich bewährt. Seit seinem Inkrafttreten am 1. Januar 2002 sind bis zum 31. Oktober 2005 immerhin 52 Pflichtangebote, 50 Übernahmeangebote und 31 sonstige Erwerbsangebote nach dem WpÜG abgewickelt worden.[3] Es ist daher zu erwarten, dass der Referentenentwurf sich im wesentlichen darauf beschränken wird, die noch fehlenden, durch die Übernahmerichtlinie vorgegebenen Änderungen umzusetzen[4] und die Regelungen des WpÜG im übrigen unverändert zu belassen, wo auch immer dies aus Sicht des Gesetzgebers möglich ist.

Diese Umstände führen zu insgesamt begrenzten Erwartungen der Praxis an die Überarbeitung des Übernahmerechtes, auch in kontroversen Bereichen wie etwa im Bereich des Drittschutzes (s.u. 1) oder beim *acting in concert* (s.u. 2).

Andererseits ist es auch von Vorteil, wenn bewährte Regeln beibehalten werden, selbst wenn diese so nicht von der Übernahmerichtlinie vorgesehen sind oder sogar über diese hinausgehen. So ist zu hoffen, dass die Möglichkeit zur Befreiung vom Pflichtangebot bei Sanierungsübernahmen (s.u. 3) ebenso beibehalten werden kann wie die Berücksichtigung des Börsenkurses beim Mindestpreis (s.u. 4). Der deutsche Gesetzgeber würde hier über die direkten Vorgaben der Übernahmerichtlinie hinausgehen, was jedoch europarechtlich zulässig ist.

Die bei dem Erlass des WpÜG und der Übernahmerichtlinie so strittige Frage der Abwehrmaßnahmen für die Verwaltungsorgane der Zielgesellschaft bei unwillkommenen Angeboten („feindliche Angebote") hat in der übernahmerechtlichen Praxis bislang wenig Bedeutung gefunden. Nur wenige Angebote haben bislang in Deutschland „feindlich" begonnen (z.B. *Barilla/Kamps*) und keines hat als solches geendet. Hier sind nur begrenzte gesetzgeberische Aktivitäten zu erwarten, zumal der deutsche Gesetzgeber seine bisherige Position nicht aufgeben dürfte, den deutschen Zielgesellschaften mangels eines europäischen *level playing field* in § 33 WpÜG bewusst bestimmte Verteidigungsmaßnahmen zuzugestehen. Der deutsche Gesetzgeber dürfte daher von den in Art. 12 Abs. 1 der Übernahmerichtlinie vorgesehenen Möglichkeiten Ge-

3 Hinzu kommen einige Angebote, die nicht durchgeführt wurden (3 in 2003, 1 in 2004 und bisher 3 in 2005), zumeist infolge des Verfehlens vom Bieter aufgestellter Mindestannahmeschwellen. In fünf Fällen (2 im Jahr 2002 und 3 im Jahr 2003) wurden Angebote untersagt.

4 Wie etwa bei dem Anwendungsbereich des WpÜG (vgl. Art. 4 der Übernahmerichtlinie).

brauch machen und von der Umsetzung der Neutralitätsregeln der Übernahmerichtlinie absehen (sog. *Opt out*). Deutsche Zielgesellschaften können sich dann freiwillig den strengeren Regeln der Übernahmerichtlinie unterwerfen (sog. *Opt in*). Auch der nach Art. 12 Abs. 3 der Übernahmerichtlinie zulässige Gegenseitigkeitsvorbehalt dürfte auf diese Weise in das deutsche Recht einfließen.

Die übernahmerechtliche Praxis wird hiermit leben können. Eine starke Marktposition bietet langfristig den besten Übernahmeschutz. Eine Gesellschaft, die zu einer Übernahmekandidatin geworden ist, wird auf Dauer kaum eigenständig bleiben, und zwar unabhängig von den einschlägigen Übernahmeregeln.

1. Der Drittschutz ist zu verbessern

Die Frage der drittschützenden Wirkung des WpÜG ist zu einem der kontroversen Themen des deutschen Übernahmerechts geworden. Auslöser für diese Diskussion waren die Frage nach der drittschützenden Wirkung von Befreiungsentscheidungen (wie z.B. bei der Übernahme der ProSiebenSat.1 Media AG durch die Saban Gruppe im Jahr 2003) und nach dem Drittschutz bei der Gestattung der Angebotsunterlage, einschließlich der Bestimmung des Angebotspreises. Im Fall der Übernahme der Wella AG durch die Procter & Gamble stand die Frage der Gleichbehandlung von Vorzugs- und Stammaktien im Mittelpunkt.

Im Fall Saban Gruppe/ProSieben Sat.1 Media AG („ProSieben") hatte die Saban Gruppe bei der zuständigen Bundesanstalt für Finanzdienstleistungsaufsicht („BaFin") einen Antrag auf Befreiung von der Abgabe eines Pflichtangebots gestellt, nachdem sie einen Kaufvertrag zum Erwerb einer Mehrheitsbeteiligung an der ProSieben mit der Kirch Media abgeschlossen hatte. Ein Aktionär der ProSieben begehrte die Hinzuziehung zum Befreiungsverfahren. Das OLG Frankfurt am Main entschied, dass das Befreiungsverfahren subjektive Rechte der ProSieben-Aktionäre nicht betrifft, da den §§ 37 Abs. 1 i.V.m. 35 Abs. 1 und 2 WpÜG – entgegen einigen Literaturmeinungen[5] – keine drittschützende Wirkung zukommt.[6] Das OLG stützte seine Entscheidung

[5] Vgl. u.a. *Cahn* ZHR 167 (2003) 262 (293 f.); *Ihrig* ZHR 167 (2003) 315 (342 ff.); *Seibt* ZIP 2003, 1865 ff.

[6] Beschluss vom 27. 5. 2003 – WpÜG 1/03, DB 2003, 1371 ff.; Anmerkung *Zschocke/Rahlf* aaO, S. 1375 f.

vorrangig auf die Intention des Gesetzgebers, der den Aktionären der Zielgesellschaft keinen Drittschutz einräumen wolle. Dies zeige sich an § 4 Abs. 2 WpÜG, wonach die BaFin nur im öffentlichen Interesse tätig werde.

Diese Ansicht des OLG Frankfurt am Main ist abzulehnen. Der Wortlaut des § 37 Abs. 1 WpÜG (wonach das Ermessen der BaFin *„unter Berücksichtigung ... der Interessen der Inhaber der Aktien der Zielgesellschaft"* ausgeübt werden muss) meint, dass die Befreiungsentscheidung der BaFin im Einklang mit den individualisierten Interessen der außenstehenden Aktionäre zu stehen hat. Die Betrachtung der betroffenen Rechtspositionen spricht für einen Drittschutz. In der übernahmerechtlichen Literatur ist anerkannt, dass § 35 Abs. 1 und 2 WpÜG, die einem Bieter bei Überschreiten der Kontrollschwelle nach § 29 Abs. 2 WpÜG die Abgabe eines Pflichtangebots auferlegen, individualschützenden Charakter haben. Für den Fall, dass der Bieter seine gesetzlichen Angebotspflichten verletzt, stehen den Aktionären der Zielgesellschaft zivilgerichtlich durchsetzbare Ansprüche, wie z.B. Schadensersatzansprüche aus § 823 Abs. 2 BGB i.V.m. § 35 Abs. 1 und 2 WpÜG, zu. Eine Befreiungsentscheidung der BaFin entzieht den Aktionären diese Rechtspositionen konstitutiv und unmittelbar. Entgegen der Auffassung des OLG Frankfurt am Main spricht auch das systematische Verhältnis von § 4 Abs. 2 WpÜG zu § 37 Abs. 1 WpÜG nicht gegen den Drittschutz der Vorschrift, da § 4 Abs. 2 WpÜG vor dem Hintergrund einer befürchteten Amtshaftung der BaFin-Mitarbeiter in das WpÜG aufgenommen wurde.

Das OLG Frankfurt hat all diese Argumente abgelehnt. Die Praxis hat daher derzeit davon auszugehen, daß ein Rechtsschutz Dritter gegen Befreiungsentscheidungen der BaFin nicht gegeben ist, trotz der unmittelbaren rechtlichen und wirtschaftliches Auswirkungen auf die Kleinaktionäre der Zielgesellschaft. Dieser Zustand wird in der Literatur zu Recht kritisiert[7] und es wäre zu begrüßen, wenn der Gesetzgeber dieser Kritik durch eine Klarstellung im WpÜG entsprechen würde.

Bei dem Übernahmeangebot von Procter & Gamble an die Aktionäre der Wella AG verlangten Minderheitsaktionäre von der BaFin eine Nachbesserung des von Procter & Gamble angebotenen niedrigeren Preises für die Vorzugsaktien im Verhältnis zu Stammaktien, hilfsweise begehrten sie die Untersagung der von der BaFin gestatteten Angebotsunterlage. Das OLG Frankfurt am Main lehnte eine Antragsbefugnis der Aktionäre ab, da weder

7 OLG Frankfurt am Main, Beschluss vom 9. 10. 2003 – WpÜG 3/03; DB 2003, 2537 ff., mit Anmerkung *Zschocke/Rahlf* S. 2540 f.; Übersicht bei *Spindler/Christoph*, BB 2004, 2197 ff. (2203).

§ 31 WpÜG noch sonstige Vorschriften des WpÜG oder der WpÜG-Angebotsverordnung ein Verfahren zur Überprüfung der Angemessenheit der angebotenen Gegenleistung vorsehen.[8] Diese Entscheidung stimmt mit der herrschenden Ansicht in der Literatur überein. Ihr ist im Hinblick auf die Struktur des Prüfungsverfahrens der BaFin zuzustimmen, welches dem Verfahren zur Prüfung von Wertpapierverkaufsprospekten ähnelt. Die BaFin prüft innerhalb kurzer Fristen, ob die Angebotsunterlage vollständig ist und ob offensichtliche Verstöße gegen das WpÜG vorliegen. Ein unmittelbarer Eingriff in eine bestehende Rechtsposition der Aktionäre der Zielgesellschaft ist hierin kaum zu sehen. Aktionäre werden durch den Ausschluss entsprechenden Drittschutzes nicht rechtlos gestellt, da sie etwaige Verstöße gegen das WpÜG, insbesondere im Hinblick auf die Angemessenheit der angebotenen Gegenleistung, im Zivilrechtsweg verfolgen können.

Das Bundesverfassungsgericht ließ in seiner Nichtannahmeentscheidung der Verfassungsbeschwerde der Wella-Aktionäre (Az. 1 BvR 1620/03) vom 2. April 2004 allerdings offen, ob nicht Drittschutz im Gestattungsverfahren zumindest dann zu gewähren ist, wenn die Angebotsunterlage offensichtlich gegen das WpÜG verstößt.[9]

Das reformierte WpÜG sollte den Drittschutz für Aktionäre in Fällen vorsehen, in denen Entscheidungen der BaFin deren Interessen unmittelbar rechtlich berühren, etwa bei einer Befreiungsentscheidung. Dies sollte auch für die vorgeschlagene Ermächtigung der BaFin zur Herabsetzung des Mindestpreises, wie z.B. in Fällen einer Sanierung der Zielgesellschaft, vorgesehen werden.

8 Beschluss vom 4. 7. 2003 – WpÜG 4/03; DB 2003, S. 1782 ff. mit Anmerkung *Zschokke/Rahlf* S. 1785 f.; ZIP 2003, S. 1392.

9 Der Nichtannahmebeschluss ist im Internet veröffentlicht unter http://www.bundesverfassungsgericht.de. *„Da Anhaltspunkte dafür nicht vorliegen, dass die in der Angebotsunterlage der P. GmbH enthaltenen Angaben über Art und Höhe der für die Wertpapiere der W. AG gebotenen Gegenleistung im Sinne von § 15 Abs. 1 Nr. 2 in Verbindung mit § 11 Abs. 2 Satz 2 Nr. 4 WpÜG offensichtlich gegen Vorschriften des Wertpapiererwerbs- und Übernahmegesetzes oder der WpÜG-Angebotsverordnung verstießen, kann nicht festgestellt werden, dass die Beschwerdeführerin als am Angebotsverfahren nicht Beteiligte in ihren Rechten aus Art. 14 Abs. 1 in Verbindung mit Art. 3 Abs. 1 oder Art. 19 Abs. 4 GG verletzt ist, weil ihr nach den angegriffenen Entscheidungen Rechtsschutz gegen die Entscheidung der Bundesanstalt über die Gestattung des Übernahmeangebots nicht zusteht.“*

2. Die Voraussetzungen für das *acting in concert* sollten präzisiert werden

Die Umsetzung der Richtlinie bietet auch Gelegenheit, die Voraussetzungen für das gegenseitige Zurechnen von Stimmrechten bei gemeinsamem Handeln von Aktionären (sogenanntes „*acting in concert*") zu präzisieren. Hierbei geht es um die Frage, ab wann Aktionäre, die alleine keine Kontrolle besitzen, aber etwaige gemeinsame Absichten im Hinblick auf die Zielgesellschaft verfolgen, zur Abgabe eines Pflichtangebotes verpflichtet sind. Dieses Thema hat bereits zu mehreren Verwaltungs- und Gerichtsverfahren geführt, zuletzt bei der diesjährigen Kontroverse um die Deutsche Börse.

Die Auslegung des § 30 Abs. 2 Satz 1 WpÜG hinsichtlich der Zurechnung von Stimmrechten, wenn Aktionäre ihr Verhalten in Bezug auf eine Zielgesellschaft „*auf Grund einer Vereinbarung oder in sonstiger Weise*" abstimmen, sowie der Ausnahme für „*Vereinbarungen über die Ausübung von Stimmrechten in Einzelfällen*" ist schwierig.

Im Fall der Beiersdorf AG hatte die Allianz im Oktober 2003 etwa 32,6 Prozent der Aktien an die Tchibo Holding, die Hamburger Gesellschaft für Vermögens und Beteiligungsverwaltung und die TROMA Alters- und Hinterbliebenenstiftung veräußert. Die BaFin prüfte, ob dieser Verkauf mit einer Kontrollerlangung dieser drei Käuferinnen im Sinne des WpÜG einherging und kam zum Schluß, dass diese zeitgleichen Erwerbe von Beiersdorf-Aktien von der Allianz nicht zur Abgabe eines Pflichtangebots an die außenstehenden Aktionäre führten. Die BaFin begründete dies damit, dass sich keine Beweise für ein abgestimmtes Verhalten der Erwerber ergeben hätten, insbesondere keine Anhaltspunkte für eine Stimmrechtsvereinbarung oder die Absicht erkennbar gewesen seien, in relevanter Art gemeinsam auf die Zielgesellschaft einzuwirken. Die BaFin konnte nicht feststellen, dass sich die drei Erwerberinnen über die mit dem Aktienkauf verfolgten Ziele, etwa die Sicherung des Standortes Hamburg, abgestimmt haben. Die Tchibo Holding war nicht zur Abgabe eines Pflichtangebots verpflichtet, da sie schon vor Inkrafttreten des WpÜG mehr als 30 Prozent der Aktien der Beiersdorf hielt und damit ein Altfall vorlag. Die BaFin wies in ihrer abschließenden Pressemitteilung darauf hin, dass ein *acting in concert* beim gemeinsamen Erwerb von Aktien nur dann vorliege, wenn ein über den Erwerb hinausgehendes gemeinsames Interesse verfolgt werde.[10]

10 Pressemitteilung der BaFin vom 23. Januar 2004, veröffentlicht im Internet unter http://www.bafin.de.

Das OLG Frankfurt am Main stellte hierzu im Fall der Pixelpark AG[11] fest, dass der gemeinsame Wille von Aktionären, ein Unternehmen in Fortführung eines bereits vorhandenen Konzepts zu sanieren, nicht ohne weiteres als *acting in concert* im Sinne von § 30 WpÜG angesehen werden könne, und zwar auch dann, wenn die Aktionäre personelle Alternativen für einen Wechsel des Alleinvorstands anstreben. Die Stimmrechte könnten wechselseitig zugerechnet werden, wenn Aktionäre bewusst zusammenarbeiten mit dem Ziel, einen dauerhaft koordinierten Einfluß auf die Zielgesellschaft auszuüben. Dies war im Fall Pixelpark jedoch nicht nachweisbar.

Dagegen wertete das OLG München im Falle der WMF AG[12] eine Vorabstimmung unter Großaktionären (Münchener Rück, Deutsche Bank und Wüstenrot) bei Wahlen zum Aufsichtsrat oder Aufsichtsratsvorsitz als abgestimmtes Verhalten zur Kontrollerlangung bzw. zum Kontrollwechsel. Das OLG München zog aus der Ausnahmeregelung in § 30 Abs. 2 Satz 1, 2. Halbsatz WpÜG für Abstimmungen im Einzelfall den Schluss, dass abgestimmtes Verhalten mit nachhaltiger Wirkung auf die Herrschaftsverhältnisse der Zielgesellschaft zur Zurechnung führe könne. In Anlehnung an die Auffassung der BaFin sah der Senat in Vorabstimmungen zur Wahl von Aufsichtsratsmitgliedern dann ein zurechnungsfähiges Verhalten, wenn die Absprache Teil eines Gesamtplans sei, der auf die Einflussnahme der Großaktionäre über die Gesellschaft ausgerichtet ist.

Im Fall der Deutsche Börse AG gab die BaFin nach Untersuchung der Vorgänge, die zum Abbruch der versuchten Übernahme der Londoner Börse und den Rücktritten des Vorstands- und des Aufsichtsratsvorsitzenden führten, nach mehreren Monaten am 19. Oktober 2005 bekannt, dass sie keine Tatsachen ermitteln konnte, die eindeutig bewiesen, dass sich die beteiligten Fondsgesellschaften (die zusammen fast 40% der Aktien der Deutsche Börse AG auf sich vereinten) untereinander koordiniert hätten, um nachhaltig und beständig Einfluss auf die Deutsche Börse AG nehmen. Die vorliegenden Indizien rechtfertigten nicht zweifelsfrei die Annahme, dass die betreffenden Fonds ein weitergehendes unternehmerisches Interesse oder einen Gesamtplan für die Deutsche Börse AG hatten.

Die obigen Fälle zeigen, dass unabhängig von der unklaren Formulierung der rechtlichen Voraussetzung die Sachverhaltsermittlung die wesentliche Schwierigkeit bei den *acting in concert*-Fällen darstellt. Hier ist für die Praxis von Bedeutung, dass – nicht zuletzt vor dem Hintergrund des Falles Deutsche Börse

11 OLG Frankfurt am Main, Beschluss vom 25. 6. 2004, ZIP 2004, 1309.

12 OLG München, Urteil vom 27. 4. 2005, DB 2005, 1264.

AG – damit zu rechnen ist, dass der Gesetzgeber mit der Umsetzung der Übernahmerichtlinie die Ermittlungsbefugnisse der BaFin verschärfen wird (insbesondere im Bereich der Auskunftsrechte und Untersuchungsrechte vor Ort). Aus der Sicht der Praxis wäre allerdings vor allem eine inhaltliche Klarstellung der Voraussetzungen wünschenswert, wann eine Zurechnung stattfinden soll. Die Reformvorschläge reichen von einer Neuformulierung von § 30 Abs. 2 Satz 1 WpÜG zur Erfassung aller Fälle des *acting in concert* bis zu einer Beschränkung des Anwendungsbereichs der Regelung auf „*Vereinbarungen im rechtlichen Sinne*". Teilweise wird die Ansicht vertreten, ein gemeinsames Handeln, das ein Pflichtangebot auslösen kann, sei künftig nur bei einem anfänglichen Erwerb der Aktien zur Kontrolle anzunehmen.[13] Letzteres dürfte allerdings wenig Aussicht auf Umsetzung haben. Es wäre auch inhaltlich schwer nachzuvollziehen, wieso späteres Parallelverhalten nicht ebenso eine Zurechnung auslösen sollte. Dies ist auch so in vergleichbaren Rechtsgebieten, bei denen der Kontrollbegriff ebenfalls ausschlaggebend ist (z. B. im Kartellrecht).

Die Klarstellung des *acting in concert* sollte nicht zu einer Verschärfung der Anforderungen führen. Andernfalls würden die auch aus *corporate governance*-Gründen gewünschten vermehrten Abstimmungen der Aktionäre untereinander konterkariert werden. Es ist normal und ergibt sich aus der Sache, dass die Aktionäre, die Eigentümer einer Aktiengesellschaft, sich miteinander über die Entwicklung der gemeinsamen Gesellschaft verständigen. Dies allein sollte keine Angebotspflicht auslösen, selbst wenn diese Abstimmung im Einzelfall zur Hauptversammlungsmehrheit führt.

Insgesamt ist damit zu rechnen, dass die Zurechnung von Stimmrechten aufgrund gemeinsamen Verhaltens auch künftig kontrovers bleiben wird. Neben dem anfänglichen Erwerb dürfte das WpÜG weiterhin den Parallelerwerb erfassen. Zusätzliche Untersuchungsrechte der BaFin dürften zu größerer Sachverhaltsaufklärung führen.

3. Die Praxis der BaFin bei Sanierungsübernahmen sollte beibehalten werden

Anders als beim Drittschutz und beim gemeinsamen Handeln besteht kein Handlungsbedarf bei den so genannten Sanierungsübernahmen, bei denen ein Bieter die Zielgesellschaft zum Zwecke der Sanierung übernimmt.

13 Offengelassen bei *Seibt* ZIP 2004, 1829 ff.

Sanierungsübernahmen haben eine erhebliche praktische Bedeutung. § 37 WpÜG i.V.m. § 9 WpÜG-Angebotsverordnung sieht eine Befreiungsmöglichkeit in Sanierungsfällen der Zielgesellschaft vor. Voraussetzung einer solchen Befreiung in Sanierungsfällen ist das Vorliegen einer Sanierungslage sowie eines plausiblen Sanierungsplans. Im Hinblick auf die Sanierungslage hat sich bei der BaFin die Rechtsauffassung durchgesetzt, dass bei der Zielgesellschaft keine Insolvenzlage notwendig ist, sondern das Vorliegen von bestandsgefährdenden Risiken ausreicht. Der Sanierungsplan muß die Ursachen der Krise darlegen und angeben, auf welche Art und Weise die Krise überwunden werden kann. Der Sanierungsplan muß einen verbindlichen Sanierungsbeitrag des Bieters beinhalten, der messbar und in bedeutsamer Weise für die Beseitigung der Krisensituation einzusetzen ist.

Hintergrund dieser Anforderungen ist die Überlegung, dass ein Kleinaktionär von einer erfolgreichen Sanierung der Zielgesellschaft profitiert und den sich daraus ergebenden Mehrwert am Markt durch Verkauf seiner Aktie realisieren kann. Der Bieter, der eine Zielgesellschaft durch seinen Beitrag saniert, soll nicht gezwungen werden, weitere finanzielle Mittel für den Auskauf der Kleinaktionäre einzusetzen.

Im Rahmen der Novellierung des WpÜG wird nun vorgeschlagen, diese Befreiungsmöglichkeiten in Sanierungsfällen zu streichen. Stattdessen soll der Bieter einen Antrag stellen können, den Mindestpreis in Sanierungsfällen herabzusetzen.

Dieser Vorschlag verschlechtert die derzeitige Rechtslage. Die Befreiung von der Abgabe eines Pflichtangebotes hat sich insbesondere in Sanierungsfällen bewährt. Die BaFin hat Befreiungen erteilt, sofern die notwendige Sanierungslage sowie ein Sanierungsplan nachgewiesen werden konnten. Der obige Gedanke, daß der Kleinaktionär von dem Sanierungsbeitrag des neuen Gesellschafters profitiert und umgekehrt der neue Gesellschafter nicht gezwungen sein soll, über den Sanierungsbeitrag hinaus einen weiteren Beitrag zum Auskauf der Kleinaktionäre zu leisten, bleibt weiterhin zutreffend.

Die BaFin sollte daher weiterhin ermächtigt sein, bei der Übernahme von bestandsgefährdeten Gesellschaften eine vollständige Befreiung von der Abgabe eines Pflichtangebotes zu erteilen. Wünschenswert wäre allenfalls die Möglichkeit, eine Befreiung vorab zu erhalten, auch wenn die flexible Praxis der BaFin bereits jetzt diesbezüglich Rechtssicherheit zu gewährleisten versucht.

4. Die Regeln zum Mindestpreis haben sich bewährt

Auch die Regelungen zum Mindestpreis haben sich bewährt. Der Mindestpreis für Übernahme- und Pflichtangebote berücksichtigte bislang neben dem höchsten Vorerwerbspreis auch den nach Umsätzen gewichteten durchschnittlichen Börsenkurs der Aktien der Zielgesellschaft während eines Zeitraumes von drei Monaten vor Ankündigung des Angebotes.[14] Dieser Durchschnittskurs ist auf der Internetseite der BAFin transparent ablesbar.[15]

Literaturstimmen halten die Aufrechterhaltung dieser Regeln für europarechtswidrig.[16] Nach Art. 5 Abs. 4 der Übernahmerichtlinie gilt als angemessener Preis bei einem Pflichtangebot der höchste Vorerwerbspreis im Zeitraum von sechs bis zwölf Monaten vor dem Angebot. Dies ändert bei Pflichtangeboten nicht nur die Berechnungsgrundlage, sondern auch den Referenzzeitraum für die Berechnung der Mindestgegenleistung.

Nichtberücksichtigung der Börsenkurse als Mindestpreis für Übernahmeangebote wäre gleichwohl bedauerlich. Die Mindestpreisregeln für Übernahmeangebote haben sich in der Praxis bewährt, und zwar unabhängig davon, ob aussagekräftige Vorerwerbe des Bieters vorliegen. Die Berücksichtigung der Börsenbewertung war ein Kernelement des WpÜG. Kleinaktionäre steigen typischerweise über die Börse – und damit zu den dortigen Bewertungen – in eine Aktiengesellschaft ein. Es ist systemgerecht, wenn die Börsenpreise auch beim Ausstieg im Rahmen eines Übernahmeangebotes als relevante Schwellenwerte angesetzt werden. Es bleibt jedem Bieter jederzeit freigestellt, ein höheres Angebot abzugeben. Ein Übernahme- oder Pflichtangebot unter Ausschluss der Bewertung durch den Kapitalmarkt ist sinnlos und höhlt die beabsichtigte übernahmerechtliche Garantie einer werthaltigen Ausstiegsmöglichkeit aus. Börsenkurse haben darüber hinaus den Vorteil der Klarheit und einfachen Berechenbarkeit gegenüber privatrechtlichen Vorerwerbspreisen, bei denen manchmal eine Vielzahl von wertbildenden Faktoren zusammenzurechnen ist.

Das Übernahmeangebot des WpÜG (das aus dem so genannten „freiwilligen Pflichtangebot“ des vorangehenden Übernahmekodex der Börsensachver-

14 § 31 Abs. 1 WpÜG; §§ 3 ff. WpÜG-AngebotsVO.

15 Auf der Internetseite der BaFin (www.bafin.de) unter „Datenbanken“: „Mindestpreise gemäß Wertpapiererwerbs- und Übernahmegesetz“.

16 Vgl. *Mülbert* NZG 2004, 633 ff.

ständigenkommission hervorgegangen ist) hat den Zweck, den Bieter von einem nachfolgenden Pflichtangebot (und damit der Pflicht, zwei Angebote in kurzer Zeit herauszulegen) zu befreien. Dieses Privileg ist nur dann gerechtfertigt, wenn die bisherigen kapitalmarktmäßigen Mindestpreisregeln auch mit dem Übernahmeangebot erreicht werden.

Es ist daher angemessen und im Interesse der Übernahmepraxis, die klare Börsenpreisregelung beizubehalten, selbst wenn das deutsche Recht hier strengere Maßstäbe ansetzt als die Übernahmerichtlinie. Ob die Berechnungsfrist drei, sechs oder zwölf Monate beträgt, erscheint demgegenüber weniger entscheidend. Allerdings ist die kapitalmarktmäßige Aussagekraft eines Durchschnittskurses auf den Zeitpunkt des Angebotes umso geringer, je länger die Durchschnittsperiode andauert.

5. Kaufangebot und gesellschaftsrechtliche Abfindung: ein unabgestimmtes Verhältnis

Im Zusammenhang mit den übernahmerechtlichen Bewertungsfragen hat sich eine weitere Frage in den Vordergrund geschoben, und zwar die Frage nach der Attraktivität eines Kaufangebots im Vergleich zu möglichen nachfolgenden gesellschaftsrechtlichen Abfindungen (etwa nach dem Aktiengesetz oder Umwandlungsgesetz). Diese Frage hat inzwischen direkte Bedeutung auch für die Erfolgswahrscheinlichkeit eines Übernahmeangebotes bekommen.

Insbesondere institutionelle Aktionäre berücksichtigen bei ihren Überlegungen, ob ein Angebotspreis angemessen ist und ob sie ein öffentliches Kaufangebot für ihre Aktien annehmen, inwiefern eine mögliche Abfindung in Folge einer erfolgreichen Übernahme aufgrund gesellschaftsrechtlicher Restrukturierungsmaßnahmen gezahlt wird. Solche Maßnahmen erfassen nicht nur den Squeeze out, sondern etwa auch den Abschluß eines Beherrschungs- und Gewinnabführungsvertrages oder eine Verschmelzung, Spaltung oder Eingliederung.

Wurde bei Einführung des WpÜG zunächst davon ausgegangen, dass spätere gesellschaftsrechtliche Abfindungen mangels Übernahmeprämie überwiegend niedriger ausfielen als der Angebotspreis eines öffentlichen Kaufangebotes, hat sich das Bild inzwischen gewandelt. Aufgrund einer Reihe von entsprechenden Präzedenzfällen hat sich inzwischen zunehmend die Ansicht durchgesetzt, dass es häufig lohnender ist, ein Übernahmeangebot nicht anzunehmen, sondern nachfolgende, bessere Abfindungen abzuwarten.

Bei der Übernahme der Wella AG durch den Procter & Gamble-Konzern wurde 2003 – entsprechend dem Interesse der Bietergesellschaft am Erwerb von Stammaktien – den Aktionären ein unterschiedlicher Preis für Stammaktien (EUR 92,25) und für Vorzugsaktien (EUR 65,00) angeboten. Beim Abschluss eines Beherrschungs- und Gewinnabführungsvertrags im Jahr 2004 betrug die angebotene Abfindung bereits einheitlich EUR 72,86 für Stamm- und Vorzugsaktien. Als 2005 der Squeeze out der Minderheitsaktionäre beschlossen wurde, lag die Abfindung schon bei EUR 80,37 je Stammaktie oder Vorzugsaktie.

Hatte bei der Übernahme der Celanese AG durch die BCP im Jahr 2004 der Angebotspreis im Frühjahr noch EUR 32,50 je Aktie betragen, wurde beim Abschluß eines Beherrschungs- und Gewinnabführungsvertrags die Abfindung bereits auf EUR 41,92 festgesetzt. Als die Hauptaktionärin in diesem Jahr die für die Überschreitung der Beteiligungsschwelle von 95 Prozent des Grundkapitals erforderlichen Aktien zum Preis von EUR 51,– erwarb, verpflichtete sie sich gegenüber den verbliebenen Minderheitsaktionären darüber hinaus zur Nachbesserung der Abfindung in Höhe des Unterschiedsbetrags zu EUR 51,00, falls jene auf ein Spruchverfahren verzichten würden.

Im Falle des Pflichtangebots der Sanofi Aventis an die Aktionäre der Hoechst AG war im Herbst 2004 ein Angebotspreis in Höhe von EUR 51,23 je Aktie angeboten worden. Während des laufenden Angebotsverfahrens wurde ein Squeeze out gegen eine Abfindung in Höhe von EUR 56,50 je Aktie beschlossen. Das Angebot wurde für insgesamt 0,1% des Grundkapitals angenommen. In diesem Jahr wurde bei einem Vergleich zur Beendigung laufender Spruchverfahren hinsichtlich der Überprüfung der Angemessenheit der Squeeze out-Abfindung ein Betrag in Höhe von EUR 63,80 je Aktie sowie eine Nachbesserung um weitere EUR 1,20 je Aktie für Minderheitsaktionäre vereinbart, die auf ein Spruchverfahren verzichten.

Die Konsequenz dieser Entwicklung ist bereits ablesbar. Die durchschnittliche Erfolgsrate der öffentlichen Angebote nach dem WpÜG, gemessen am Erwerb außenstehenden Kapitals durch das Angebot, sank zwischen 2002 und 2004 von über 60% auf unter 40%.[17]

Diese Entwicklung vermindert die Effektivität des WpÜG und vereitelt das gesetzgeberische Ziel, Unternehmensübernahmen auf einer fairen und sicheren rechtlichen Basis zügig abzuwickeln.

Es wäre daher zu wünschen, daß der Gesetzgeber durch eine Abstimmung und Harmonisierung der übernahmerechtlichen und gesellschaftsrechtlichen Bewertungsregeln die Spekulation auf spätere höhere Abfindungen unterbinden und damit die Attraktivität von öffentlichen Kaufangeboten stärken

17 Bad Homburger Kreis Forum für Übernahmerecht: 2002: 60,46%; 2003, 53,13%; 2004: 36,57%.

würde. Ein erster Schritt ist die zu erwartende Einführung der in der Übernahmerichtlinie vorgesehenen Möglichkeit, die Angemessenheit einer Squeeze out-Abfindung unwiderleglich zu vermuten, wenn 90% der außenstehenden Aktionäre ein vorangegangenes Übernahme- oder Pflichtangebot zu diesem Preis angenommen haben.

Die Überarbeitung der Bewertungsrichtlinien[18] allein kann dies nicht gewährleisten, selbst wenn diese – wie derzeit angenommen – tendenziell zu niedrigeren Unternehmenswerten und damit zu niedrigeren gesellschaftsrechtlichen Abfindungen für die Aktionäre führt.

Insgesamt handelt es sich bei diesem Themenkreis um ein ungelöstes Problem, das im Spannungsfeld zwischen dem kapitalmarktrechtlichen WpÜG und dem traditionellen Aktienrecht und Umwandlungsrecht liegt. Es ist nicht zu erwarten, dass die WpÜG-Novelle dieses Spannungsfeld erfolgreich auflösen wird.

6. Der übernahmerechtliche Squeeze out und das neue Andienungsrecht

Mit der Umsetzung der Übernahmerichtlinie neu in das deutsche Recht eingeführt wird der zu erwartende übernahmerechtliche Squeeze out sowie das dem deutschen Recht bisher fremde Andienungsrecht für Minderheitsaktionäre (*Sell out*).[19] Das Andienungsrecht soll es Aktionären, die ein Angebot nicht angenommen haben, ermöglichen, ihre Aktien in einer bestimmten Frist nach Ablauf des Angebotes an den Bieter zu veräußern, wenn bei diesem die Voraussetzungen für einen Squeeze out vorliegen.

Wenig wahrscheinlich erscheint die Einführung eines gattungsmäßigen Squeeze out,[20] auch wenn die Möglichkeit eines solchen Squeeze out (etwa für

18 Das Institut der Wirtschaftsprüfer in Deutschland e.V. (IDW) veröffentlichte am 30. Dezember 2004 den Entwurf einer Neufassung des IDW-Standards „Grundsätze zur Durchführung von Unternehmensbewertungen“ (IDW ES 1 n.F.); Stand: 9. Dezember 2004. Gegenüber der bisherigen Fassung enthält der Bewertungsstandard eine Neuorientierung insbesondere hinsichtlich der Ermittlung des Kapitalisierungszinsfußes und der Vollausschüttungsannahme.

19 Art. 15 und 16 der Übernahmerichtlinie.

20 Nach Art. 15 Abs. 3 Satz 2 der Übernahmerichtlinie können die Mitgliedstaaten bei Zielgesellschaften mit mehreren Wertpapiergattungen vorsehen, dass das Aus-

stimmrechtlose Vorzugsaktien) für viele Aktiengesellschaften interessant wäre. Ein auf eine Aktiengattung beschränkter Squeeze out würde die verfassungsrechtliche Eigentumsdiskussion[21] erneut entfachen, da ein Squeeze out – bezogen auf das Gesamtkapital einer Aktiengesellschaft – mit einer Kapitalbeteiligung des Bieters von weniger als 95% möglich würde.

Eine offene Frage ist das künftige Verhältnis zwischen dem übernahmerechtlichen Squeeze out und den geltenden Regeln im Aktiengesetz. Dies ist insofern von Bedeutung im Hinblick auf die bereits erwähnte Vermutung, dass eine Squeeze out-Abfindung als angemessen gilt, wenn 90% der außenstehenden Aktionäre ein vorangehendes Kaufangebot zu diesem Preis angenommen haben. Diese Regel ist im derzeitigen Recht nicht vorgesehen. In die Berechnung der 90% sollten auch solche Erwerbe des Bieters zählen, die der Bieter zeitgleich außerhalb des Angebotes (z.B. über die Börse) zu diesem Preis erzielt. Es wäre im übrigen zu begrüßen, wenn die 90%-Regel auch für einfache öffentliche Kaufangebote gelten würde, sofern diese die Mindestpreisvorschriften für ein Übernahmeangebot einhalten. Dies würde es Unternehmen, die bereits jetzt Kontrolle an der Zielgesellschaft besitzen, ermöglichen, durch ein vorangeschaltetes attraktives Kaufangebot langwierige Spruchverfahren im Rahmen des aktienrechtlichen Squeeze out zu vermeiden.

Aus diesen Gründen sollte die Durchführung des übernahmerechtlichen Squeeze out auch ohne gesonderten Hauptversammlungsbeschluß möglich sein (etwa durch ein gerichtliches Antragsverfahren). Auf diese Weise könnten die Missbräuche, die nach wie vor im Bereich der Anfechtungsklagen gegen Squeeze out-Beschlüsse bestehen, von vornherein vermieden werden.

Es bleibt abzuwarten, welche praktische Bedeutung die neuen Instrumente des übernahmerechtlichen Squeeze out und Andienungsrechtes erlangen werden. Für beide muß der Bieter die 95%-Schwelle an der Zielgesellschaft erreichen. Dies dürfte in der Praxis schwer werden, wenn sich die erwähnte Entwicklung fortsetzt, wonach höhere gesellschaftsrechtliche Abfindungen die Erfolgsaussichten von Übernahmeangeboten beeinträchtigen. Zwischen 2002 und 2004 sank die nach einem öffentlichen Angebot nach dem WpÜG erreichte durchschnittliche Beteiligung eines Bieters an der Zielgesellschaft

schlussrecht nur in der Gattung ausgeübt werden kann, in der eine Beteiligung des Bieters von 90–95% der Stimmrechte erreicht ist.

21 Vgl. BVerfGE 100, 289ff.

bereits von etwa 89% auf unter 80%.[22] Diese Entwicklung kann nur dann dauerhaft umgekehrt werden, wenn das bereits erwähnte Spannungsverhältnis zwischen übernahmerechtlichem Angebotspreis und gesellschaftsrechtlicher Abfindung beseitigt wird.

7. Zusammenfassung

Die Umsetzung der Übernahmerichtlinie wird nur zu den notwendigen Änderungen des WpÜG führen, da dieses wesentliche Kernelemente bereits vorweggenommen und sich im übrigen bewährt hat. Diese Umstände führen zu insgesamt begrenzten Erwartungen der Praxis an die Überarbeitung des deutschen Übernahmerechtes.

Wünschenswert wäre eine Verbesserung des Drittschutzes sowie eine Klärung der Voraussetzungen gemeinsamen Handelns (*acting in concert*). Bewährte Regeln, wie die Möglichkeit zur Befreiung vom Pflichtangebot bei Sanierungsübernahmen oder die Berücksichtigung des Börsenkurses beim Mindestpreis, sollten beibehalten werden. Bei den Vorschriften zu den Abwehrmaßnahmen für unwillkommene Übernahmeangebote dürfte der deutsche Gesetzgeber von der Umsetzung der Neutralitätsregeln der Übernahmerichtlinie absehen *(Opt out)* und es den Zielgesellschaften überlassen, sich freiwillig den strengeren Regeln der Übernahmerichtlinie zu unterwerfen (*Opt in*). Auch der Vorbehalt der Gegenseitigkeit dürfte Eingang in das deutsche Übernahmerecht finden.

Ein neuer übernahmerechtlicher Squeeze out sowie ein Andienungsrecht (Sell out), beides für den Fall, dass der Bieter eine 95%ige Beteiligung an der Zielgesellschaft erreicht, werden neu in das deutsche Recht eingeführt werden. Sollten mehr als 90% der außenstehenden Aktionäre ein vorangegangenes Übernahmeangebot angenommen haben, so gilt der dafür angebotene Preis als angemessene Abfindung. Hiermit wird zum ersten Mal die übernahmerechtliche Bewertung mit nachfolgenden gesellschaftsrechtlichen Abfindun-

22 Bad Homburger Kreis Forum für Übernahmerecht: 2002: 88,72%, 2003: 77,12%; 2004: 79,37% und in den ersten neun Monaten des Jahres 2005: 68,51% (Angaben zu 2005 berücksichtigen durchgeführte Angebote, bei denen die Angebotsunterlage bis einschließlich 30. September 2005 veröffentlicht wurde. Dabei erfolgte die Berücksichtigung der Angaben zu Axel Springer AG/ProSiebenSat.1 Media AG unter dem Vorbehalt, daß die tatsächliche Durchführung des Angebots noch von Angebotsbedingungen abhängig ist.).

gen verknüpft. Unabhängig, inwieweit diese 90%-Regel praktische Bedeutung erlangen wird, ist sie ein begrüßenswerter erster Schritt, der sich derzeit abzeichnenden Entwicklung gegenzusteuern, wonach die Spekulation auf höhere gesellschaftsrechtliche Abfindungen die Attraktivität, und damit die Effektivität, von Übernahmeverfahren zu beeinträchtigen scheint.

Anlage

Statistische Übersichten zur Entwicklung der Angebote nach dem WpÜG:

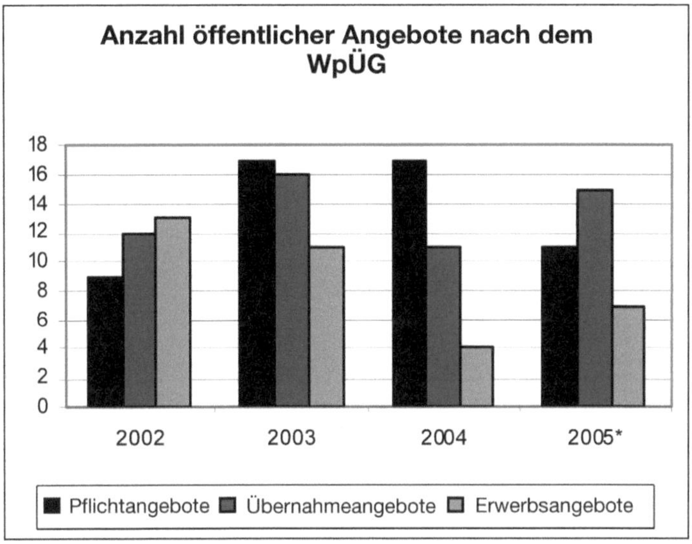

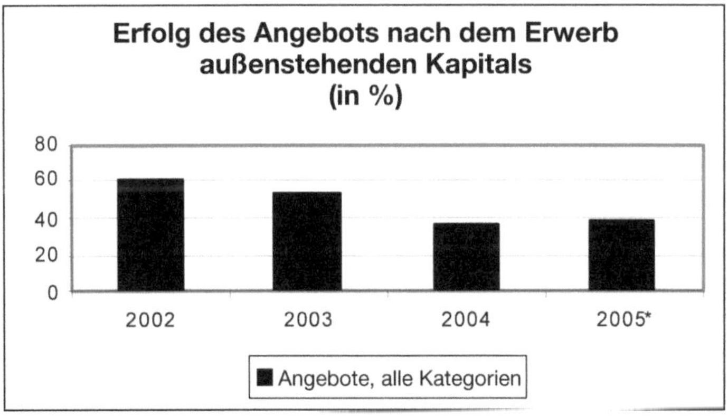

Quelle jeweils: Bad Homburger Kreis Forum für Übernahmerecht.

* Angaben zu 2005 berücksichtigen durchgeführte Angebote, bei denen die Angebotsunterlage bis einschließlich 31. Dezember 2005 veröffentlicht wurde (Berücksichtigung

der Angaben zu Axel Springer AG/ProSiebenSat.1 Media AG unter Vorbehalt der Angebotsbedingungen). Die Ergebnisse einiger Angebote, deren Annahmefrist im Jahre 2006 noch lief, konnten bisher nicht berücksichtigt werden.